The Closing of the American Heart

Other Books by Ronald Nash

Christianity and the Hellenistic World

Christian Faith and Historical Understanding

Social Justice and the Christian Church

Choosing a College

Faith and Reason: Searching for a Rational Faith

Process Theology (editor)

Liberation Theology (editor)

Evangelicals in America

Evangelical Renewal in the Mainline Churches (editor)

Poverty and Wealth

The Concept of God

The Word of God and the Mind of Man

Freedom, Justice and the State

Ideas of History (editor)

The Light of the Mind:
St. Augustine's Theory of Knowledge

The Case for Biblical Christianity (editor)

The Philosophy of Gordon H. Clark (editor)

The New Evangelicalism

Dooyeweerd and the Amsterdam Philosophy

The Closing of the American Heart

What's Really Wrong With America's Schools

Ronald H. Nash

Foreword by R. C. Sproul

PROBE Books

Distributed by Word Publishing

Copyright   © 1990 by Probe Ministries International

Library of
Congress
Cataloging-
in-Publication
Data

Nash, Ronald H.
   The closing of the American heart: what's
really wrong with America's schools/Ronald
H. Nash: foreword by R. C. Sproul
     p.   cm.
   Includes bibliographical references.
   1. Public schools—United States. 2. Moral
education—United States. 3. Christian education—Philosophy. 4. Education—United
States—Aims and objectives. I. Title.
   LA217.N354   1990   90-30823
   370'.973—dc20   CIP

ISBN   0-945241-11-9

Place of
Printing

Printed in the United States of America

Editor   Steven W. Webb

Design   Cover design by Rick Dembicki
Cover illustration by Keith Condon
Book design by Meisje Johntz Connor

*To the Memory
of My Father*

About the Author

For more than twenty-five years, Dr. Ronald Nash has been professor of philosophy and religion at Western Kentucky University. For twenty of those years, he also served as head of the department of philosophy and religion. Dr. Nash is a graduate of Brown University and of Syracuse University, where he earned his Ph.D. in philosophy. Nash is the author or editor of twenty books, including: *Christianity and the Hellenistic World; Christian Faith and Historical Understanding; Social Justice and the Christian Church; Choosing a College; Faith and Reason; Process Theology; Liberation Theology; Evangelicals in America; Poverty and Wealth; The Concept of God;* and *The Word of God and the Mind of Man.* He has lectured extensively at colleges and universities throughout the United States and Great Britain. He also serves as an advisor to the United States Civil Rights Commission.

Table of Contents

Foreword   **9**

Preface   **13**

CHAPTER 1
The Closing of the American Heart   **19**

CHAPTER 2
Reason and Virtue   **33**

CHAPTER 3
Three Kinds of Illiteracy   **45**

CHAPTER 4
Three Enemies of "the Permanent Things"   **61**

CHAPTER 5
The Educational Establishment   **75**

CHAPTER 6
Four Essential Steps   **97**

CHAPTER 7
The Separation of School and State   **113**

CHAPTER 8
The Christian School Movement   **127**

CHAPTER 9
American Higher Education and the Radical Left   **141**

CHAPTER 10
Strengths and Weaknesses of the Evangelical College   **159**

CHAPTER 11
Renewing Christianity's Links to Its Past   **177**

CHAPTER 12
Reopening the American Heart and Mind   **189**

APPENDIX 1
Curriculum Proposal   **203**

Notes   **207**

For Further Reading   **223**

Index of Persons and Works   **233**

Foreword

Perhaps our minds are jarred when we read the words of the Proverb:

"As a man thinks in his heart, so is he."

What is jarring about this verse is the conjunction of the words "thinks" and "heart." We are accustomed to associating thinking with the mind and feeling with the heart. Has the author of Proverbs slipped into a faulty view of human nature by which he confuses feeling with thought?

By no means. Indeed there are occasions when the Bible uses the term "heart" to refer to one's feelings, but in this case (as in many others) the term heart refers to the center, root, or core of one's being. A fair paraphrase of this verse may read, "As a man thinks in the depths of his being, so is he."

What we think, what we believe, what captures our consciences determines what we become. Therefore, what we think and how we think are crucial to life itself.

In ancient Greece an impasse occurred in theoretical thought when the struggle to gain ultimate truth was not resolved. The debate between monists and pluralists, corporealists and incorporealists, Heraclitus and Parmenides ended with the rise of skeptical humanism, or, if you prefer, humanistic skepticism.

The dramatic influence of skepticism was seen in the arena of education. Abandoning the quest for ultimate, normative truth, education came under the control of the Sophists. The Sophists sought wisdom of a more practical type. The science of rhetoric, for example, turned away from questions of how to speak the truth, to questions of how to persuade people of something whether it was the truth or not. Here, in ancient Greece, Madison Avenue was born.

The work of these men was unabashedly superficial, though clever. It engendered a sophisticated sophistry. Ultimately it was, and had to be, a world view of relativism wherein practical and/or expedient concerns swallowed up a quest for objective reality. Preferences replaced laws, personal gratification replaced virtue, and truth was slain in the streets. The supreme motto was found in the credo of Protagoras: *Homo mensura*—man is the measure of all things. Close behind Protagoras came the creed of the relativistic skeptic, Gorgias, who declared that "all statements are false."

Gorgias's claim, of course, is self-contradictory. If all statements are false then the statement "all statements are false" is equally false. No matter. One of the virtues [*sic*] of relativism is that we can convert its propositions to their contraries and have just as much, or just as little truth. It matters not if we say all statements are false or that all statements are true; either way the relativist is satisfied.

At least one Athenian was not so satisfied with the Sophists. In fact he was so convinced that the issues raised by such an educational philosophy were so important that he said, "the unexamined life is not worth living." Yet Socrates was so convinced that the examined life was worth living for, that he was willing to forfeit his own life to combat the educational philosophy of the Sophists.

When Socrates drank the hemlock rather than submit to the dominant educational philosophy of his day, he did so with the full conviction that in this battle nothing less than Western civilization was at stake. Indeed it was more than Western civilization, it was human civilization that was at stake. Socrates understood that without an eternal and unchanging ground for virtue, man *qua* man cannot survive. The theological significance of this was understood by Dostoevsky when he declared, "If there is no God, then all things are permissible."

There is a gadfly loose in the land. His name is Ronald Nash. In this book, Nash lucidly exposes the current American educational systems as being as deeply rooted in relativism as anything the ancient Sophists ever dreamed of.

Nash is profoundly concerned with how people think. Yet he is equally concerned with what people think. He cares deeply about the content of education. He demonstrates irrefutably that there is no such thing as a neutral educational philosophy. Every educational philosophy, every educational system, every educational curriculum has an ultimate concern. In this sense, every educational system is inescapably religious. As man is incurably religious so is he also *fabricum idolarum*. We are idol-factories, though our production plants are not so often automated industrial plants as they are university and high school classrooms.

Nash pinpoints the arena of the modern clash of civilization as the schoolroom. Here the thinking is shaped, formed, and altered that determines what we become. Here the heart is injected with the drugs that heal or destroy.

In this book, Dr. Nash explores the network of convictions that link education with politics, economics, science, philosophy, and religion. His analysis excises not only the tissue of secular education but cuts into the alternate forms of education offered in the Christian school movement. His scalpel penetrates to the heart of the matter.

I can hardly wait for this manuscript to be published and released to the public. I will secure at least enough copies of it to present as gifts to every member of the board and administration of the Christian school my grandchildren attend. I want to put copies in the hands of every faculty member of the seminary where I teach and every member of the Board of Ligonier Ministries.

I rarely get as excited about a book as I am about this one. Please, dear reader, read on. Examine Nash's content, get its message into the depths of your own heart. This book is radical in the sense that it gets to the root of the crisis we face in education.

Orlando, 1989   R. C. SPROUL

Preface

The state of education in America does anything but bring joy to the minds of most parents these days. Even many teachers and administrators are worried that American education is beyond repair. Learning itself should be inspiring to young people as they seek to explore and conquer the challenges they encounter in literature and letters, the sciences, history, philosophy, and religion. But our young are not learning, and in this book we will explore the reasons why.

Unfortunately, due to the tragic condition of American education at all levels today, this book cannot generate much in the way of joy, pride, or even hope in regard to our current state of affairs. The proper response to any report card about American education must include such emotions as anger, resentment, despair, and grief. We should feel grief and despair at the millions of young lives that have been deprived of a proper education and at what those individuals, their families, and our nation will lose as a result. But we should also feel real anger and resentment at those people and institutions that are responsible for all this. These were people and institutions that readily took billions of dollars in public and private money, profited personally from the system, and have through their incompetence, ignorance, greed, and assorted other intellectual and moral vices created the intellectual and moral crisis that now afflicts every level of American education.

If learning and education are ever again to inspire our young, we must solve the current crisis. In this book I'll offer *some* hope. But remember, my purpose here is to evaluate the state of education in America, so there will be a lot of grief along the way—such is the nature of the case.

This preface will take care of several preliminary matters. The first concerns the book's subtitle, "What's *Really* Wrong With America's Schools?" There is much that is wrong with our schools and it is important that every American understand how bad things are. Plenty of people have offered their own diagnoses of the problem. Because there is so much that is wrong, it would be difficult for anyone to discuss the subject and not hit part of the target. Unfortunately, many of these diagnoses are superficial or incomplete. And most of them miss the most serious causes and hence, fail to recognize the most important remedies. I readily admit that not *every* problem in the education crisis is discussed, but I do believe you'll have a much better grasp of the major issues after reading this book.

Some readers will be puzzled by my use of the word "heart" in the book's major title. The best way to grasp this meaning is to give chapter 1 a careful reading. Other than that, the best help I can provide is simply to say that I use the word "heart" in much the same way the Bible uses it in passages like the following:

> "Blessed are the pure in heart, for they will see God" (Matt. 5:8).

> "For where your treasure is, there your heart will be also" (Matt. 6:21).

> "For out of the overflow of the heart, the mouth speaks. The good man brings good things out of the good stored up in him, and the evil man brings evil things out of the evil stored up in him (Matt. 12:34–35).

> "For out of the heart come evil thoughts, murder, adultery, sexual immorality, theft, false testimony, slander" (Matt. 15:19).

> "Jesus replied, 'Love the Lord your God with all your heart'" (Matt. 22:37).

What these passages refer to is the center of a person's being. Many people recognize the propriety of such a usage but persist in thinking of the "heart" only in terms of emotions and feelings. It is that to be sure. How could *the* center of our being possibly be separated from emotions and feelings? But the heart is much more than this; it is also the *religious* and *moral* center of our being that plays a role in determining our ultimate commitments. It is the center of our valuing self.

As the argument of this book unfolds, it will become clear that I believe that evangelical Christians in America already have hold of the key to much of the solution to America's educational crisis. But other hands also have hold of the same key. The evangelical Christian has important allies in this struggle against educational incompetence and malfeasance. This is not a time for evangelicals to ignore these allies. One can still find many conservative Roman Catholics who share important religious and moral values with evangelicals. This is equally true of many conservative Jews.

Being an evangelical Christian myself, I have written this book from the perspective of my personal heritage and world view. In the spirit of tolerance, it is my hope that many readers outside my circle of theological and personal convictions will grasp the *substance* of my claims and apply them to their own context.

Evangelicals suffer from weaknesses found less often in the camps of our allies. One of these is a stubborn proneness to anti-intellectualism and superspirituality. These unfortunate traits often lead to a disparagement of logical reasoning and to a failure to give proper attention to such things as philosophy, the arts, and other important aspects of culture. Superspirituality leads many conservative Protestants to sit on their hands while society and our educational system go to hell.

This book has five objectives. (1) It analyzes the contemporary crisis in American education; it reports what is wrong and offers what I think are the correct reasons why things are so bad.

(2) It seeks to do this from a distinctly Christian perspective. To get more specific, it does this from the perspective of American evangelicalism.[1] Obviously, one does not have to be an evangelical Christian to recognize the nature and scope of the crisis nor to understand what must be done to solve our problems. But if this book is correct when it argues that an essential but frequently overlooked element of the education crisis is religious and moral in nature, the importance of the Christian stance I adopt should be obvious.

(3) The inadequacies of contemporary education are not exclusively matters of the mind, or so this book argues. I also examine the extent to which traditional religious and moral values are under assault at every level of public and higher education. Protestants, Catholics, and Jews who care about such values, norms, and standards need a clearer picture of what our educational system is doing to undermine these values. Increased understanding will then hopefully translate first into concern and then into action.

(4) But concern and action won't accomplish much without a blueprint for action. Hence, my fourth goal is to discuss what can

and should be done to improve the quality of education at every level. In pursuit of this goal, the importance of increasing educational opportunities for our children is discussed. One essential step in this requires a strengthening of the private school movement, which includes evangelical, Roman Catholic, and Hebrew schools. This book addresses important changes that must be made in the way our teachers are trained. I examine the importance of litigation that will change the way our courts presently think of religion, values, and the schools, as well as the importance of changing the ways state and federal legislators approach the funding of education. I also offer advice both to families that want their children in public schools and the families that believe their children must attend private, religious schools. But you will not hear this book repeating the old nonsense that what education needs is more federal money. That issue doesn't even come close to being relevant.[2]

(5) Finally, I must identify the enemy. I don't like the word "enemy" and I hope my use of it doesn't alienate people who, while presently part of the problem, might be open to switching sides and becoming part of the solution. But when you're involved in a war—in this case, a war for the hearts, minds, and souls of our children—you can hardly help your cause by mistaking the enemy for a friend. In some cases, the "enemy" includes institutions or structures that have been set in place. In still other instances, the "enemy" includes specific people, sometimes acting alone, but often working together in organizations or networks of one kind or another.

Before I bring this preface to a close, some acknowledgments are necessary. The first acknowledgment must go to Steve Webb of Probe Books who kept pestering me to do this book until I finally acquiesced. Others at Probe who deserve thanks are Don Closson, Meisje Johntz Connor, Lou Whitworth, and Jimmy Williams. Second, a word of appreciation to Susan Gore and the interlibrary loan department at Western Kentucky University is long overdue. This is my twentieth book, and that department has played a helpful role in many of them. Much of the research for this book was done during June, July, and August of 1989 while I taught short summer school courses at Trinity Evangelical Divinity School, at Reformed Theological Seminary, and at the San Francisco extension of Fuller Theological Seminary. I owe a word of thanks to people like Walt Kaiser and Ken Kantzer at Trinity, Luder Whitlock and Richard Watson at Reformed, and to Art Patzia at Fuller for making our stay at their schools such a pleasant time. I also want to thank Tom and Kipp Gutshall for making their lovely California home available to us during my teaching stint in San Francisco. Finally, several readers deserve thanks: Mike Beidel, Dan Russ, and Rob Gustafson.

And one final word: During the busy summer of 1989, my father died. With his passing, I lost both a father and a friend. I dedicate this book to his memory.

At an early age I came to believe that the life of culture (that is, of intellectual and aesthetic activity) was very good for its own sake, or even that it was the good for man.

—C. S. Lewis, *Christian Reflections*

The Closing of the American Heart

Education at all levels in the United States has reached the crisis stage. Of course, the situation didn't arise yesterday; it has developed over a period of decades. Nor is the crisis news to people who have been paying attention to what's been going on in the country.

One event that helped bring the plight of American education to public attention was the 1983 publication of a report from the National Commission on Excellence in Education. The report carried the ominous title, "A Nation at Risk." The most widely quoted paragraph from the report warns that: "The educational foundations of our society are presently being eroded by a rising tide of mediocrity that threatens our very future as a nation and as a people." The report goes on to say, "If an unfriendly foreign power had attempted to impose on America the mediocre educational performance that exists today, we might well have viewed it as an act of war. As it stands, we have allowed this to happen to ourselves."

A number of people have raised their voices to report this crisis, to protest the conditions, people, and ideas that have created it, to warn about even more serious consequences ahead, and to identify the things that must be done to turn things around. Writing about American public schools, Samuel Blumenfeld has stated: "The plain, unvarnished truth is that public education is a shoddy, fraudulent piece of goods sold to the public at an astronomical price. It's time the American consumer knew the extent of the fraud which is victimizing millions of children each year."[1]

Critics of American colleges and universities have been just as direct. According to Charles J. Sykes, the modern American university is "distinguished by costs that are zooming out of control; curriculums that look like they were designed by a game show host; nonexistent advising programs; lectures of droning, mind-numbing dullness often to 1,000 or more semi-anonymous undergraduates herded into dilapidated, ill-lighted lecture halls; teaching assistants who can't speak understandable English; and the product of all this, a generation of expensively credentialed college graduates who might not be able to locate England on a map."[2]

"Behind its ivy-colored camouflage," another writer observes, "American higher education is a fraud—untrue to its students, untrue to itself. It has displaced moral truth with a melange of 'values,' and forsaken reason for the trivial pursuit of 'relevance.'"[3]

It is no longer possible to ignore the academic vacuum that exists at all levels of American education nor the social, cultural, and moral disorder that has accompanied this intellectual bankruptcy. One can find a number of studies that focus on such obvious matters as why high school students cannot read, write, or do basic math. Recently, however, an increasing number of studies have begun to examine what Joseph Baldacchino calls "the deeper and more philosophical questions about the nature and purpose of education in Western society."[4]

But even while some writers are probing these deeper and more fundamental issues, they are encountering opposition from groups who obviously care more about other things than the quality of education. "In place of qualitative and substantive issues," Baldacchino explains, "these groups—which enjoy great influence in the academy, the foundations, and the dominant news media—prefer to confine the discussion to the level of process, procedure, and quantity, while granting to the great 'whys' and 'wherefores' of education the shortest shrift."[5] What Baldacchino implies—and what many sources that will be noted later in this book confirm—is that our present plight in education was not some kind of accident for which no one is liable. It was not impersonal forces or structures that created this situation. At every stage, human beings—including educators, politicians, judges, and parents—made decisions that have brought us to our present crisis.

Allan Bloom's *The Closing of the American Mind*

No discussion of the education crisis has received more attention and stimulated more recent debate than Allan Bloom's best-selling 1987 book, *The Closing of the American Mind*. Sales of the book have long since passed the 750,000 mark.

The burden of Bloom's book is the claim that American civilization is threatened by the very people who control the education of its young. In his words, "[T]he crisis of liberal education is a reflection of a crisis at the peaks of learning, an incoherence and incompatibility among the first principles with which we interpret the world, an intellectual crisis of the greatest magnitude, which constitutes the crisis of our civilization."[6] As one of Bloom's reviewers explains, "Instead of being havens of independent thought, universities have become channels of indoctrination, inculcating attitudes regarded as respectable by the majority of American intellectuals and confirming the prejudices of those who control the agenda of public discourse."[7]

Bloom's specific indictments of higher education include the following: (1) American colleges have permitted their curricula to deteriorate. This can be seen in the watering down of essential courses. (2) Colleges have also allowed the removal of important courses or the addition of trivial courses to the core curriculum. (3) They have permitted the inflation of grades so that higher grades mean less and lower grades have become almost nonexistent. (4) They have opened wide the doors to trendy and faddish courses, such as courses in pop culture where students get university credit for looking at the pictures in comic books. (5) Our colleges now make it easy for students to ignore the difference between love and easy sex. (6) Academicians have let loose an avalanche of meaningless jargon within their academic disciplines. (7) A similar flood of meaningless language (for example, words like "lifestyle" and "commitment") in non-academic areas tends to camouflage the moral emptiness of the typical student's life. And finally, (8) university communities have become the fountainhead of the loss of taste in the arts and its replacement by a surrender to the vulgar.

College students are surrounded by an allegedly academic setting in which the things that they find most obvious are confusion, conflicting claims, and the absence of any fixed points of reference. Whereas students used to go to college in the hope of discovering wisdom and virtue, these have been replaced by colleges that seek to train them in socialization and sociability. College, Russell Kirk states, has become a boring means to job-certification. It is a "temporary sanctuary for the aimless and the neurotic . . . an alleged instrument for elevating the 'culturally deprived.'" The university world has become "an industry, employing hundreds of thousands of people at good salaries [that supplies] 'research' services to the state or to private industry, furnishing public entertainment through quasi-professional sports and other diversions."[8]

America's colleges and universities are centers of intellectual disorder. No longer will students find integration and ordering of knowledge; instead, all is in a state of flux. Other signs of this disorder include

the cafeteria-style curriculum, presently becoming the "open" curriculum; "discipline" reduced to a devil-term; the swelling empire of Educationism, formerly called pedagogy, with its frequent contempt for "subject matter"; the popularity of soft and often shallow "social science" degrees; the repudiation, by a growing number of professors and students, of the traditions of civility and of all concepts not born yesterday; the compartmentalizing of knowledge, leading at best to the development of elites unable to communicate one with another; the retreat of able or clever professors into "research," as distinguished from teaching; the substitution of ideological infatuation for the old philosophical habit of mind, particularly in the Sixties.[9]

All of this disorder at the university level is aided and supported by the equally bad state of affairs in the elementary and secondary grades. What Kirk calls "the enfeeblement of primary and second schooling" means that "the typical freshman [enters] college wretchedly prepared for the abstractions with which college and university necessarily are concerned."[10] And so, Kirk concludes,

[T]oday's college has something for everybody—except for those students who still sense that the higher learning ought to be concerned with wisdom and virtue, and for those professors who obdurately profess, despite the intellectual promiscuity of the time, their belief in some coherent body of knowledge. Funds and energies are squandered upon those students (or inmates, rather) and those programs which show the most slender promise. In our time, we have seen the speedy degeneration of the higher learning into aimless sociability on the one hand, and into anti-intellectual ideology on the other.[11]

What is the point to Bloom's title, *The Closing of the American Mind?* Bloom approaches his subject by noting, in the very first paragraph of his book, the uncritical and easy way in which today's students accept relativism:

There is one thing a professor can be absolutely certain of: almost every student entering the university believes, or says he believes, that truth is relative. If this belief is put to the test, one can count on the students' reaction: they will be uncomprehending. That anyone should regard the proposition [affirming relativism] as not self-evident astonishes them, as though he were calling into question $2 + 2 = 4$. [12]

Bloom goes on to note that students today believe somehow that this kind of relativism is inseparably linked to tolerance and an open mind. After all, who wants to approach life with a *closed* mind? A closed mind is even less suitable when it belongs to a college student, is it not? And so, Bloom explains: "Relativism is necessary to openness; and this is the virtue, the only virtue, which all primary education for more than fifty years has dedicated itself to inculcating."[13] Every college student wants to believe that her mind is open, not closed. This kind of openness and the relativism upon which students think openness is grounded is one thing—and perhaps the only thing—that some of them pick up in college. Today's students have come to believe that "The true believer is the real danger. . . . The point is not to correct the mistakes [of the past] and really be right; rather it is not to think you are right at all."[14]

When challenged, today's students are unable to defend their relativism. Their commitment to "openness," Bloom explains, is a product of indoctrination. "The best they can do is point out all the opinions and cultures there are and have been. What right, they ask, do I or anyone else have to say one is better than the others?"[15] The major virtue—perhaps the *only* virtue—their indoctrinators (otherwise known as teachers) wish them to acquire is openness.

But this alleged openness is not openness at all. Instead of opening the American mind, this set of cleverly and attractively packaged opinions has effectively *closed* the American mind. Relativism extinguishes "the real motive of education, the search for a good life."[16] Openness actually produces a shallow conformism since it leads students to believe that "out there in the rest of the world is a drab diversity that teaches only that values are relative, whereas here we can create all the life-styles we want. Our openness means we do not need others. Thus what is advertised as a great opening is a great closing. No longer is there a hope that there are great wise men in other places and times who can reveal the truth about life."[17]

Bloom is arguing, then, that there are really two kinds of openness, what we might call True and False Openness. The false type of openness follows from the kind of relativism already described; it is promoted, Bloom says, "with the twin purposes of humbling our intellectual pride and letting us be whatever we want to be, just as long as we don't want to be knowers."[18] A true openness, on the other hand, "invites us to the quest for knowledge and certitude, for which history and the various cultures provide a brilliant array of examples for examination."[19] True openness is a virtue that allows and encourages us to use our reason in pursuit of the good. False openness leads its followers to deny the power of reason and accept virtually anything. And so the relativism that grounds so much that passes as education these days only appears to produce open minds; its real consequence is the closed mind referred to in the title of Bloom's book.

Some of the more interesting criticisms of Bloom's book have come from conservatives. This fact surprises many people since the book had been widely perceived as a conservative work. But, some conservatives think, this is one of those times when appearances can be deceiving.

One conservative critic who has warned of the inadequacies of Bloom's argument is Donald J. Devine, who puts his point this way:

> Americans, especially today's students, enter college without firm ideas based on their upbringing. They are open to all beliefs openly. What they should do (according to Bloom) is come to college with the traditional beliefs and myths earlier generations of students used to bring with them. They should then spend their lives studying philosophy and only then end up like real philosophers (presumably like Allan Bloom): rejecting their prejudices and concluding like Socrates, that they do not know anything—that there is not any truth, except that you cannot know anything. Bloom has an unlikely thesis because he asks students to go though a great amount of onerous study to arrive at a relativism towards truth he believes they already hold. If one accepts Bloom's view of knowledge, do not American college students already have the wisdom of Socrates? They know nothing. So why go through the bother?[20]

Charles Kesler, another critic, makes much the same point when he complains that "Bloom objects to American nihilism not because it is immoral, but because it is thoughtless; and he does so without giving any account of whether a thoughtful morality exists or in what it might consist."[21] Many conservatives and Christians alike seem to have misread Bloom because they've made a very simple error. They have noted that Bloom seems to be an enemy of some of their enemies. They then jump to the conclusion that anyone who's an enemy of my enemies must be on my side. Since Bloom is a critic of a certain kind of relativism, they reason, that must mean Bloom is an absolutist. But contemporary academicians, Bloom included, seldom operate in terms of such an elementary either-or mentality.

The German philosopher Hegel talked a lot about "the Absolute," but was really a relativist. Another German thinker, Friedrich Nietzsche, attacked "nihilism" (a philosophy that denies any validity to value judgments), but then offered his own relativistic alternative to the "absolutism" of the past. Bloom appears to be much more at home in the camp of such neo-relativists than in an intellectual world where there really are objective and unchanging standards of truth and goodness.

Much of the confusion about Bloom's book results from the fact that it is really two different books that are joined in a rather strained and artificial manner. Most people seem to have read only the first 137 pages, the section that contains the argument about how modern educators have brought about the closing of the American mind. But after this first section, Bloom embarks on a highly eccentric reading of Western thought designed to support some theories he has about the influence of German thinking upon American universities. It can easily look as though he combined one manuscript (part one) that he wrote for a more general audience with some other manuscripts in which he plays around with some exotic theories about some of his favorite philosophers. As Joseph Baldacchino explains, the message in the last 250 pages of the book is less than inspiring:

> When one cuts through the book's dense rhetorical fog, the burden of Bloom's position is that love of country is beneath serious philosophers since what differentiates countries is "convention," not "nature" or true reality; that religion is mere "superstition" and wholly inimical to any genuine search for truth; and that aristocratic institutions or customs, which traditionally accorded considerable significance to a person's family and related duties and station, have been exposed by Enlightenment thinkers as inherently "unjust" and, thanks to those thinkers' salutary influence, play little role in contemporary society. As for "ideas of civilization" and "sentimental and historical forces," Bloom dismisses them as largely mythical (i.e., untrue) or arbitrary, hence undeserving of influence on discerning individuals.[22]

Bloom appears to side with Plato and Aristotle when he identifies reason as the highest part of a human being and when he states that the search for the Good is the real reason for philosophy. But, Baldacchino warns, the similarity is deceptive since Bloom gives terms like "reason" and "good" new meanings that put his position at odds with Plato and Aristotle.

> Thus, for Plato and Aristotle, reason meant reflection on or contemplation of the universal good. To be able to contemplate the good was the highest activity, the

crowning achievement, of man. But before man could be ready to philosophize, he first had to embody in his character the virtues of "aristocracy," by which was meant not titled nobility but the qualitatively best life. . . . It was this preoccupation of the Greek philosophers with the ethical and their sense that the ethical for man has its source in the transcendent that became assimilated to Christianity and helped in large measure to shape the development of Western civilization and culture.[23]

Hence, what Bloom's book really does is to sever the classical tie between reason and ethical virtue. When Bloom uses the word "reason," he does not mean it in Plato's sense of a reason that has an essential ethical dimension (wisdom). And so, Baldacchino notes, Bloom "misses or distorts the heart and soul of [Plato's and Aristotle's] teaching, which, as it concerns how men should live, is ethical. Whether this is intentional or not, it is hard to say."[24] But one thing is clear to Baldacchino; Bloom's book is not the conservative treatise many have taken it to be. "At best," he writes, *The Closing of the American Mind* is a confused book. At worst, it is deliberately subversive, intended to undermine some of the strongest pillars of Western civilization."[25]

If these critics of Bloom are correct, we would be rash to assume that Bloom himself has done much more than point out ways in which other representatives of higher education have helped produce a closing of the American mind. It is ironic, these critics suggest, that Bloom is playing his own role in the crisis.

Forgetting for the moment whether Bloom's own position is really superior to the relativism and false openness he critiques, it is also necessary to examine his major recommendation to improve American education. What is it and will it do the job?

After all the dust has settled, Bloom has but one recommendation to make by way of improving higher education in America. He writes,

Of course, the only serious solution is the one that is almost universally rejected: the good old Great Books approach, in which a liberal education means reading certain generally recognized classic texts, just reading them, letting them dictate what the questions are and the method of approaching them—not forcing them into categories we make up, not treating them as historical products, but trying to read them as their authors wished them to be read.[26]

Is this really all that Bloom has to offer? At this point, many of Bloom's critics find themselves agreeing with Charles Kesler when he writes: "For all his talk of facing up to hard choices, Bloom never makes explicit just what is at stake educationally and politically."[27]

The problem is not that there is anything wrong with having students read the Great Books. They have a deserved place in the experience of anyone who wants to be counted among the truly educated. The problem is that people need some kind of comprehensive, overarching philosophy to guide them through the maze of conflicting ideas. The wise educator will not simply turn unprepared students loose among the Great Books; she will provide the student with a map or guide.

One condition of being an educated person is that he or she have a single, unified world and life view, something not to be found in the Great Books. As philosopher Gordon Clark once put it, "[I]f someone wishes to unify education, it is not enough to say that a philosophical base is necessary. To accomplish such a result, it is essential to provide the philosophy."[28] What distinguishes a Christian in all this is the recognition that "there is only one philosophy that can really unify education and life. That philosophy is the philosophy of Christian theism."[29]

John Robbins compares Allan Bloom to a doctor "who diagnoses the disease but never prescribes a cure." Or, even worse, Bloom is like a doctor who "prescribes a treatment that will exacerbate, not meliorate, the disease."[30] It is one thing to tell the patient he's sick. The more important and more difficult task is to tell the patient how to get better. But in order to do that, "what is needed is a comprehensive unifying philosophy of education, and [Bloom] offers none. Could anything speak more eloquently of the intellectual bankruptcy of humanism than this?"[31]

People concerned about the serious decline in American education at every level can thank Bloom and his book for helping to raise the level of consciousness, to some degree at least. But it does appear that those interested in solutions for that problem will have to look elsewhere.

The Closing of the American Heart

Some writers have drawn attention to what they call the religious roots of human theoretical thought. According to such writers, human thoughts and actions have religious roots related to the human heart, the center or religious root of our being.[32] Human beings are never neutral with regard to God. Either we worship God as Creator and Lord, or we turn away from Him.[33] Because the heart is directed either toward God or against God, theoretical thinking is never as pure or autonomous as many would like to think. It seems clear then that some people who appear to reject Christianity on rational or theoretical grounds are, in fact, acting under the influence of nonrational factors, that is, more ultimate commitments of their hearts. The arguments they want the rest of us to think were the grounds of their unbelief are in fact simply an exercise in self-justification. The unbelief came first; then came the arguments.[34]

Much of this book will examine the manifold ways in which various individuals and movements have sought to remove matters of the heart (belief in God, in the doctrinal and moral content of Christianity, in the importance of other values) from education. I want the reader to consider that the grounds for this elimination of the matters of the heart from education is often a consequence of religious commitments.

Every so often, some reformer may speak about the importance of higher standards in education. But even when they do, Joseph Baldacchino points out, they say "virtually nothing about the concrete shape those standards should take or the criteria upon which they should be based. Instead, nearly exclusive attention is devoted to quantitative and procedural matters, such as proposals for raising teachers' salaries, giving teachers greater control of school administration, and relieving them of routine chores through heavier reliance on technology and paid aides or assistants."[35] In other words, there is absolutely no recognition of the real causes of educational decline. At the same time, other groups attempt to alter the content of traditional education, either by diluting it or changing it in ways that cut out the core of traditional learning and replace it with a radical content.

One of this book's major contentions is that America's educational crisis is not exclusively a crisis of the mind. As the title of Bloom's best-seller suggests, our educational crisis represents to some extent a closing of the American mind. But it also represents something more profound, a closing of the American heart. People in control of education have, to be sure, stripped away important content, leaving many of our students functionally and culturally illiterate. But in an even more sinister way, ideologues committed to their own secular, humanistic agenda have succeeded in cutting traditional moral and religious values from what our students learn while cleverly making it appear that the substitute (which is really simply a different religion) is a neutral alternative. Like Allan Bloom, I want my readers to understand that there has been a closing of the American mind; I also want them to understand why. But it is important to go beyond what Bloom and others have said and realize that something else, something equally fundamental, has also occurred, namely, a closing of the American heart. No real progress towards improving American education can occur until all concerned realize that an education that ignores moral and religious values cannot qualify as a quality education.

Bloom does talk about how modern education has "impoverished the souls of today's students," as his book's subtitle indicates. Unfortunately he never makes any connection between the soul and the mind, nor does he explain what moral values should feed the soul (again, diagnosing the problem, but failing to clearly state the cure).

The ancient Greeks recognized that excellence is not intellectual alone. The good man or woman is the well-rounded individual, sound of mind, strong in body, and healthy in spirit. A good education will be concerned with the whole human being, and this requires that something be said about moral and spiritual values.

It was Aristotle who pointed out that the worst human being is not the evil individual who lacks knowledge. However evil this person may be, he is too stupid to do much harm. The person who concerned Aristotle more was "the astute rascal," the individual who had all the practical knowledge to achieve what he wanted but lacked the moral character to seek the right ends. Contemporary American education almost appears designed to produce precisely this kind of human being.

Socrates and Plato warned against the inadequacies of an education that only taught people how to select the best means to achieve their ends or goals. It was far more important, they thought, that humans come to recognize the importance of selecting the right ends. But the subject of right ends, good ends, noble ends, is precisely what contemporary American education seeks to avoid. The educational enemies of Socrates and Plato were called Sophists. What Americans have done for too long now is turn the control of their educational systems over to twentieth-century Sophists.

Bloom is correct when he challenges the processes and people who have brought about a closing of the American mind. But this is only a small part of the problem. The Sophists of our age have also severed the link between reason and virtue, between the mind and the heart. There is objective truth "out there," which it is our duty to pursue and discover. But there is also an objective moral order "out there," as well as "in here," within the structure of each human consciousness. An adequate education will, to be sure, seek to bring about a new, a true openness with respect to truth. But it will also seek to bring about an end to the processes that have produced a closing of the American heart. The question of values, standards and norms must once again be given center stage in the educational process.

CHAPTER

2

I know that we live in an age where the homely or psychological detail is considered all-important. We like heroes in shirtsleeves, or, in other words, we don't like heroes. But things were not always that way, and today is not forever.

—Louis Auchincloss

Reason and Virtue

Modern education in the United States has largely separated virtue and knowledge. But things have not always been this way; nor should they be now. One necessary condition of America's being delivered from its present educational crisis is a recovery of the belief that there is a transcendent, universal moral order. This moral order must once again be restored to a central place in our schools. "To apprehend this reality," Joseph Baldacchino writes, "and to act in the light of the transcendent purposes with appropriate reverence and restraint, is the essence of wisdom; and to help deepen and strengthen this apprehension—through philosophy, history, literature, and the arts and sciences—is the overarching purpose of any education worthy of the name."[1]

One supporter of this view earlier in the twentieth century was the Harvard professor and author, Irving Babbitt. Baldacchino explains that Babbitt believed that "teachers—if they are doing their job correctly—form the great link in the chain of civilization without which it cannot hold. They are both the conservators and the transmitters of culture. It is from them that future generations come to appreciate the ideals of their country and the wider civilization of which it is a part: justice, for example, and equality, and ordered liberty."[2] While modern teachers, judges and politicians seek to separate virtue and knowledge, a growing number of people agree with Babbitt and others like him that "the development of the intellect and moral character are intimately related."[3]

Russell Kirk, a well-known representative of Babbitt's position, explains that for Babbitt, "the great end of education is ethical. In the college, as at all other levels of the educational process, the student comes to apprehend the differences between good and evil. It is this humane tradition and discipline which makes us true human persons and sustains a decent civil social order."[4]

The transcendent order of what T. S. Eliot called "the permanent things" includes "the body of knowledge not undone by modern winds of doctrine or by modern technology." The Ten Commandments and the moral precepts of the New Testament are examples of these permanent things. So too is any transcendent truth. "The truths of the fifth century before Christ, or of the first century of the Christian era, possess as much meaning today as they did many centuries ago."[5] It is these "permanent things," Kirk insists, that are the proper objects of study in what is termed "the higher learning."

Just as there is an order in nature (the laws of nature), in reason (the laws of logic), and in the realm of numbers (the laws of mathematics), so too is there a moral order. Baldacchino describes its importance:

> Insofar as men act in accordance with this [transcendent moral] order, they experience true happiness and are brought into community with others who are similarly motivated. But men are afflicted with contrary impulses that are destructive of universal order. When acted upon, these impulses bring suffering and a sense of meaninglessness and despair; the result is disintegration and conflict—within both the personality and society at large. Yet so tempting are the attractions of these impulses—to yield is effortless and the payoffs in terms of short-term pleasure and ego gratification are alluring—that they frequently prevail and must be taken into account in any realistic assessment of human affairs.[6]

Baldacchino is describing what every student of Plato or Augustine or C. S. Lewis is familiar with. When any individual or collection of individuals acts in disobedience to the moral order, short-term gratification may be experienced; but such behavior produces an inevitable deterioration of the personality and leads to a long term loss of what is truly worthy. And when this occurs, as it must, there cannot help but be a loss of happiness (understood in Aristotle's sense as well-being or the good life).

And so, we have seen, important thinkers throughout history have contended that there is a higher order of permanent things, that human happiness is dependent on living our lives in accordance with this transcendent order, and that peace and order within human society requires similar conduct.[7] And, to underscore the point most relevant to this book, *the most important task of education is to continually remind students of the importance of this transcendent order and of its content.*

It is not difficult to find an assortment of people who give lip service to this moral order. Too often, however, a more careful analysis reveals that the apparent friends of the permanent things are not friends at all. One recent book that represents this circle of scholars is *Habits of the Heart: Individualism and Commitment in American Life* by Robert Bellah and others.[8]

Some of Bellah's criticisms of American society have value. But much of this material is also rather banal and trite; the authors describe things we have known about for years. One reviewer of the book, Wilfred McClay, complains that what we need "is not yet another repetition of stale formulae, but a sense of what is to be done." McClay's point is reminiscent of criticisms of Allan Bloom's failure to recommend positive steps to improve American education. "On that score," McClay continues, "Bellah's book hardly begins even to address the problem, relying instead on the incantation of abstractions that remain conveniently disembodied and unexplained."[9] McClay pursues this weakness still further by writing:

> One would think that a book dedicated to a revival of public morals and communal values would have something to say about some of the pressing moral issues of our time, particularly those—such as abortion, divorce, adultery, homosexuality, and pornography—which bear upon sexuality, that most intimate point of intersection between the public and the private, the communal and the individual. But *Habits of the Heart* does not, for the simple reason that, for all of its authors' putative commitment to a post-liberal moral vision, they would

never dream of being caught taking an illiberal position on such questions.[10]

In other words, the authors have no desire to jeopardize their
standing among their liberal peers by appearing to take a position
on any moral issue that would make them seem somehow less
than liberal. And so they waffle or remain silent on any issue that
might earn them disapproval from the Left. As McClay notes:

> The book repeatedly dwells on the need to recover a
> "framework of values," upon which we all can agree
> and upon which we can build a rich and renewed
> social life together. But these values remain conve-
> niently unspecified, for the authors clearly did not
> want to ruffle anybody's feathers or challenge any-
> body's sensibilities [although they are quick to fault
> the "unreflective" rigidity of evangelical Christians].
> Thus, their call for moral revival is little more than
> empty posturing and vague uplift, reminiscent of
> Norman Vincent Peale or Bruce Barton, with some
> Walter Rauschenbusch thrown in for good measure.[11]

A growing number of evangelical academicians have endorsed
Bellah's book uncritically. They want to be accepted by their
liberal peers, and probably for good reasons like maintaining a
good testimony to the secular community, and keeping the dialogue flowing between scholars of different traditions. But this
does not excuse their uncritical acceptance of books like Bellah's,
and it does not inspire much confidence in their judgment.
Fortunately, the nonevangelical McClay displays sounder judgment in this case by showing clearly what the basic flaw of the
Bellah book is:

> The book calls for a return to our "republican" and
> "Biblical" traditions, to counterbalance the danger-
> ously amoral, selfish, radical-individualist tendencies
> of unrestrained liberalism. . . . [However] it gradually
> emerges that Bellah and Co. do not really want to
> revive these traditions as they actually existed. He
> wants them *mutatis mutandis*, purged of any elements
> that might run contrary to the conventional liberal
> political agenda. He wants us to avail ourselves of
> them piecemeal, picking and choosing what parts are

appropriate to the 1980s and what parts are not, re-making the tradition as we feel necessary. . . . Bellah wants all the benefits of these traditions without paying the price for them. He wants to have strong moral values without the taint of discipline or intolerance, strong communal values without insularity, strong commit-ments without punishments for those who disdain them, national pride without patriotism, and so on.[12]

"But," McClay concludes, "this wish list is composed of in-substantial word-combinations, the fond pipedreams of tender-minded academics. They have no relationship to reality, no precedent in history."[13] Books like Bellah's *Habits of the Heart* deserve more probing, critical analysis from evangelical scholars and less uncritical adulation. For although such dialogue be-tween evangelicals and thinkers from other traditions (Bellah is reported to be a devout Catholic) is admirable, its pursuit cannot be effective if the evangelicals disenfranchise their own position and heritage in the process.

Education's Inescapable Component

It is now time to add another factor to the equation we're working with. I have sided with those who argue for the in-separability of knowledge and virtue, who insist that transcen-dent norms and standards are an essential part of any quality education. I now wish to go further and maintain that education, like any important human activity, has an inescapable *religious* component.

Religious faith is not just one isolated compartment of a per-son's life—a compartment that we can take or leave as we wish. It is rather a dimension of life that colors or influences everything we do and believe. John Calvin taught that all human beings are "incurably religious." Religion is an inescapable given in life. Whatever we may think of other things he said, Paul Tillich was right when he defined religion as a matter of "ultimate concern." Obviously religion is more than this, but it cannot be less. Every person has something that concerns her ultimately and whatever it is, that object of ultimate concern is that person's God. What-ever a person's *ultimate* concern may be, it will have an enormous influence on everything else the person does or believes; that, after all, is one of the things *ultimate* concerns are like.

The human activities we group under the heading of educa-tion cannot help but reflect the influence of our ultimate or religious concerns. As Rockne McCarthy and his team of writers state, "At bottom all public policy is shaped by some 'ultimate concern'.... The dichotomy between the private as religious and the public as secular therefore draws through life a wholly arbitrary and unreal line of demarcation. The public affairs of society and the state, including its governmental schools, are not less religiously qualified than the so-called private affairs of personal, church, home, and non-governmental school life."[14]

This view was shared by the late Henry Zylstra who pointed out its implications for education:

> The fact is that education is a human affair. It represents a human awareness of reality and a human appropria-tion of it. And this is a further fact; whatever is human is religious. ... To be human is to be scientific, yes, and practical, and rational, and moral, and social, and artis-tic, but to be human further is to be religious also. And this religious in man is not just another facet of himself, just another side to his nature, just another part of the whole. It is the condition of all the rest and the justifica-tion of all the rest. This is inevitably and inescapably so for all men. No man is religiously neutral in his knowl-edge of and his appropriation of reality.[15]

No man is religiously neutral, Zylstra states. This is a sentence worth repeating, worth pondering. Whether the person in ques-tion is an atheistic philosopher offering arguments against the existence of God, or a psychologist attributing belief in God to some cognitive malfunction, or an ACLU lawyer attempting another tactic to remove religion from the public square, no human is religiously neutral. The world is not composed of religious and non-religious people. It is composed rather of religious people who have differing ultimate concerns, different gods, and who respond to the Living God in different ways. Each human life manifests different ways of expressing our allegiances and our answers to the ultimate questions of life. All humans are incur-ably religious; we simply manifest *different* religious allegiances.

It is absurd, then, to think that the choice in public education is between sacred and secular. Whatever choice the state makes under the current modes of thinking will only establish one person's set of ultimate concerns at the expense of others. An education that pretends to be religiously neutral is a fraud. Secular Humanism, as we should all know by now, is a *religious* world view as certainly as Christianity and Judaism. It expresses the ultimate commitments and concerns of its proponents.

One of the challenges of Christian education at all levels is bringing Christians to see the implications of all this. Zylstra hinted at his own frustration in this regard when he wrote:

> It is so easy in the name of Christianity to turn one's back to art, to science, to politics, to social problems, to historical tensions and pressures, in one word, to culture, if you will. But once the conviction seizes on you that these all, precisely because they are cultural realities, exhibit a religious allegiance and ultimate loyalty, that none of them is neutral but rather that all of them are faith-founded, all laid on an altar, all dedicated to a god, then you realize that they are at the very least important. Then you realize, too, that the true discernment of the God behind the culture, the assumption underlying the thought, the dogma beneath the action, the soul in the body of the thing, are precisely what it is the business of our schools as schools to disclose and to judge. In that lies the strengthening of the moral sinews of our young Christians.[16]

Any putative education that strips the religious element out of its subject matter is a travesty, a perversion of the word "education." When religion is removed from history, what is left is a distortion of the historical record. And yet this is precisely what most textbook publishers have done in an effort to enhance their sales. Whenever this kind of censorship is practiced, education ceases to be education and becomes something else, something dark, sinister, incomplete, and subhuman. And the textbook committees and the publishers who become participants in this act of censorship must be viewed as traitors to their culture.[17]

But now something else must be recognized. The question of moral and religious values must be broadened to include the larger issues of world views. One Christian writer who spent more than thirty years trying to get others to see this was Francis Schaeffer. According to Schaeffer, "The basic problem of the Christians in this country in the last eighty years or so, in regard to society and in regard to government [and we might add, in regard to education], is that they have seen things in bits and pieces instead of totals."[18] Schaeffer explains how this inability to see the larger picture weakens Christian efforts to combat social evils. Christians, he writes,

> have very gradually become disturbed over permissiveness, pornography, the public schools, the breakdown of the family, and finally abortion. But they have not seen this as a totality—each thing being a part, a symptom of a much larger problem. They have failed to see that all of this has come about due to a shift in the world view—that is, through a fundamental change in the overall way people think and view the world and life as a whole. This shift has been *away* from a world view that was at least vaguely Christian in people's memory (even if they were not individually Christian) *toward* something completely different— toward a world view based upon the idea that the final reality is impersonal matter or energy shaped into its present form by impersonal chance. They have not seen that this world view has taken the place of the one that had previously dominated Northern European culture, including the United States, which was at least Christian in memory, even if the individuals were not individually Christian.[19]

There are several reasons this has happened. First, Christians as a whole don't pay much attention to philosophy. This inattention to the important matters of the mind is often a product of a persistent streak of Pietism and anti-intellectualism in their past. Second, thinking in holistic terms, in terms of world views, is difficult. It requires effort, and often means that Christians will have to read serious books and then *think* about what they've read. Up to now, it appears this has been too much to ask of many Christians. All of this is unfortunate. Among other things, it means that evangelical Christians often allow the enemy to win by default; either the Christian doesn't show up or, when he does, he shows up improperly prepared.

Each human being has a world view. These world views function like eyeglasses; they are interpretive conceptual schemes that explain why we "see" the world as we do, why we think and act as we do. World views are double-edged swords. An inadequate world view (or conceptual scheme) can, like poorly prescribed eyeglasses, hinder our efforts to understand God, the world, and ourselves. The right world view can suddenly bring everything into proper focus.

A world view is a set of beliefs about life's most important questions. Examples of these questions include: Is there a God? What is God like? Did God create the world or is the world eternal? Is God in control of the world or is everything that exists part of a huge, impersonal, cosmic machine in which everything that happens is predetermined by laws and conditions over which God has no control? Are there universal, transcendent moral laws? Because so many elements of a world view are philosophical in nature, Christians need to become more conscious of the importance of philosophy. Though philosophy and religion often use different language and often arrive at different conclusions, they deal with the same questions, which include questions about what exists (metaphysics), how humans should live (ethics), how they think (logic), and how they come to know (epistemology). Philosophy matters because the Christian world view has an intrinsic connection to philosophy and the world of ideas. It matters because philosophy is related in a critically important way to life, to culture, and to religion. And it matters because the systems opposing Christianity use philosophical methods and arguments.

Earlier I stated that it is impossible to separate education from a human being's ultimate concern (religion). It is just as important to recognize that it is also impossible to separate one's view of education from his or her world view. A teacher's world view, for example, influences her educational philosophy which influences her educational policy which in turn influences her educational practice. One's philosophy of education will always be a reflection of a more general world and life view.

A Christian philosophy of education is based unapologetically upon a Christian view of life and the world. A Christian philosophy of education recognizes that all human knowledge is distorted and fragmented. It knows that education is never neutral; its ultimate dependence on philosophical and religious presuppositions is a fact of life. What sets a truly Christian education apart is the Christian's acceptance of the biblical perspective (that is, the framework of convictions found in Scripture) as normative and authoritative.

While the Bible does not teach physics or astronomy, it does provide a structure for human thought, a perspective on reality. The biblical perspective can, among other things, inform us of the limitations and proper aims of theoretical inquiry. For example, it tells us that the pursuit of knowledge, while important, is not the sum total of human life. The biblical perspective also provides a basis on which we may evaluate the non-Christian presuppositions and conceptual schemes often operative in the various disciplines. For example, the view of some sociologists and psychologists that human evil is exclusively a result of defective conditions within human society is unacceptable to people who accept the biblical perspective.

A Christian philosophy of education is also grounded on a particular view of the Christian's faith and life. The Christian life is a response of one person to the activity of another person, God. The activity of God is revealed through the structure of creation and through the events of salvation-history, the latter including the revelation of God in Scripture.

Another foundation of this philosophy of education is a view of the Christian community. The Christian does not exercise her faith in an exclusively private way, in a way that seeks total isolation from others. Her faith is fulfilled in communion and association with others. Within this community of believers, no vocation is more important than any other. All vocations make their contribution to the development of a Christian culture. Every vocation is a calling from God. Therefore, Christian higher education must be seen as a project of the Christian community through which its youth are prepared to assume their places as mature members of the community, each one aiding the community to perform its purpose on earth. Whatever the Christian community needs in order to fulfill its program should be a goal of Christian education.

The Christian community's relation to its society is also important. There are two tendencies Christians should avoid in their relations with society: withdrawal and accommodation. Christians are not to flee the society in which they find themselves and set up a separate society. They are to exercise their faith within society. There is much that the Christian can learn from non-Christians. While she may have to place what she thus learns in a new framework or context, she can still learn.

But neither should the Christian accept uncritically every element of non-Christian society. Paul's words in Romans 12:1–2 apply here: "Be not conformed . . . but be ye transformed." Thus Christian education must serve the Christian community at the same time it seeks to achieve Christian goals in the midst of society. Its aim: to prepare the student to live out her faith in the surrounding society. This requires that the student understand society and learn to criticize it. Christian higher education must equip her to perform both tasks.

According to Michael Peterson, "The starting point for a Christian philosophy of education is the innate human tendency to seek understanding. This divinely created tendency finds sophisticated corporate expression in formal education. . . . [T]he school can be interpreted as a divinely ordained, human institution" designed to meet the needs of the human desire to know.[20]

Peterson also sees important implications for education in the Christian doctrine of creation. For one thing, the doctrine of creation implies that the world God created is real. This contrasts with some Asian world views that regard all of reality as an illusion. The reality of the world means not merely that it exists but that there is something there for us to investigate and know. The second thing that follows from the doctrine of creation is that the world is intelligible; it can be known. "Since nature is a creature of a supremely creative mind, it is open to rational investigation by finite minds."[21] Finally, the doctrine of creation implies that God's creation is good. Hence, Christian education approaches its subject matter in disagreement with other systems that view the world as illusory, unintelligible, or evil.

A Christian philosophy of education also contains a theory of knowledge. In this case, Peterson explains:

> A complete Christian view of knowledge recognizes that reality is complex and that each of its domains must be known on its own terms. There is no single way to discover all the different truths there are. We must discover empirical truths through observation and experiment, historical truths through records and artifacts, logical and mathematical truths by abstract reasoning, and so forth. Christians have no shortcuts

in these areas, but share the same basic noetic capabilities as other humans.[22]

Peterson ends his discussion with a ringing endorsement of the Christian world view and the essential grounding it provides for a Christian philosophy of education. "What Christians have," he writes, "is a world view which gives truth an appropriate residence. Christian theism affirms that the world is real and that there can be a genuine knowledge of it. Since there is such a thing as truth, one of the deepest longings of our being can be satisfied. . . . Moreover there is a Christological center for knowledge. . . . the very heart of reality is rational, and that all other knowledge takes on proper perspective through relationship to Christ."[23]

When the Christian encounters people who argue that education should be free of any religious content, she should recognize that this is not a religiously neutral claim. Rather, it is an assertion that reflects the religious commitments of the person making it. Education is an activity which is at its root religious, since like all meaningful human activities, it reflects the ultimate commitments of the person engaged in the activity. There is no such thing as removing religion from education; any attempt that claims to be such is merely a substitution of one set of ultimate commitments for another. Efforts to remove the Christian faith from subjects like American history distort the content of the subject. Just as wrong is the idea that an evangelical textbook publisher should make it appear that evangelicals played a major role at every point in the history of the U.S. All such efforts are a travesty of history. And finally, this chapter has argued, education has an indispensable link to moral considerations. The rescue of American education therefore requires more than a reopening of the American mind; equally important—perhaps even more important because of the essential link between knowledge and virtue—is an all-out effort to reopen the American heart, an effort that will once again return moral and religious values to their rightful place at the heart of the educational process. To whatever extent it is possible, this restoration of values should be attempted in the case of the public schools of the land. But while that effort is continued, Americans should support the private schools of this nation that recognize the importance of both mind and heart, of both knowledge and virtue.[24]

Educationists are entertaining. We can always find a good laugh in their prose, with its special, ludicrous combination of ignorance and pretentiousness. It's always amusing to watch them reinventing the wheel every few years and announcing ... that children who know the sounds of letters can actually read words they've never seen before, by golly.

—Richard Mitchell, *The Graves of Academe*

Three Kinds of Illiteracy

America's educational crisis is manifested in three levels of illiteracy: functional illiteracy, cultural illiteracy, and moral illiteracy. This chapter's examination of illiteracy uses the word in a broader sense than is usually the case. Typically, to say that a person is illiterate means that the person cannot read or write. But the word does have other senses. It is sometimes used of someone who is ignorant of the fundamentals of a particular art or area of knowledge. It is this broader meaning that is in view when, for example, we say that a person is musically illiterate. The word can also be used to describe a person who falls short of some expected standard of competence regarding some skill or body of information. In this last sense, a person who falls short of our commonly expected standard of competence in mathematics can be described as illiterate, even if he or she is quite competent in language skills.

Functional Illiteracy

To be functionally illiterate is to fall short of what we typically regard as the minimal level of competence with regard to such basic functions as reading, writing, and mathematics.

According to Samuel Blumenfeld, America's "public schools are falling apart and academic standards are at their lowest. At least a million students emerge from high school each year as functional illiterates thanks to the educational malpractice rampant in American public schools."[1] A recent issue of *Time* reports that 13 percent of American seventeen-year-olds are functionally illiterate. *Time's* estimate for minority seventeen-year-olds is 40 percent.[2] The United States Department of Education estimates that our educational system has left us with 24 million functionally illiterate people. These are not people who never went to school; they are for the most part, individuals who have spent eight to twelve years in public schools.

Writing in the monthly *Commentary*, Chester E. Finn, Jr., a professor at Vanderbilt University, cites the dismal findings of the National Assessment of Education Progress. "Just five percent of seventeen-year-old high school students can read well enough to understand and use information found in technical materials, literary essays, and historical documents."[3] Imagine then how hopeless it is to get the other 95 percent to read Plato or Dante—or the Bible. "Barely 6 percent of them," Finn continues, "can solve multi-step math problems and use basic algebra."[4] We're not talking difficult math here but rather something as elementary as calculating simple interest on a loan.

Clearly incompetence of this magnitude is not the result of accident. There must be forces, structures, ideologies, and above all, people who are responsible for this kind of disaster. And indeed there are; in later chapters, I will identify some of them. Tragically, they include the same people and institutions and movements that continue to receive billions of dollars of taxpayer's money to support the same kinds of educational malfeasance that produced our present crisis.

Finn goes on to cite a recent report from the Southern Regional Educational Board to the effect that 30 percent of the colleges and universities in the fifteen-state region that was surveyed report that at least 50 percent of their new students are academically unprepared for college. Sixty percent of the responding schools report that at least one-third of their freshmen require remedial work, a fact that implies they should never have been graduated from high school. According to a 1987 survey of New Jersey state colleges and universities, 73 percent of all entering freshmen were *not* proficient in verbal skills while 69 percent fell short of minimal standards in computation.

While he uttered the words several years ago, Karl Shapiro, a respected poet-philosopher at the University of California, Davis, described a situation that has only gotten worse. In his words, "What is really distressing is that this generation cannot and does not read. I am speaking of university students in what are supposed to be our best universities. Their illiteracy is staggering.... We are experiencing a literacy breakdown which is unlike anything I know of in the history of letters."[5]

Eighty years ago, in 1910, only 2.2 percent of American children between the ages of ten and fourteen could neither read nor write. It is important to remember that the illiteracy of 1910 reflected for the most part children who never had the advantage of schooling. The functional illiterates of 1990 are "the result of the way we actually teach children to read in our schools, for our teachers today, whether they know it or not, have been deliberately trained to produce functional illiteracy."[6] In 1910, only one child out of one thousand in the state of Massachusetts was illiterate. According to the Boston Globe (March 11, 1984), 40 percent of the adults in Boston are functionally illiterate. "Never," writes Samuel Blumenfeld, "have we had more reading experts, remedial specialists, and doctors of education devoted to reading. Never has more money been poured into reading 'research,' and never have we had more illiteracy affecting every level of society."[7]

Not too long ago, critics of American education were bemoaning the fact that thousands of functionally illiterate young people were being allowed to graduate from high school. A large number of them, regrettably, have since been admitted to universities across the country. Not even that problem seems as scandalous as it once did. Functionally illiterate men and women are now walking the streets of this nation with college degrees in their hands. Some of them, as we will see, even hold teaching positions in public schools. In one recent book, an author reports that the College of Education at the University of Massachusetts (Amherst) has a history of admitting functional illiterates to its graduate program and then allowing them to "graduate" with master's and doctor's degrees.[8]

Cultural Illiteracy

Even when the students in our public schools and colleges are functionally literate, they often suffer from a different problem—*cultural illiteracy*. According to E. D. Hirsch, Jr., the person with whom the term is most closely associated, "To be culturally literate is to possess the basic information needed to thrive in the modern world."[9] As William J. Bennett explains, being culturally literate

> entails more than recognizing the forms and sounds of words. It is also a matter of building up a body of knowledge enabling us to make sense of the facts, names and allusions cited by an author. This background knowledge [is what we mean by] cultural literacy. For example, someone who is unsure who Grant and Lee were may have a hard time understanding a paragraph about the Civil War, no matter how well he reads. Likewise, a reader who isn't familiar with the *Bill of Rights* will not fully understand a sentence containing the words "First Amendment." Understanding the subject, then, involves not just the possession of skills; it also depends on the amount of relevant prior knowledge a reader has, on his cultural literacy.[10]

To be culturally illiterate is to be deficient in one's understanding of the basic terms and concepts that a person needs to function properly in our society. In his book *Cultural Literacy: What Every American Needs to Know,* Hirsch provides a long list of the names and terms that one must know if she is to be culturally literate.[11]

Cultural illiteracy is also the burden of another recent book, this one titled *What Do Our 17-Year-Olds Know?* A more accurate title might have been *What Do America's 17-Year-Olds NOT Know?* The book, co-authored by Diane Ravitch and Chester E. Finn, Jr., reports what has been learned from the first nation-wide assessment of what American seventeen-year-olds know about history and literature. The national average of right answers for the history questions was 54.5 percent; the average for the literature questions was even lower, 51.8 percent. The authors point out that if we approach these percentages from the commonly accepted view that 60 percent is the line between passing and failing, American students are in deep trouble. As Ravitch and Finn observe, "If there were such a thing as a national report card for those studying American history and literature, then we would have to say that this nationally representative sample of eleventh grade students earns failing marks in both subjects."[12]

A few examples from the Ravitch and Finn book may help underscore how bad things really are. Take the matter of history, for example. An astonishing 31.9 percent of seventeen-year-olds do not know that Columbus discovered the New World before 1750! Forty percent are ignorant of the fact that the Japanese attack on Pearl Harbor occurred between 1939 and 1943. Almost 75 percent could not place Lincoln's presidency within the correct twenty-year span. More than two-thirds could not place the American Civil War in the fifty-year span between 1850 and 1900. Forty-three percent did not know that World War I occurred during the first half of the twentieth century. Almost 50 percent could not place Franklin Roosevelt's presidency in the years between 1929 and 1946. These are not difficult or trivial matters of information. This cultural illiteracy about history is not something the authors found in the backwoods of some third-rate nation. This abysmal ignorance exists among American youth who have had eleven years of public school education, who are one year away from getting a high school diploma, and who soon will be college students. Just for the record, I ought to state that I asked several large college-level classes I teach the same questions and found almost the same degree of ignorance.

Things didn't get any better when the students surveyed in the Ravitch-Finn book were tested about geography. Almost one-third of them could not locate France on a map of Europe while less than half could locate the state of New York on a map of the United States.

The test also examined seventeen-year-olds' familiarity with important literature. The results were equally depressing. Almost 35 percent did not know that "We hold these truths to be self evident..." are words from the Declaration of Independence. Forty percent were ignorant of the basic plot of *Tom Sawyer*. More than 40 percent did not know that Dickens' *Tale of Two Cities* described events occurring during the French Revolution. I suppose there is something fitting and prophetic about the fact that the last item on the literature test indicates that almost 87 percent of American seventeen-year-olds are ignorant of the content of John Bunyan's *Pilgrim's Progress*.

As this chapter was being written, a local newspaper carried a story about a recent book describing the tainted athletic program at a well-known East Coast university. One of those reports concerned one of the school's prize athletes who was being tutored in the hopes of prolonging his athletic eligibility for another semester. The tutor asked the athlete to name the country immediately south of the United States. His answer was Canada. "No," the tutor replied, "let me give you a hint. This is a country where the people speak Spanish." The athlete's eyes brightened as a smile of recognition appeared on his face. "The country must be Spain."

Is the reader beginning to get the picture? This nation has thousands of public schools and colleges; it has millions of citizens who own high school diplomas and college degrees that mean practically nothing. The cost of these almost useless diplomas and degrees totals billions of dollars.

Has anything been done to identify the causes of this cultural literacy? E. D. Hirsch, Jr., author of the major book on the subject, knows where much of the blame rests. He writes,

> The theories that have dominated American education for the past fifty years stem ultimately from Jean Jacques Rousseau, who believed that we should encourage the natural development of young children and not impose adult ideas upon them before they can truly understand them. Rousseau's conception of education as a process of natural development was an abstract generalization meant to apply to all children in any time or place; to French children of the eighteenth century or to Japanese or American children of the twentieth century. He thought that a child's intellectual and social skills would develop naturally without regard to the specific content of education. His content-neutral conception of educational development has long been triumphant in American schools of education and has long dominated the "developmental," content-neutral curriculum of our elementary schools.[13]

The twentieth-century thinker who popularized this contentless approach to education in the United States was John Dewey, about whom Hirsch has this to say:

> Believing that a few direct experiences would suffice to develop the skills that children require, Dewey assumed that early education need not be tied to specific

content. He mistook a half-truth for the whole. He placed too much faith in children's ability to learn general skills from a few typical experiences and too hastily rejected "the piling up of information."[14]

But, Hirsch counters, it is only as children do pile up "specific, communally shared information" that they can "learn to participate in complex cooperative activities with other members of their community."[15] We can thank Dewey and his followers for much of the cultural illiteracy that afflicts America's youth.

Diane Ravitch and Chester Finn, Jr., agree with Hirsch that the thing most responsible for the widespread cultural illiteracy in America is an approach to education that eliminates culture from the curriculum and replaces it with an emphasis on learning skills. "There is a tendency," they write, "in the education profession to believe that *what* children learn is unimportant compared to *how* they learn; to believe that skills can be learned without regard to content; to believe that content is in fact irrelevant so long as the proper skills are developed and exercised."[16] While the acquisition of skills has a place in our schools, it is only part of the total educational process.

There is an important lesson in this for Christian schools. Christian schools work hard to help their students achieve functional literacy, and they certainly emphasize the importance of moral literacy. But they must be very careful that they not shortchange their students in the important matter of cultural literacy.

While the older traditional approach to education had its faults, it contained something that is missing from the new developmental approach. From the old approach, one could learn "who we were as a people, what battles we had fought, what self-knowledge we had gained." In short, one acquired "a point of view that could be disputed, attacked, or controverted. What took its place was not a reformulated and modernized literary tradition that embraced the rich variety of our culture, revealing to us how we had changed during a critical period of our history. The old tradition was dead, but in its stead there was merely cafeteria-style literature, including the written equivalent of junk food."[17]

Our new educational approach has now given us several generations of students who are functionally illiterate. Those who managed somehow to squeak through our public schools while still attaining a degree of functional literacy have had to make their way through an educational system that seems designed to make cultural illiteracy a way of life for millions. But many educators were not satisfied. Many of them regard the pursuit of moral illiteracy for their students as their proudest accomplishment. They will deny culpability with regard to functional illiteracy; they will claim innocence with regard to cultural illiteracy; but their contribution to their students' moral illiteracy is something many of them actually claim with pride.

Moral Illiteracy

According to Paul Vitz, a professor of psychology at New York University, the struggle over American education is more than a battle to end functional and cultural illiteracy. The real conflict reflects a cultural war "between those who are religious and support traditional values and those who are secular and advocate antitraditional or modernist values."[18] Those on the side of religious, traditional values include conservative Protestants and Catholics and Jews. "They have in common the same God, the same commitment to family, and the same general moral values. Today, America is dividing into a new two-class society—one committed to religion and conservative, traditional values and the other committed to secular and liberal, modernist values."[19] The real war over American education, then, is between these two camps. Of course, the effective participants in the struggle understand this. But the majority of Americans do not and hence often misunderstand what is really going on.

While it is difficult to get some people to believe that anyone involved in education or public life would intentionally act in ways that would induce functional illiteracy, it is hard to overlook the educational philosophy that is responsible for the kinds of cultural illiteracy noted earlier. But no informed American can possibly doubt that there has been an all-out campaign at many levels of our society to cut moral and religious values from our schools. There is an unmistakable bias again religious and moral values in our public schools and in higher education; this bias runs deep and can no longer be corrected by anything as simple as a reform of our present system.

Russell Kirk observes that even some college students sense that something important is missing from their education. "Not a few undergraduates," he writes, "complain that their college offers them no first principles of morality, no ethical direction, no aspiration toward enduring truth."[20]

According to Jewish scholar Will Herberg: "We are surrounded on all sides by the wreckage of our great intellectual tradition. In this kind of spiritual chaos, neither freedom nor order is possible. Instead of freedom, we have the all-engulfing whirl of pleasure and power; instead of order, we have the jungle wilderness of normlessness and self-indulgence."[21] It is plain that, for Herberg, the wrecking of our intellectual tradition is linked inseparably to the loss of moral order.

John Silber, president of Boston University, has also taken note of this generation's moral illiteracy. In his powerful book, *Shooting Straight*, he writes:

> In generations past, parents were more diligent in pass-ing on their principles and values to their children, and were assisted by churches and schools which empha-sized religious and moral education. In recent years, in contrast, our society has become increasingly secular and the curriculum of the public schools has been denuded of almost all ethical content. As a result universities must confront a student body ignorant of the evidence and arguments that underlie and support many of our tradi-tional moral principles and practices.[22]

This elimination of values has resulted from several factors. One has been the apathy, indifference, and inaction of people who should have been on guard. This includes the majority of conservative Protestants, Catholics, and Jews who failed to say or do anything. Like the people in Jesus' parable of the wheat and the tares (Matt. 13), they slept while the enemy came and sowed tares in their field.

But the plague of moral illiteracy is also due to the greater commitment, dedication, and cleverness of the people who gained control of public education. It was their zealous dedication and specious arguments that won over enough politicians and judges to seal their victory. That victory has been a defeat for education in this nation and an irreparable loss for the millions of young people who had the misfortune of going to schools controlled by their philosophy.

The Values-Clarification Boondoggle

One of the more disturbing signs of the moral vacuum in America's educational system is the misleadingly named "values-clarification" movement. One of the early books touting this movement was a 1970 work, *Moral Education,* co-edited by Theodore Sizer, then dean of the Harvard School of Education, and his wife, Nancy F. Sizer. Readers got an informative preview of the book's contents by noting the ease with which the editors blasted what they called the morality of "the Christian gentleman," "the American prairie," and the McGuffy *Reader.* The preface also condemned the hypocrisy of teachers who still terrorize their students by using a grading system. One must pause a bit and contemplate what kinds of graduates the Harvard School of Education would set loose on the land. According to the Sizers' preface, every author in their anthology agreed that there was no place in America's new schools for "the old morality."

In one of the more helpful articles written about the values-clarification movement, philosopher Christina Hoff Sommers explains that the leaders of the movement "do not worry about credentials." In other words, it does not matter if spokespersons for the movement have any academic credentials in the field. When one's approach to morality is nihilistic (denying value to anything) and contentless, there is no need to know anything. "They are convinced," Sommers explains, "that traditional middle-class morality is at best useless and at worst pernicious, and they have confidence in the new morality that is to replace the old and in the novel techniques to be applied to this end."[23] It is no wonder then that courses that purport to teach values-clarification are essentially contentless.

Perhaps the most basic assumption of the movement is that no one should think they have the right set of values to pass on to children. This statement applies to teachers as well as parents. Parents reading this book may wish to pause and reflect a bit on this last statement.

The proponents of values-clarification are not content to tell parents they have no business imposing their own values on their children. They clearly see the implications of their nihilism for education. Sommers explains:

> Western literature and history are two traditional alien-
> ating influences that the values clarification movement

is on guard against. [Sidney Simon, educationist at the University of Massachusetts] has written that he has ceased to find meaning "in the history of war or the structure of a sonnet, and more meaning in the search to find value in life." He and his colleagues believe that exposure to one's cultural heritage is not likely to be morally beneficial to the "average student."[24]

Sommers often sounds as though she can hardly believe what she is reporting. As a university philosophy teacher who specializes in ethics, she advises that "Young people today, many of whom are in a complete moral stupor, need to be shown that there is an important distinction between moral and nonmoral decisions. Values clarification blurs the distinction."[25] It does this in the following way: "The student has values; the values clarification teacher is merely 'facilitating' the student's access to them. Thus, no values are taught. The emphasis is on *learning how*, not on *learning that*. The student does not learn *that* acts of stealing are wrong; he learns *how* to respond to such acts."[26] Parents should reflect a while on what a sex-education course taught by such a person will do for their child. If Christian parents need any help in this regard, Kenneth Gangel draws an insightful picture:

> Values clarification in secular education centers on inviting impressionable children and young people to make a choice among options without any consideration of absolute truth and absolute values. Is lying acceptable? Is stealing permissible? Should premarital sex be approved? Well, "it depends." Situations differ. If young people have "clarified" their own value systems and have chosen to do or not to do these things, education has been achieved.[27]

Gangel also provides a valuable analogy of this bizarre movement and the strange people who propagate it:

> The contemporary values-clarification movement is a bit like giving teenagers a driver's license without a handbook or training, placing them in a car and telling them, "Anything you do on the freeway is okay, just as long as you understand why you're doing it. The important thing is that you have made the decisions." The destructive result of such a philosophy would

create automotive lunacy on the highways. On the moral highway of life, values clarification is educational lunacy.[28]

Gangel warns that this movement may be the most serious factor in America's educational crisis. He writes, "Perhaps the number one problem in public education is the attempt to educate students without a moral point of reference. With a floating target of truth and the desertion of absolutes, the entire system has abandoned its base."[29] It is time to question the common sense of families who turn the education of their children over to people who might have felt right at home teaching values-clarification to the guards in Nazi death-camps. It is interesting to speculate what such teachers would have thought about this movement if they had been inmates in such a camp.

Many modern educationists would leave our children adrift on a sea of moral illiteracy, it seems. The refusal to recognize the necessity of ethical absolutes and basic moral values, much less teach such (lest it be considered propaganda) has left our culture loosed from its most important moorings. Without the necessary anchor of moral values, our children are cut loose from any complete and adequate understanding of objective reality. The personal experiences of eight-year-olds, unfortunately, are not sufficient for deciding the future of a nation.

The desertion of absolutes that Ken Gangel warned against above has escalated far beyond the mere teaching of values-clarification, however. We can see moral deterioration all through society as a result of such relativistic nonsense. But others have eloquently warned of the consequences of such moral decay.

We find a most creative expression of such concern in the writing of the nineteenth-century poet, essayist, and thinker, Matthew Arnold. He saw the need for reform in education and the danger of losing moral values in the educational process not long after it began to be popular to promote relativism in the schools of his day.

Matthew Arnold was the son of Dr. Thomas Arnold, Anglican clergyman and headmaster of Rugby School. Dr. Arnold became an educational reformer, and his son followed his father's lead. Matthew became an inspector of schools in his native England, serving in such a capacity for thirty-five years. He believed that the people of the middle classes were the future of the world (though he was quite critical of them and their lifestyles) and thus they needed to be adequately educated for their future responsibilities.

Arnold saw the Bible as a great work of literature and a means of advancing culture, though he did not hold to personal faith in Christ. But he recognized the importance of the Christian faith as a guide for society and saw the waning of faith as a loss for society. He believed that culture and education would have to fill the void left by the retreat of biblical faith as the integrating force in society.

In the poem *Dover Beach* Arnold presents the reader with a couple in a room on the cliffs of Dover. The night scene is beautifully described. The immediate feeling is one of quietness and near solitude. The scene is viewed through the window of the couple's room. The man calls the woman to the window and as they listen, the sounds of the sea are artistically created by Arnold's words. We seem to hear the ocean in our mind's "ear." With words such as "only," "draw back," "begin and cease," and "tremulous cadence," our peaceful, tranquil feelings (perhaps with mild melancholy) give way to feelings of uneasiness or apprehension or deeper melancholy. This is made plain by the expression, "eternal note of sadness."

This thought is linked to the reference to the Greek writer of tragedies, Sophocles, and the "turbid ebb and flow of human misery."

This sadness brings to mind the melancholy fact that though once full, the sea of faith (Christian belief) has ebbed. Once it was at high tide, piled up in ripples and waves like a furled garment at the waist. Now the sea of faith has ebbed, retreated, withdrawn. The Christian faith is waning, and its retreat has left an even greater sadness and melancholy. The world has become dreary and naked because we are exposed and alone. Secular man is "free" but irrevocably lonely.

Finally the man calls his lover to be true. Nothing in the world is certain now that the Christian faith is in retreat. Confusion now creeps in; war and conflict spread. All that remains is love and personal relationships.

Arnold believed that culture could take the place of Christian faith as the basis for society. Yet as his famous poem plainly shows, the loss of the Christian faith in the West left the world a more fearful, lonely, and confusing place. Culture and education are not adequate grist for the mill of society, and Arnold's poetry clearly reveals the loss his heart feels at the inadequate solution his secular mind has suggested.

Dover Beach

The sea is calm tonight.
The tide is full, the moon lies fair
Upon the straits—on the French coast the light
Gleams and is gone; the cliffs of England stand,
Glimmering and vast, out in the tranquil bay.
Come to the window, sweet is the night air!
Only, from the long line of spray
Where the sea meets the moon-blanched land,
Listen! you hear the grating roar
Of pebbles which the waves draw back, and fling,
At their return, up the high strand,
Begin and cease, and then again begin,
With tremulous cadence slow, and bring
The eternal note of sadness in.
Sophocles long ago
Heard it on the Aegean, and it brought
Into his mind the turbid ebb and flow
Of human misery; we
Find also in the sound a thought,
Hearing it by this distant northern sea.
The Sea of Faith
Was once, too, at the full, and round earth's shore
Lay like the folds of a bright girdle furled.
But now I only hear
Its melancholy, long, withdrawing roar,
Retreating, to the breath
Of the night wind, down the vast edges drear
And naked shingles of the world.
Ah, love, let us be true
To one another! for the world, which seems
To lie before us like a land of dreams,
So various, so beautiful, so new,
Hath really neither joy, nor love, nor light,
Nor certitude, nor peace, nor help for pain;

And we are here as on a darkling plain
Swept with confused alarms of struggle and flight,
Where ignorant armies clash by night.

Conclusion

Matthew Arnold recognized the incredible loss that the secularization of our educational system creates. The loss of Christian values has marched on, though, despite Arnold's poetic harbinger. In the chapters that follow, I will identify and discuss the ideas, ideologies, people, and movements who, to use Russell Kirk's apt phrase, have served as our generation's "enemies of the permanent things," those values that have been replaced with the relativistic nonsense, irrational ideas, and moral bankruptcy that sent Arnold into eternal sadness. The restoration of functional, cultural and moral literacy requires that we know who the enemies are. We must find ways to loosen their destructive control over the education of future generations of young people. And we must then act in cooperation with others in our society who want to see an end to the crisis of American education.

CHAPTER

4

We have too readily blamed shortcomings in American education on social changes (the disorientation of the American family or the impact of television) or incompetent teachers or structural flaws in our school systems. But the chief blame should fall on faulty theories promulgated in our schools of education and accepted by educational policymakers.

—E. D. Hirsch, Jr., *Cultural Literacy*

Three Enemies of
"The Permanent Things"

More than twenty years ago, Jewish scholar Will Herberg described modern man as a resident of a "metaphysical wasteland." As Herberg went on to explain: "We are surrounded on all sides by the wreckage of our great intellectual tradition. In this kind of spiritual chaos, neither freedom nor order is possible. Instead of freedom, we have the all-engulfing whirl of pleasure and power; instead of order, we have the jungle wilderness of normlessness and self-indulgence."[1]

According to Herberg, three intellectual movements pushed us into this intellectual wasteland: relativism, positivism, and secularism. Herberg described each of these movements as a *creeping conviction*. What he meant was to suggest "not merely the insidious, almost underground, workings of these forces, but also that what has affected the modern mind in the West has not been an array of intellectual arguments, but the unremitting operation of mind-setting attitudes, often hardly noticed, but doing their remorseless work by cultural pressures and compulsions. While the results have amounted to a drastic change in the metaphysical climate, the forces have been very largely social and cultural."[2]

Even though Herberg wrote during the crazy days of the sixties and early seventies, the three movements of relativism, positivism, and secularism have become even more entrenched in the educational world. This is due in large measure to the fact that individuals who were indoctrinated by others who were relativists, positivists, and secularists are the professors of the nineties who are now busy indoctrinating their own students.

Relativism

As Allan Bloom states, "There is one thing a professor can be absolutely certain of: Almost every student entering the university believes, or says he believes, that truth is relative."[3] While this relativism is seldom, if ever, supported with arguments, it nonetheless travels in the company of a number of other theories and beliefs—equally untenable—that help provide psychological support for students and professors who want to believe that there are no objective standards of truth or morality or, indeed, of anything. In other sections of the book, I look at some of its close relatives: deconstructionism and the perversely-titled position already identified as "values-clarification." It is enough for now to get some initial idea of how confused the advocates of relativism are.

As a first step, we must determine what relativism is. Herberg once defined it as "the *creeping conviction*[4] that there is no such thing as truth or right, but only the varying beliefs of varying cultures, each apparently justified in its own terms; no fixed norms, but merely shifting opinions."[5] Relativism is not simply the view that different people hold different beliefs about what is true and false or right and wrong. That such disagreements are widespread is too obvious to require further comment. In order to be a bona fide relativist one must go beyond mere observation of such disagreements and make the astounding claim that all of these conflicting beliefs are correct at the same time and in the same sense. Ethical relativism then is the view that conflicting ethical standards are correct for all the different people who hold them. Epistemological relativism is equally generous to parties who disagree over the truth or falsity of conflicting beliefs.

Relativists love to draw attention to real and serious disagreements among people, as though the mere existence of these disagreements proves the relativity of what it is that people quarrel over. Absolutely nothing follows from the fact that two individuals or two cultures disagree over the morality of a particular action any more than that their disagreement over some nonethical issue might be thought to imply the absence of any objective truth. When person A says the world is flat and person B claims the world is round, it hardly follows that there is no objective truth about the matter. Similarly, when person A says that abortion on demand is morally acceptable and person B says it is wrong, it does not follow that the morality of the practice is purely a matter of taste. In both cases, we are dealing with beliefs. A believes the world is flat while B believes otherwise. As we know, there is an objective truth on this issue; therefore, one person's belief is correct and the other's is not. Likewise, ethical disputes involve conflicting beliefs. Even in especially difficult cases where we may have trouble knowing which belief is correct, it is hard to see what would justify the conclusion that in ethical disputes, *no* beliefs are objectively and universally true.

We have all heard people say something like, "That may be true for you but it isn't true for me." As Mortimer Adler explains so nicely, talk like this rests on a serious confusion. The confusion is "between the truth or falsity that inheres in a proposition or statement and the judgment that a person makes with regard to the truth or falsity of the statement in question. We may differ in our judgment about what is true, but that does not affect the truth of the matter itself."[6]

As an example, Adler considers

> a difference of opinion about the number of peaks in the Colorado Rockies that exceed 14,000 feet. One person sets the number at fifty; the other says, "Not so." The number of peaks in Colorado exceeding 14,000 feet is some definite integer, and so the statement that sets it as fifty is either true or false, regardless of what the persons who dispute this matter of fact may think about it. . . . We do not make statements true or false by affirming or denying them. They have truth or falsity regardless of what we think, what opinions we hold, what judgments we make.[7]

Adler's conclusion holds with equal force to judgments we make about morality. To paraphrase his earlier claim, we do not make actions good or bad by the judgments we make about them. They are good or bad regardless of what we think, what opinions we hold, what judgments we make.

Of course, many relativists attempt to counter this by claiming that what we believe about morality results from learning or conditioning. Philosopher Ed Miller of the University of Colorado notes the serious weakness in such thinking. The fact, he writes,

> that something is learned is hardly evidence against its objective truth and validity. We learn that two plus two equals four, and that war is bad, and we learn all kinds of things which we believe to be nonetheless true. Is there, in fact, anything that we claim to know that we have not learned in one way or another? And though people may disagree about their interpretation of "good," it does not follow from this that there *is* no objective good. We may just as easily conclude from the fact that people often disagree in their interpretations of the world that the world does not exist, or from the fact that some people cannot see that two plus two equals four that perhaps it doesn't.[8]

And so Miller brings us back to the same problem we encountered before. Just because people disagree over something, it does not follow that there is no objective truth or goodness. Where two people hold directly opposing beliefs, there is one thing we are entitled to conclude, namely, that one of them is right and the other is wrong.

I do not want to leave the impression that the case for the objectivity of moral laws rests solely on the weakness of arguments against such objectivity. "If we did not believe," Miller writes,

> that there is an objective and unchanging foundation of moral values and ideals, then we would not bother to make such judgments, at least not seriously. On the contrary, that we continue to exercise moral judgment, not only in reference to ourselves but also to others, is clear evidence that we do, in fact, take such judgments as counting for something and as being ultimately and objectively significant. In this way, it may be argued, it is self-contradictory (practically speaking) to make judgments of moral value and to deny at the same time that there is any objective basis of morality. What can be more comical than someone who spends the day

fanatically and passionately crusading for the eradica-
tion of certain evils, while in the evening he delivers
cool lectures on the relativity of all ideas?[9]

British philosopher and long-time professor at Princeton University, W. T. Stace, drew attention to the same absurdity:

[I]f taken seriously and pressed to its logical conclusion, ethical relativism can only end in destroying
the conception of morality altogether, in undermining
its practical efficacy, in rendering meaningless many
almost universally accepted truths about human affairs, in robbing human beings of any incentive to
strive for a better world, in taking the life blood out of
every ideal and every aspiration which has ever en-
nobled the life of man.[10]

If there are no objective standards of morality, we can never
be justified when judging the ethics of one culture to be better
than another; we have no grounds on which we may compare
the standards of one age to another; and the very notion of moral
progress is an illusion. Will Herberg was correct when he noted
that "a thoroughgoing relativism is logically incoherent, since
some fixed point of reference is obviously required on which to
hang any system of relativity. In effect, any system of relativism
that claims to be thoroughgoing is driven to the premature
absolutization of some merely relative value or truth."[11]

Relativism, then is a position for which the world still awaits
an argument. It is also self-defeating in the sense that every
self-styled relativist is forced, sooner or later, to appeal to absolutes of his own making. And it is a theory that robs life of
elements needed for any life to have meaning.

Positivism

Herberg defines *positivism* as "the *creeping conviction* that the
only kind of reality and truth is the kind [allegedly] revealed by
and verifiable in terms of, positive science."[12] It is the belief that
human knowledge cannot be extended beyond what can be
discovered by use of the scientific method.

Positivism should be distinguished from *Logical Positivism*, an
extreme and rather fanatical version of positivism that exercised
enormous influence from about the mid-1930s to the mid-1950s.

Most of the old Logical Positivists have either died off or admitted they were wrong.[13] But the disappearance of Logical Positivism from the academic scene should not mislead anyone into thinking that the more general positivistic movement has lost any of its vigor. The spirit of positivism still exists in the form of an arrogant, quasi-religious devotion to the scientific method.

Many people believe that science is the only area of human study (other than mathematics and logic) that is true. Anything else can only be a matter of opinion. If some belief cannot be tested by the scientific method, it cannot be true; belief in it cannot be rational. Of course, it is interesting to ask if *that* claim (the positivists's own thesis) can be tested by the scientific method. Obviously, it cannot. And so, the positivist's own claim turns out to be neither true nor rational. This observation of the self-defeating nature of positivism opens the door to a number of similar criticisms. As J. P. Moreland points out, "[T]he aims, methodologies, and presuppositions *of* science cannot be validated *by* science. One cannot turn to science to justify science any more than one can pull oneself up by his own bootstraps. The validation of science is a philosophical issue, not a scientific one, and any claim to the contrary will be a self-refuting *philosophical* claim."[14]

The truth and rationality of science is grounded on a number of assumptions which cannot be verified by the scientific method. The scientist assumes, for example, that knowledge is possible and sense experience is reliable, that the universe is regular, and that scientists should be honest. Without assumptions like these—assumptions that the scientist cannot justify within the limitations of his methodology—scientific inquiry would soon come to a screeching halt. Calvin College philosopher Del Ratzsch notes the implications of all this:

> If we then are justified in accepting the foundational principles of science (that is, if accepting those foundations is legitimate or rational), then that justification must rest on something other than scientific method. Thus, either accepting science itself is not justifiable or else there is some nonscientific, justifiable basis for accepting science. Therefore, not only can science not validate its own foundation (implying that there *are* areas outside the competence of science), but if we do

accept science, including its foundations, there must be some other sort of grounds for accepting at least some beliefs. This implies that science cannot be the only legitimate basis for believing something. Those who claim either that science is competent for dealing with all matters or that science is the only legitimate method for dealing with any matter are seriously confused.[15]

The widespread but uncritical propensity of so many to worship at the shrine of the scientific method is an act of blind faith. The positivist movement is intellectually indefensible.

Secularism-Naturalism-Humanism

The third intellectual movement that has helped to create the intellectual wasteland Herberg deplored is one he identified under the label of *secularism*. Herberg defined the term to mean "the *creeping conviction* that human life can be lived and understood, in its own terms, without regard to any higher order of reality, that is, without regard to God."[16] Herberg is certainly correct in identifying secularism as a major contributor to our contemporary intellectual crisis. He is also right when he treats secularism as a by-product or consequence of relativism and positivism combined. Since this movement is essentially a rejection of all that previous generations have regarded as the Sacred, it seems fitting to refer to it under the title of secularism. But for once, I must find fault with Herberg's analysis. The position he is struggling to explain contains other important elements. Unless those other elements are seen to be part of the mix, we'll fail to understand secularism properly. Hence to indicate the three-fold nature of this movement, I choose to call it *secularism-naturalism-humanism*. While clearly related, while seldom separated, the three key elements in this mix emphasize different points.

As we've seen, secularism is the rejection of the Sacred. "To maintain," Herberg explains, "that human life is to be lived and understood as if there is nothing beyond means, in effect, to exalt to divine status, that is, to absolutize, some this-worldly (hence, merely relative) reality, value, or truth. Considered historically, this absolutization of a social ideal, or program, or movement, riding roughshod over everything, has been mainly responsible for the indescribable dislocations and disasters of the past two centuries, beginning with the Enlightenment and the French Revolution, and moving with catastrophic fatality through German Nazism and Russian and Chinese communism in our time."[17]

The second ingredient in this mix is *naturalism*. The basic claim of naturalism is that *nothing exists outside the material, mechanical, natural order*. For naturalists, the universe is a closed, self-explanatory system. The naturalists' universe is analogous to a box. Everything that happens inside the box is caused by or is explainable in terms of other things that exist within the box. Nothing (including God) exists outside the box; therefore, nothing outside the box we call the universe or nature can have any causal effect within the box. Since what exists within the box is properly studied by science, it is easy to see how positivism and naturalism fit together so easily. The scientific method has to be the mainline to truth since there is nothing that cannot be discovered by science; likewise, there is nothing outside the box we call "Nature."

Given such a naturalistic world view, it is small wonder that people who are naturalists object to major elements of the Christian world view. Any naturalist is precluded from believing in God, spirit, soul, angels, miracles, prayer, providence, immortality, heaven, sin, and salvation, as Christians normally understand these notions, for one simple reason: Such beliefs are logically incompatible with the naturalist's world view.

It is important to notice that no naturalist ever bothers to prove that naturalism is true (just as no positivist can prove that positivism is true). Indeed, as more than one book argues, it is impossible to prove the truth of naturalism.[18] The commitment that some people make to a system like naturalism is similar in important respects to the commitment that other people make to Christianity. It is important to realize that people do not become naturalists because they are somehow more in tune with modern science. Their rejection of miracles and other elements of the historic Christian faith is a reflection of their ultimate religious commitment to a naturalistic world view.

Moving from secularism and naturalism to *humanism* is less like taking a small step than it is to looking at another side of the same coin. One way to define humanism is to let its advocates speak for themselves:

Humanists regard the universe as self-existing and not created. Humanism asserts that the nature of the universe depicted by modern science makes unacceptable any supernatural cosmic guarantees of human value. [This is simply an admission that humanists are also naturalists.] Religious humanism considers the complete realization of human personality to be the end of man's life and seeks its development and fulfillment in the here and now.

In the place of the old attitudes involved in worship and prayer the humanist finds his religious emotions expressed in a heightened sense of personal life and in a cooperative effort to promote social well-being. Man is at last becoming aware that he alone is responsible for the realization of the world of his dreams, that he has within himself the power for its achievement.[19]

What these statements make clear is that humanism is a religion, albeit a religion without God. Or to put it another way, it is a religion in which human beings assume the place of God. Humanism is, in the word of an ancient Greek philosopher, the belief that man (and not God) is the measure or standard of all things.[20]

Lutheran scholar Richard John Neuhaus has called this mix of secularism-humanism-naturalism the "bootleg religion" of the public schools.[21] What he means is that while the courts of this country continue to rule that Christianity and Judaism have no standing in the public schools, they continue to permit another religion, the avowed enemy of Jewish and Christian supernaturalism, to have ready access to students in public schools. Indeed, major tenets of this alien religion show up repeatedly in even the most casual examination of public school textbooks. Rockne McCarthy and other contributors to the book, *Society, State and Schools* document this charge.[22] New York University professor Paul C. Vitz reveals the other side of the coin and shows how humanistic censorship has succeeded in eliminating any religious content (other than secularism-humanism-naturalism) from most textbooks.[23] "The upshot of this evidence," Rockne McCarthy and his colleagues point out, "is that the public schools are not neutral; they reflect a religious perspective as defined by the courts. Naturalistic humanism is that religion, and the courts, if faced with the evidence, must conclude that the public schools stand in violation of the Supreme Court's present interpretation of the establishment clause."[24]

Statements made by a Harvard University educator at a 1973 teacher's seminar provide a disturbing insight into the mindset of humanists interested in using public education to advance the cause of their own religion:

> Every child in America entering school at the age of five is mentally ill because he comes to school with certain allegiances toward our founding fathers, toward our elected officials, toward his parents, toward a belief in a supernatural Being, toward the sovereignty of this nation as a separate entity. It's up to you teachers to make all of these sick children well by creating the international children of the future.[25]

And so we learn that the practitioners of secular humanism see the children of Christian parents as sick and therefore proper targets for the "healing" influence of their indoctrination.

Where Do We Go From Here?

It is instructive to see what Will Herberg thought would follow Western civilization's ensnarement in the metaphysical wasteland to which relativism, positivism, and secularism-naturalism-humanism have brought us. Ironically, Herberg suggests, a philosopher usually regarded as an arch-enemy of Christianity saw clearly the dangerous situation that would follow the rejection of the Judeo-Christian world view on which Western civilization had been built. That philosopher is Friedrich Nietzsche (1844–1900), who wrote the following prophetic words:

> In the end, there is a metaphysical faith at the base of our faith in science. . . . We all, atheists and anti-metaphysicists, take our flame from the great fire which has been kindled by faith—the Christian faith and also that of Plato, the faith that claims that God is Truth. What are we going to do when all this becomes unbelievable?[26]

Nietzsche's point is explained by a passage in one of his writings, *The Gay Science*, in a section titled "The Madman."[27]

Have you not heard of that madman who lit a lantern in the bright morning hours, ran to the market place, and cried incessantly, "I seek God! I seek God!" As many of those who do not believe in God were standing around just then, he provoked much laughter. Why, did he get lost? said one. Did he lose his way like a child? said another. Or is he hiding? Is he afraid of us? Has he gone on a voyage? Or emigrated? Thus they yelled and laughed. The madman jumped into their midst and pierced them with his glances. "Whither is God?" he cried. "I shall tell you. *We have killed him*, you and I. All of us are his murderers.... God is dead. God remains dead. And we have killed him."

Here the madman fell silent and looked again at his listeners; they too were silent and stared at him in astonishment. At last he threw his lantern on the ground, and it broke and went out. "I come too early," he said then; "my time has not come yet ... this deed is still more distant from them than the most distant stars— *and yet they have done it themselves*."

Nietzsche's startling statement that God is dead was not an assertion of his own personal atheism. It was not so much a piece of speculation about the nonexistence of God as it was a diagnosis of the civilization of his day. What Nietzsche meant was that men no longer believe in God. For all practical purposes, Western man has destroyed his faith in God; he has killed God.

It is interesting to note that the very men in Nietzsche's story who began by ridiculing the madman's search for God were also shocked by his apparent blasphemy. Nietzsche's point has even more force in our own society, where, with few exceptions, men and women live their lives as if there were no God and yet still carry on a profession of being religious. In Nietzsche's dramatic picture, there is something tragically absurd about the man who is shocked by someone else's atheism when it is impossible to discover any genuine religious faith in him. For the average American today, as for the average individual in Nietzsche's Germany, it simply makes no practical difference whether God exists or not. This is true in spite of those polls that show that 98 percent of Americans believe in God.

However, Nietzsche's main concern was not religion but ethics. Even though men no longer believed in God, they had not yet become fully conscious of the extent of their unbelief. Moreover, the morality of the Western world was still grounded on the principles of the Christian faith. Nietzsche realized that if civilization were to survive, humanity needed standards and values by which to live. But he also realized that traditional morality, that is, the morality of Western Europe, went hand in hand with the Christian faith. What will happen, Nietzsche was asking, when men see the inconsistency between their rejection of God's existence and their acceptance of a morality grounded on the nature and being of God? What will happen when men finally understand that the foundations of Western morality are no longer solid rock but only sinking sand? Nietzsche feared what would happen when modern man finally realized that he was continuing to cling to a morality, the foundations of which he had abandoned years before. Nietzsche's special term for what would happen next is *nihilism*.

Nihilism is a condition in which all ultimate values lose their value. That is, traditional moral values will become obsolete with the knowledge that their logical ground (God) is nonexistent. Thus, Nietzsche feared, when men awaken from their sleepwalking, civilization will collapse and nihilism will result. If Nietzsche's diagnosis is correct, what is needed is a new foundation of morality; the old one has been destroyed. Much of his philosophy should be understood as an attempt to provide just such a new foundation—in Nietzsche's terms, "a revaluation of all values." In one of his books, Nietzsche has his prophet Zarathustra say, "To value is to create; hear this, you creators! Valuing itself is of all valued things the most valuable treasure. . . . Change of values—that is a change of creators. Whoever must be a creator always annihilates."[28] In other words, the creation of new values must be accompanied by the annihilation of old ones. And so Nietzsche attacked traditional morality like a man possessed. Christian morality, he wrote, is the morality of weak, decadent people. What we need in its place is a morality of strength and power—*the will to power*. In place of what he called the "slave-morality" of Christianity, Nietzsche proposed to substitute a "master-morality" in which the chief virtues would be strength, dominance, and the will to power.

"What is good?" Nietzsche asks. "Everything that heightens the feeling of power in man, the will to power itself. What is bad? Everything that is born of weakness. What is happiness? The feeling that power is growing, that resistance is overcome."[29]

The final result for the few who would understand Nietzsche and were able to follow him would be the Superman *(Ubermensch)*. This term which occurs so often in Nietzsche's writings is better translated as the "Overman." What Nietzsche was trying to say is that man in his present condition is only a bridge to a higher form of life. "I teach you the Overman. Man is something that shall be overcome. What have you done to overcome him?"[30] Again he wrote: "Man is a rope, tied between beast and Overman—a rope over an abyss. A dangerous across, a dangerous on-the-way, a dangerous looking-back, a dangerous shuddering and stopping. What is great in man is that he is a bridge and not an end."[31] Behind man is the beast from which he came; ahead is the being he can become if only he allows Nietzsche to guide him. But if man should falter, look back, and fail to move ahead to the Superman, he will fall from his precarious perch into the bottomless pit of nihilism.

But it is still not clear what Nietzsche meant by "the will to power" and "the Superman." The Superman, or Overman, is the strong man whose will refuses to submit to the values and standards of others, *especially God*. He is the powerful man who creates his own values. Nietzsche's strong man never says, "I ought." That is, he never submits to rules laid down by God or anyone else. Rather, the Superman is the person who says, "I will!" It is a mistake to read an advocacy of moral libertinism into Nietzsche's words. Nietzsche would warn that a man who is dominated by his lusts, who cannot control his passions, is not a strong man—is hardly a model of the will to power. The Superman will be master both of himself and of his environment. Actually, Nietzsche taught the value of an action lies in the agent and not in what he does. Nietzsche did not really care whether a man lived a life of self-control or licentiousness as long as it was done out of strength and power, *as long as it was a reflection of his autonomy!* Nietzsche's Superman begins to remind us of the ethics of the early Jean-Paul Sartre who did not care what choices people made so long as they were their own choices.

Nietzsche's parable of the madman who proclaims the death of God is an apt picture of the religious bankruptcy of the West. In spite of pious professions to the contrary, most men and women go on acting as if God does not really exist. In such a condition, for all practical purposes, God *is* dead, since men and women don't really believe in Him. In an effort to save society from the nihilism that would follow the discovery of the death of God, Nietzsche was willing to destroy the old Christian foundation of morality and substitute a new naturalistic, autonomous basis of value.

While Nietzsche then was no friend of Christianity, he saw, in Herberg's words, "the abyss toward which Western thought was heading. We can find in [his] insights, however ambiguous, the flash of illumination we need to understand our time. Modern man is at the end of his rope, metaphysically as in so many other respects. His relativist, positivist, secularist faith, however thoroughly it has pervaded his being, is no longer really believable."[32]

When any culture reaches the point that God becomes dead (because the people in that culture no longer believe or act like they believe in God), the only way to save that culture is to confront its men and women with their unbelief and secularism and challenge them to place their faith in the living God who is there. If contemporary Christians will let this truth be burned into their souls, they will no longer passively submit to the domination of their culture by relativists, positivists and secularists. They will no longer acquiesce to control of their children's education by advocates of the anti-Christian religion of secular humanism. They will strike back. They will found and support private Christian schools in which children of any religious persuasion can receive the quality education no longer available in public schools—an education that at the same time contains essential moral and spiritual values at its core. They will challenge through litigation the Supreme Court's discriminatory stand for one religion and against all others. They will seek, again through litigation, ways of ending the injustices that force parents who prefer the quality of a private school for their children to bear a double financial burden, especially when the portion they are coerced into paying supports schools that undermine traditional values.

CHAPTER

5

Rigorous teachers seized my youth,
And purged its faith and trimmed its fire,
Showed me the high, white star of Truth,
There bade me gaze and there aspire."

—Matthew Arnold

The Educational Establishment

The search for the causes of America's educational crisis won't be complete until we examine the role of the people most closely related to the problem, America's public school teachers and the educationists who have assumed the task of preparing these teachers. Many discussions of the educational problem stop before this point is reached. That is often the case because the people doing the talking either are members of the educational establishment or have close ties to it.

My examination of the educational establishment will proceed via four steps. First, I will take a brief look at the individual teacher and the growing body of evidence that suggests that many of them are woefully under-educated. I will then look at the major reason for this widespread incompetence, namely, the departments and colleges of education that have been given the power to determine what future teachers will be taught. These same people, in most states, also help set the qualifications that people who wish to teach must meet. Not surprisingly, those qualifications include an indefensibly high number of courses taught by educationists. Thirdly, I will discuss the goals and activities of the largest teacher's union in America, the National Education Association. No picture of our educational crisis can possibly be complete without an understanding of the NEA's contribution to the disaster. Finally, I will examine some elements of the ideology that underlies the thinking, attitudes, and actions of many contemporary educationists and how that ideology translates into educational policy.

Before I begin, a couple of qualifications seem advisable. First, it is important to recognize that there are thousands of excellent, dedicated teachers in America's public schools. The fact that there are incompetents in the profession and that this chapter will focus attention on them should not be taken as a lack of respect for the good ones. There are also many fine people across the country who belong to the class of professional educationists. I will be saying some rather uncomplimentary things about this class which, I hope, will not be taken as a personal attack on any of them. Many members of this profession are genuinely concerned about the quality of education received by future teachers. Some of them may even admit that courses in professional education lower the overall quality of this training by preventing prospective teachers from including more content courses in their programs. In some cases, these good people are victims of their own limited education. The fact that they were forced to spend so much of their college career in education courses kept them from taking liberal arts courses that might have changed their perspective on things. I regret that some may be offended by what this chapter says about their profession. But I have no choice but to state what I believe. They are welcome, in return, to say anything they wish about the philosophy profession. Some of what they say may even be correct.

Incompetent Teachers

Are there incompetent teachers in America's classrooms? Even though the evidence is not nearly as complete as we would like, it looks as though there are lots of them.

For one thing, there is embarrassing evidence that suggests that many of the college students presently electing education as their field of study are significantly weaker than the average college student. In 1988, the SAT scores for students planning to study education averaged 855, forty-nine points below the mean of 904 for all U.S. students planning to attend college. In 1989, things got even worse. The average SAT scores for prospective education students in this year fell to 846, fifty-seven points below the national average of 903. During my twenty-six years as a teacher and administrator in a university that used to be a state teacher's college, I've talked to enough students to know that many who concentrate on education do so with the full understanding that it is one of the easier fields in which to get a degree. Students these days who know they're not especially intelligent are smart enough to know an easy path to a college degree when they see it.

And so the quality of the people presently selecting education as a college major or area of concentration is a legitimate cause for concern. When the personal shortcomings of many of these students are married to the essentially contentless courses in education they're forced to take, it is easy to see why so many poorly prepared people are ending up in our nation's classrooms.

In recent years, disturbing signs of how widespread this incompetency is have come to light. In 1983, for example, school teachers in Houston, Texas, were required to take a competency test. More than 60 percent of the teachers failed the reading part of the test. Forty-six percent failed the math section while 26 percent could not pass the writing exam. As if this weren't bad enough, 763 of the more than 3,000 teachers taking the test cheated.[1] While competency testing seems to be an important stage towards the improvement of education in America, the National Education Association, our nation's most powerful teacher's union, opposes it for people already in the profession. Dr. John Silber, president of Boston University, makes an interesting observation about competency tests for teachers. He writes, "Against certifying teachers on the basis of competence, it is frequently argued that no test will demonstrate competence, much less excellence, in teaching. This is true, of course. But this inability to test exhaustively an individual's ability to teach should not obscure the fact that there are many tests on which failure demonstrates the inability to teach."[2]

In its issue of June 16, 1980, *Time* magazine carried a cover story titled, "Help! Teacher Can't Teach!" The fact that the story is now ten years old is no cause for comfort. In the intervening years, other national magazines have carried similar stories that make it clear that the situation today has not improved. A few examples from the *Time* story will suffice. *Time*, for example, tells about a Chicago public school teacher who answers the question of a television news reporter with the words, "I teaches English." A third grade teacher in Chicago writes the following sentence on a blackboard: "Put the following words in alfabetical [sic] order." A fifth grade teacher in Mobile, Alabama, the proud holder of a Master of Education degree from one of this nation's teacher's colleges, sends the following note home to one of her students' parents: "Scott is dropping in his studies [no punctuation] he acts as if he don't care. Scott want pass in his assignment at all, he a had a poem to learn and he fell to do it." This is a precise copy of the note.

Is it any wonder that, with teachers like these, our students are illiterate? How did this teacher ever get out of high school, let alone graduate with a bachelor's and then a master's degree in education? What must we think about the competence of her college teachers, to say nothing about the people who judged her qualified to teach? It should be obvious that people this incompetent could not end up as teachers without there being something terribly wrong with the people, institutions, and programs that control teacher education in this country.

Professional Educationists

"It is not too much to say that in the past fifty years public education in the United States has been in the hands of revolutionaries."[3] These shocking words were written by a respected University of Chicago professor named Richard Weaver. According to Weaver:

> This came about when state bureaucracies were created to set the terms and supervise the working of the expanding public school system. State legislators felt that they had to turn the actual administration of affairs over to a body of "experts." In course of time these state departments of education became virtually autonomous in their power to define the goals, methods, and materials of public instruction. The final step came when they were able to require all prospective school teachers through the high school level to take a set number of course in a subject called "Education," wherein the philosophical premises and aims of [a new approach to education] were taught. . . . Here was an educational system within the educational system, committed to a body of methodology whose goals were defined by a philosophical sect.[4]

As one consequence of this, almost all of the control of American public education rests in the hands of an educational "establishment." Samuel Blumenfeld explains:

> A vast army of professionals and careerists populate this establishment, from lofty professors of education to lowly first-grade teachers, not to mention the bureaucrats in the state departments of education and the administrators who run the schools. A network of teachers' colleges—like a system of religious seminaries—has been built to train all of those who would become professionals in the educational establishment. In these colleges future teachers and administrators are indoctrinated in the dogma of the public religion. The combination of vast sums of [taxpayers'] money, sacrosanct institutions of learning, and an army of professionals make up this formidable establishment.[5]

It's difficult to be on the campus of any American university for very long without realizing how little respect professional educationists have among professors in legitimate academic fields. One such professor, philosopher Gordon Clark, once wrote that what little value may really be found in professional education courses "has been diluted, padded, and stretched to make several courses instead of being assembled into a single one the equal of courses in mathematics or history. It is not surprising, therefore, that Departments of Education must depend on legislative compulsion rather than on intrinsic merit to obtain students. In all the curriculum no other subject is so widely condemned as Education."[6]

An event from my own past supports Clark's negative verdict. Many years ago, near the beginning of my own teaching career in a state university that had for years been a state teacher's college, I found myself in a situation where my philosophy department had to employ a recently retired educationist to replace a professor who would be gone for a year. In hindsight, it was a horrible mistake. The gentleman had taught professional education courses at another state university for years. Someone thought it would be a good idea if he taught one more year in my department. Since he had taken some courses with a few well-known philosophers, we thought it possible that he'd get through two semesters without doing any harm. Besides, we had no real alternative.

In those days, registration for every semester took place on the floor of our huge basketball arena, each student seeking a card that would admit her to the courses she wanted to take. Normally at registrations, we used to get fairly excited when the line of students wanting a philosophy course got to be two or three people long. But after the visiting educationist's first semester, registration was different. Then the line of students wanting a philosophy course stretched all the way across the arena and out the door.

At first I thought these poor students had finally discovered how important philosophy was. But then I learned that each student in the long line wanted a course with only one member of the department, the retired educationist. They refused to take courses from any other teacher. That seemed like a good time to have a little talk with the educationist. It began with a question from me: "What kinds of grades did you give the first semester?" His reply went like this: "Well, I did have one student who never came to class. I had no choice. I had to give him a 'B.'" When word got out that this visiting philosophy teacher had given every other student an "A" (for doing what, no one knows), every student in the university wanted to take his course. What I remember to this day was the educationist's surprise that anyone would question his giving every student a grade of "A."

I know that many people will have difficulty believing this story, but it happened exactly as described. For all I know, the only "B" that educationist gave in his entire career went to the one student from my university who never attended class. This event illustrates why professors in solid, academic fields have so little use for professional education courses. They are courses with little or no content, that require little or no significant work, and that result in highly inflated grades for every student smart enough not to antagonize the teacher.

What makes the presence of these sorts of educationists in the academic world even worse is the fact that they somehow have gotten the politicians in their states to dictate that no one can become a public school teacher in that state without taking an inordinate number of courses in professional education. This enormous overemphasis in such courses might not be so bad, except that most education students take the courses in place of content courses. While they may learn how to teach (a debatable claim), they end up having little or nothing to teach. The Master of Education degree in many states is an excellent example. A teacher of English, let us say, who wishes to earn a Master of Education degree may do so by taking as few as three or four English courses as part of her program. The rest of the program can be satisfied with professional education courses in which the teacher learns such urgent things as how to get along with a grumpy principal.

For more than ten years, Reginald Damerell was a teacher in the College of Education at the University of Massachusetts at Amherst. The study of his experiences at Amherst is told in his book, *Education's Smoking Gun: How Teachers' Colleges Have Destroyed Education in America*.[7] It is not a pretty or comforting picture. For those who might care, Damerell was a member of the committee that was charged to evaluate the dissertation for which Bill Cosby received his well-publicized Doctor of Education degree. But that's a story Damerell should tell for himself.

Damerell tells the story of one graduate student that is relevant to this chapter. The young lady who is the subject of the story had received an especially low score on the Graduate Record Exam. For some reason, most colleges of education require applicants to take this test, then they ignore the results. In this case, the lady's score was practically zero. But like others with equally bad scores, she was admitted to the Master of Education program. According to Damerell's account, the young lady was functionally illiterate. Even though she continued to get high grades in her other education courses, Damerell was confident she would never graduate. It seems that she had received one or two "incompletes" in his courses, and he knew she was incapable of completing the work. Since such incompletes automatically become "F's" after a certain amount of time, Damerell naturally believed that the "F's" she had gotten in his courses would prevent her from graduating.

One day, to his amazement, Damerell learned that the lady had graduated after all. He discovered that someone in the College of Education had, in violation of university rules, tampered with her transcript by removing the incomplete grades he had given her. The now missing courses which should have shown up as

"F's" had been replaced with other education courses for which she received "A's". The functionally illiterate young lady was now the proud holder of a Master of Education degree. For all anyone knows, this unearned and unmerited degree may have helped her get a job in education where she could pass on the qualifications of prospective teachers who, like her, were functionally illiterate. Perhaps one day, one of those teachers might even have said something like, "I teaches English." (I don't use this example to be offensive; I'm only quoting the *Time* article cited earlier.)

We should hardly be surprised, then, to hear Vanderbilt University professor Chester E. Finn, Jr., say:

> The higher-education system . . . is awarding a great many diplomas to individuals whose intellectual attainments are meager, even at the end of college, and for minority graduates this is happening so often that the academy may be faulted for massive deception. It is giving people degrees which imply that they have accomplished something they have not in fact achieved. Like driving a new car home from the dealer only to discover that it is a lemon, the owners of such degrees are likely one day to think themselves cheated rather than aided by the hypocrisy and erratic quality control of the academic enterprise. The taxpayers who now underwrite most of that enterprise are apt to feel much the same.[8]

Reginald Damerell states that "Empty credentials are all that any school or department of education in any university in the United States gives to its graduates. The education field is devoid of intellectual content, has no body of knowledge of its own and acts as if bodies of knowledge do not exist in other university departments."[9] The noted American economist, Thomas Sowell, calls schools and departments of education "the intellectual slums" of American academia.[10] James B. Koerner has identified "the inferior intellectual quality of the Education faculty" as "the fundamental limitation of the [education] field."[11] Clearly, the educational impoverishment of the people who control teacher education is a major factor in America's education problem. A problem equally great is the fact that "it never seems to occur to many modern teachers that the primary business of the teacher is to study the subject that he is going to teach. Instead of studying the subject that he is going to teach, he studies 'education'; a knowledge of the methodology of teaching takes the place of a knowledge of the particular branch of literature, history or science to which a man has devoted his life."[12]

Educationists have not been content to force the students, America's future teachers, to take their contentless courses in place of more important courses in the liberal arts. According to Damerell, educationists

> have actively promoted the decline in the 3 Rs. They have aggressively attacked them. They have trained teachers-to-be as attackers and dispersed them to schools throughout the United States. . . . It would be a mistake to ascribe to education professors any intellectual understanding of the consequences of their actions. They do not recognize that the literature of Greece, Rome, and modern Europe made today's culture possible. . . . Educationists' attacks on the 3 Rs have been made out of ignorance compounded by self-interest. Having no body of knowledge of their own and having never made a positive contribution to public schooling, educationists have had to keep putting out new notions to justify their existence.[13]

We have heard some of the voices of people who believe that an important part of the educational crisis is the professional education establishment. A related part of the problem is the required certification without which otherwise qualified individuals are not permitted to teach. Given all that we know about the dismal state of professional education in this country, it is beyond belief that the standards of certification are, by and large, left in the hands of the same educationists whose major contribution to education is the mass production of unqualified teachers. Not surprisingly, these same educationists have made the major condition of certification to be the taking of an inordinately large number of their own education courses. It has been a highly successful gambit in the sense that it guarantees them an unending stream of students and, as a result, guarantees them a livelihood.

University president John Silber argues that the educationists' stranglehold on teacher certification should be terminated. He regards this as one necessary step in easing the educational crisis. In Silber's words,

> [W]e must break the monopoly of schools of education on teacher certification. For a long time certification standards for teachers have been, in many states, almost entirely in terms of education courses—that is, courses having little to do with education—and this has given education schools their virtual monopoly on the supply of teachers. In doing so, it has also placed almost insurmountable obstacles in the way of highly intelligent students and highly intelligent adults out of school who will simply not accept the intellectual and spiritual indignity of the typical school of education curriculum. The willingness to endure four years in a typical school of education often constitutes an effective negative intelligence test.[14]

Readers who thought the earlier discussion of educationists was a bit harsh should pause and reread Silber's words. He urges states to remove the monopolistic control educationists have been given over the preparation and certification of teachers. Surely, he writes, some state

> will have the wisdom and the courage to take the lead in breaking the monopoly of Schools of Education by passing a ten-year moratorium on certification requirements. During the decade of this moratorium, schools would be free to recruit qualified college graduates with majors in academic subjects whether or not they had any education courses. From a vastly increased pool of talent, made up of persons attracted by the ideals of the teaching profession, by its calendar, by the quality of life of teachers, and by intellectual and moral challenge, schools would be able to develop a teacher corps of significantly increased quality.[15]

The respected president of Boston University believes that if just one state would demonstrate the wisdom to experiment with his suggestion, the resulting improvement in that state's educational programs would be so dramatic and receive so much national attention that concerned parents and taxpayers in other states would call for similar changes in their own areas.

Some voices can be heard in support of even stronger measures than Silber's recommendation that teacher certification be completely removed from educationists' control. They are urging that America's departments and colleges of education be abolished and the little important work that has to be done in this area be turned over to the respective academic departments such as English, history, and math.[16] Writing in 1985, Reginald Damerell estimated that the elimination of departments and colleges of education would result in a minimal saving of 1.5 billion dollars a year![17] This enormous sum of money could then be used by state and local governments to upgrade facilities or raise teacher's salaries, if they wished. Or this money could be put to even better use by adding it to other monies that could be used to increase parental choice in education by making available vouchers or tax credits, a step that this book will soon identify as the most crucial step in improving American education.

What is the best undergraduate preparation for future teachers? One thing is clear: the answer is not to be found in the schemes and machinations of the educationists. The answer is not to be found in majors in this or that area of professional education. The best preparation for teachers "is a rigorous liberal arts education. The humanities are the most likely to produce a literate person, a critical person, a person who can think for him or herself, and can act accordingly."[18] This wise answer points the way to changes in teacher training that must be taken if this nation is serious about dealing with its education crisis.

The National Education Association

The National Education Association (NEA) is another of the major obstacles to significant reform and improvement of American education. With a membership of approximately two million[19] (more than 70 percent of America's public school teachers) and a total of about $375 million received from dues to spend each year, it is a powerful organization. It uses its clout and financial muscle to elect politicians who support its causes. It carries on an aggressive lobbying campaign.

The NEA uses its money and power on behalf of goals that reflect its secular and far-left political ideology. Connaught Coyne Marshner identifies what the NEA stands for, namely, "More bureaucracy, more federal aid (aid that specifically discriminates against private or religious education), teacher (not parent or community) evaluation of school boards and administrators, teacher (not parent or community) say-so on 'learning experiences and teaching techniques' and 'instructional materials' and 'controversial issues.'"[20]

But what do NEA members and authorities themselves say about some of the results of NEA policies? Former NEA officials Bill Boynton and John Lloyd write: "Most school districts are characterized by adversarial relationships, which run counter to creating healthy environments in which students can learn."[21]

Perhaps more dangerous than NEA policies, however, are the instructional materials for teachers. According to Chester Finn's analysis of NEA materials, "It includes the delegitimizing of all authority save that of the state, the degradation of traditional morality, and the encouragement of citizens in general and children in particular to despise the rules and customs that make their society a functional democracy."[22]

The NEA frequently uses some of the union dues it collects from its members to pay for television commercials that boost its public image. To judge from those commercials, the NEA is a patriotic organization that has only one reason for existing, namely, offering every student in America the very best possible education. The truth turns out to be something quite different. According to W. A. John Johnson, editor of the *Daily News Digest*, the NEA is "an educational Mafia" that "captured the high ground of American public education in the late 1800's." The real and often hidden agenda of this group "has deliberately steered the public schools, its teachers and children down a disaster road to socialism, secular humanism, radicalism, planned failure in reading and writing, suffocation of Christianity, the trashing of basic values and the establishment of one of the most powerful and dangerous unions, the National Education Association (NEA)."[23]

Perhaps the most vocal of the NEA's rapidly growing list of critics is Samuel Blumenfeld, who begins his book-length investigation of the union with these words:

> Over the past decade Americans have become slowly aware that something is happening in their political life which has never happened before. Public school

teachers, once loved and respected for their devotion
to their profession, have become militantly politicized
and are now the most active and powerful advocates
of the political and social agendas of the radical Left.
The National Education Association, which represents
1.7 million teachers, has decided that its members are
no longer satisfied with merely being public servants.
They want to become political masters.[24]

The problem is that the NEA does not really represent the rank
and file teachers that make up its own membership. Numerous
critics have substantiated that the union has stopped representing the real interests of America's teachers and American
education. Instead, NEA leaders have taken every opportunity
to "advocate left-wing social programs which in no way reflect
the views of their members. But, most important, they have been
uncompromising in struggling to increase their own power at
the expense of the power of the NEA rank and file."[25] Even NEA
president Mary Futrell has admitted, "Instruction and professional development have been on the back burner to us compared
with political action."[26] And it has been clearly documented that
the NEA spends millions each year to elect the candidates it
favors.[27]

Blumenfeld presents evidence to support his contention that
"the radical left [has] decided that the best way to achieve power
in America is through the organized political action of public
school teachers."[28] He believes that "American teachers are being
used by clever political activists to bring the radical left to power."[29]
It is ominous that such a powerful organization with such a
partisan political agenda should be in control of America's schools.
This agenda coupled with the NEA's enormous power makes it
extremely unlikely that any reform of public education can occur
without that power being challenged.

Blumenfeld identifies some of the strategies the NEA is using
to achieve a monopoly of control over public education. The first
strategy is control over the teaching profession, primarily through
control over the process of teacher certification and secondly
over teacher's colleges. Regarding the latter, Blumenfeld states,
"[T]he NEA wants complete control of all teachers' colleges so
that what is taught in them will conform with NEA policies."[30]
This statement is not the result of an overactive imagination;

Blumenfeld quotes directly from NEA resolutions that have been made public. As far as teacher accreditation is concerned, Blumenfeld warns that the "NEA wants the power to screen all candidates for the teaching profession and keep track of them during their training."[31] If the NEA has its way, he continues, "it will be illegal for virtually anyone to teach anything in America without a license. Every teacher, public or private, will be licensed, every teacher of teachers will be licensed, every substitute will be licensed, every teacher of remedial reading will be licensed, and schools, public and private, will be required to hire only licensed teachers. And who will control the licensing? Why, the NEA, of course!"[32]

Blumenfeld elaborates on this abuse of power. It is the goal of the NEA, he states, "to control all teacher certification in the United States and, through the agency shop, control the hiring and firing of teachers."[33] This exclusive union control will give the NEA a virtually limitless source of income from non-voluntary dues from people who are forced into membership; it will have the power to prevent anyone from securing a teaching position who does not share its ideology and submit to its control. This is the NEA's goal.

In addition to its aim to control who will teach and who will teach the teachers, in addition to its intention of gaining the exclusive right to represent teachers as well as a closed shop, the NEA has made it clear that it wishes to control the content of education, what our children are taught. Its preferred curriculum is unmistakenly secular and naturalistic.

Another NEA strategy is influencing elections to insure the election of candidates who support its agenda. It has been doing this for years through involvement in the Democratic Party, through its own PAC (political action committee) and through PACs affiliated with state organizations. Its own publication, *NEA Today,* boasts that "in 1980 and once again in 1984, NEA had more of its members elected as delegates to the Democratic and Republican national conventions than any other membership organization or state delegation. This year [1988] NEA expects as many as 500 Association members will be on hand at the conventions to fight for party platform planks reflecting the Association's agenda for quality education. . . . This sort of Association-wide organizing in support of a candidate is what separates the political hacks from the achievers. . . . The Association works to deliver the resources no one else offers."[34]

The next time the Democratic Party has a convention on either the state or local level, pay attention to the enormous power the NEA exercises. When the NEA speaks, liberal politicians listen and tremble. The NEA also attempts to influence such governmental agencies as the U.S. Department of Education and state departments of education. The fact that Ronald Reagan's promise to abolish the federal Department of Education was never fulfilled can be attributed to the NEA's influence, as well of course as to the indifference and incompetence of assorted officials in his administration.

The last NEA strategy to be mentioned here is the influence it seeks to exert on federal funding. It seeks control over the disbursement of tax dollars to schools. It opposes the use of tax dollars to support private schools at every turn. It opposes all efforts to increase parental choice in education that include private schools. The NEA, Blumenfeld explains, "views private education as its most serious competitor, its barrier to a total monopoly, and it has vowed to bring it under NEA control through teacher certification and state accreditation laws. . . . [T]o the NEA, any private school, no matter how small or poor seems to be a threat to its monopolist plans."[35]

The NEA has also gone on record stating that it is opposed to any form of home-schooling unless performed by certified teachers who use a state-approved curriculum.[36]

Americans who care about quality education must do everything possible to resist NEA efforts to weaken private schools, especially Christian schools. They should become activists on behalf of Christian schools and challenge attempts by educationists to extend their certification powers over teachers in private schools. They should identify politicians who have sold out to the NEA for the mess of pottage they call a campaign contribution; and they should then work to defeat politicians like this at every level of government—federal, state, and local. Americans who care about quality education should find ways of challenging the educationists' monopoly over teacher accreditation. Efforts to change or eliminate existing certification requirements that include large numbers of useless education courses should be supported and encouraged.

Frankly, the power that professional educationists and the NEA have attained over public education is so complete and so unchallenged that the recommendations of the last paragraph do appear unrealistic. But there were times when other causes appeared equally hopeless. What is needed are leaders in each community and each state who will start the process, along with others who will provide the same kind of financial support and dedicated willingness to make personal sacrifices that have come to characterize the pro-life movement.

Up to this point in the chapter, I have been talking about some of the people, institutions, and organizations that are responsible for America's educational disaster. Before this chapter ends, it is also important that I say something about some of the ideas and theories that provided much of the intellectual underpinning for the actions and policies that we've examined. A major source for these ideas has been the philosophy of John Dewey and the philosophy of education that grew out of his system. There is no doubt that Dewey's influence has diminished greatly in some respects. He is almost totally ignored by contemporary American philosophers, and few living educationists seem to be interested in acknowledging his indispensable role as midwife to the contemporary theories of education that are at the root of our problems. Nor should we ignore such predecessors of these theories as Jean Jacques Rousseau. But Dewey is the most important proximate source of these waters. If we want to know how the waters got polluted, his system is as good a place to look as any.

John Dewey's Instrumentalism

After graduating from the University of Vermont, John Dewey (1859–1952) taught high school for three years. He then did graduate work in philosophy at Johns Hopkins University, following which he taught at the universities of Michigan, Minnesota, and Chicago. In 1905, he went to Columbia University where he taught until his retirement in 1929. During his lifetime, Dewey first developed and then became the spiritual and political leader of a system in which relativism, positivism, secularism, humanism, and naturalism merged into a position which, in spite of its inadequacies, helped change the face of American education. The system goes by several names: pragmatism,[37] instrumentalism[38] and/or experimentalism.[39]

For Dewey, everything turns on the ever-changing relationship between humans and their environment. Thinking is not a search for some "truth" that exists statically "out there," independent of us. Thinking rather is an *instrument* that we use in our attempt to solve problems. Reflective thinking is always related, for Dewey, to some transformation of a practical situation. Thinking never occurs in isolation from particular problems that need solving. Ideas then are instruments or plans of operation that aid us in our attempts to solve problems. Ideas are working blueprints of action, invented to benefit some practical interest or eliminate some discomfort. It follows then that what Dewey regards as truth is simply an idea that works, that is, that helps us solve some problem. Thinking therefore is a way of reconstructing situations in ways that will aid us in attaining certain desired ends. I will have more to say shortly about the importance that ends and the means to those ends play in Dewey's system.

Dewey was a prototype of the twentieth-century secularist. He once wrote that "faith in the prayer-hearing God is an unproved and outmoded faith. There is no God and there is no soul. Hence, there are no needs for the props of traditional religion. With dogma and creed excluded, then immutable truth is also dead and buried. There is no room for fixed, natural law or moral absolutes."[40] As the last two sentences of the quote make clear, Dewey was also the consummate relativist.

Dewey was a thorough-going naturalist. He viewed humans only in their capacity as biological organisms. He subordinated what others regarded as the mental and spiritual aspects of the human person to the physical and biological. Human thinking is not the product of an immaterial soul. It is simply a different aspect of man's functioning as a biological being.

Dewey denied the existence of any fixed truth. But while he denied the fixed and unchangeable character of the laws of logic, he nonetheless used those laws to argue for his own position. He expected his readers to follow *his* train of thought to his conclusions, thus conveniently ignoring the fact that his repudiation of logic invalidated his own reasoning.

An earlier paragraph introduced Dewey's emphasis on the importance of humans selecting the best means (here, once again, is the notion of instrumentalism) to our desired ends or goals.

Dewey rejected the traditional philosophical distinction between intrinsic values (values that are good in themselves) and instrumental values (values that are good as a means to something else). He denied that there are any intrinsic ends or values in life; everything that can be said to be good can only be good in an instrumental sense, as a means to something else. All humans can do is pursue instrumental values; they can never arrive at anything that possesses intrinsic value.

Dewey's position here is clearly defective. Unless there were at least one thing that possessed intrinsic value, that was good in itself, nothing else could possess instrumental value. The picture of humans spending their entire lives in the pursuit of transitory, changing values which are only means to something else, coupled with the claim that there exists nowhere anything of enduring and intrinsic value, makes our moral quest either a bad joke or an exercise in futility. As so often happens with thinkers like Dewey, he failed to practice what he preached. Even though he denied the fixity of any moral standards, he urged the importance of "moral growth." But the notion of moral growth appears meaningless without some kind of fixed end toward which "growth" can progress.

One need not look beyond Plato to find what's wrong with Dewey's view. Plato saw that the basic question in life is not the selection of the best *means* to something else. Rather, Plato argued, the important thing in life is to make certain that one has selected the right *ends*. Long before any human starts worrying about whether she has the best *means*, she should reflect about whether her *ends* or goals in life are the ones she should be seeking. She should ask: Is this the sort of thing I should be seeking? Dewey's system is powerless to help humans discover if their ends are correct. Indeed, on his analysis, no end can ever be intrinsically good.

Science (and the scientific method) is sometimes indispensable when we are dealing with the present, that is, with what *is* the case. If a person's end is simply "getting high," the scientific method (and Dewey's experimentalism and instrumentalism) can help a person discover which means (for example, which drug and which method of using that drug) is best. But values (that is, the permanent things) point beyond the present to the *future*. How can we identify the value that will continue to satisfy in the future? How can we recognize the end that we *ought* to seek? Don't expect any answer from Dewey on this more vital question.

Unlike many earlier philosophers who were content to spin their theories in ivory towers isolated from society, Dewey recognized the importance of getting his ideas into society. There is no quicker way to do this (an end) than to make your views the dominant theory of education (his means). The Teachers College of Columbia University became the major instrument through which Dewey's philosophy of education came to be accepted, in many parts of the nation, as the foundation of an entirely new approach to education. While it would be a drastic oversimplification to equate Dewey's system with the whole of what came to be known as "progressive education" (Dewey himself often criticized elements of it), nonetheless it is not difficult to see the close connection.

Since Dewey believed that education cannot occur via any direct transfer of information, he thought that teachers should provide students with the appropriate experiences. What is an appropriate experience? For Dewey, an experience contributes to a student's education if it contributes to that student's "growth." The teacher "educates" by changing the student's environment in ways that help the student to grow. But what, one must ask, constitutes *growth*? Is there any criterion of growth? How can there be growth and progress without some fixed end or ends by which growth and progress can be measured? Can one be faulted for seeing a resemblance between Dewey and the charlatans who pretended to be making the emperor's new clothes in the Hans Christian Anderson story? In the story that we all remember so well, it was finally a child who blurted out, "The emperor is naked." Dewey and his followers fooled most of the education profession (not a difficult thing to do, as it turns out) and lots of powerful people in high places into thinking they were putting together an approach to education that we could build a society upon. What should have been obvious from the start was that it was a charade. The emperor is still naked.

From Theory to Practice

In his book, *Visions of Order*,[41] Richard M. Weaver provides a list of the assumptions and tenets of the philosophy of education that came to dominate the teaching of American young people. Earlier, I stated that John Dewey's philosophy was a mixture of relativism, positivism, secularism, naturalism, and humanism. The theory of education described by Weaver is a consequence of those ideas.

The first assumption that has captured the people who gained control of public education since World War II is the view that "there is no such thing as a body of knowledge which reflects the structure of reality and which everyone therefore needs to learn. Knowledge is viewed as an instrumentality which is true or false according to the way it is applied to concrete situations or the way it serves the needs of the individual." Relativism is king, Weaver warns. And thus, "there is no final knowledge about anything. The truths of yesterday are the falsehoods of today and the truths of today will be the falsehoods of tomorrow."

It follows then that it is not the purpose of education to teach knowledge; what the progressive educator does, in this new view of things, is teach students. This translates into a situation where everything must be adapted to the particular student and to the group in ways that take account of their limitations. There are no longer any standards by which the "learning" of the student or the performance of the teacher can be measured. In a world without standards, what the student studies should be up to him. The student's interests should be the major consideration in what he studies and when he studies it.

In such an approach to education, it is obviously wrong to think of the teacher as some kind of authority figure. "[A]uthority is evil. The teacher is there as a 'leader,' but the duty of the leader is only to synchronize and cooperate with the work of the group." Anything like grades and other forms of competition in school are bad; they help lead students to feel superior or inferior to others, and such feelings are inconsistent with Dewey's vision of democracy. Sensory learning should be placed on an equal footing with intellectual learning. The last thing the "good" teacher will do is place undue importance on the mind, as opposed to the senses. "Consequently there should be less education through symbols like language and figures [notice the denigration of reading, writing, and arithmetic] and more through using the hands on concrete objects. It is more important to make maps than to learn them, said John Dewey, the grand pundit of the revolutionary movement." This helps to explain why so many students are geographically illiterate in the sense that they cannot point out England on a map of Europe or the Mississippi River on a map of the United States. It is hardly surprising, then, that we learn that the major aim of educators who believe all this is not to train students to know anything but to help them adjust to the society around them.

For such educators, Weaver explains, "knowledge, which has been the traditional reason for instituting schools, does not exist in any absolute or binding sense. The mind, which has always been regarded as the distinguishing possession of the human race, is now viewed as a tyrant which has been denying the rights of the body as a whole." This results in a situation where "the student is to be prepared not to save his soul, or to inherit the wisdom and usages of past civilizations, or even to get ahead in life, but to become a member of a utopia resting on a false view of both nature and man."[42]

We should not be surprised when we discover that students haven't been learning much recently. Part of the reason is that the professional educationists who have taken over the vital task of preparing teachers have persuaded those teachers that *what* a student knows is no longer important. As Weaver puts it, "This set of propositions practically inverts our traditional idea of education, which venerates mind, recognizes the moral and practical value of discipline, and regards competition as the indispensable spur to outstanding achievement. Yet these are the very propositions which have been systematically taught by educationists for about fifty years and which have strongly affected education on all . . . levels."[43]

Conclusion

Since it's impossible to pretend that the education crisis doesn't exist, educationists and the NEA have taken it upon themselves to instruct Americans about the proper way to solve the problem. According to them, the answer is simple: more money. What is the source of this money that will, they say, finally put an end to our problem? Their answer is the seemingly bottomless pit called the treasury of the United States. Their allies in seeking massive new amounts of public funds are the politicians, the Washington bureaucrats, and the liberals who control the media. How is this money to be used? It is to be entrusted to the very people who helped create this crisis. And what should we expect if they succeed? Without question, we can expect the education crisis to get worse.

What we need to do is ignore the hysterical reporting we hear each night on the evening news that suggests that a U.S. president who opposes giving more money to education (i.e., to the educationists) is somehow betraying America's children. We need to elect a different group of congressmen who are not in the pocket of the education establishment. We need to end the educationists' stranglehold on teacher preparation and certification. And we need thinking people who are able to challenge the destructive philosophy of education upon which the crumbling house of American public education has been erected.

CHAPTER

6

Skillful observation and controlled thoughtfulness. . . .
those are the habits of literacy. The attentive and patient
observer, therefore, must come to see at last that school
is not 'something else over there.' School is America. If
you want to predict the future of our land, go to school
and look around.

—Richard Mitchell, *The Graves of Academe*

Four Essential Steps

The last chapter noted several causes for the educational mess
in the United States and suggested courses of action to deal with
these causes. With regard to incompetent teachers in the classroom, several things must be done. There must be appropriate
competency testing of all teachers, new and old (such testing will
be discussed later). Appropriate steps should then be taken to
remove those who fall below a certain level of competency. This
will create an obvious need for qualified teachers to replace those
found incompetent.

The certification requirements that presently exist in almost all
states should be abandoned. They are unwisely slanted towards
individuals who have frequently been less able academically and
who were coerced into taking large numbers of education courses
that reduced their opportunities in the kinds of humanities courses
that are the backbone of any quality education. I also argued that
the monopoly power professional educationists presently have
over certification requirements should be ended. I agreed with
experts who urge that departments and schools of education be
abolished and that the relatively insignificant amount of worthwhile material to be found in the bloated educationist curriculum be handled by other departments. And finally I argued
the need for greater awareness of the serious threat that the
militant, far-left ideologues running the NEA pose, not only to
the education of America's youth but also to our stability as a
society. Politicians who sell their consciences and their votes for

NEA money and votes should be identified and defeated. NEA power should be challenged at every opportunity.

In this chapter, I want to discuss four additional factors in the overall solution to our educational crisis. The first three will be covered rather briefly since, once recognized, they should be obvious. The last point will deal with the importance of increasing parental choice which may be the most vital step of all. Because of its significance and the urgency to expanding family choice with regard to schools as rapidly as possible, the topic of family choice will be continued in the following chapter.

The Educational Role of the Family

Writing in *Christianity Today*, Ernest L. Boyer, president of the Carnegie Foundation for the Advancement of Teaching, urges his Christian audience to "view moral education as a partnership, not an obligation for the schools to carry alone."[1] All of the evidence suggests, he continues, "that, in the end, parents matter most, and it is unfair to families—as well as to schools—to expect classrooms to do the whole job. I am not trying to take schools off the hook. They have an important role to play in the moral development of children. But we cannot expect schools to do what families have not been able to accomplish."[2] While Boyer's remarks dealt primarily with moral education, they apply with equal force to all aspects of a child's education. As the late Presbyterian theologian, J. Gresham Machen, once said: "The most important Christian education institution is not the pulpit or the school, important as those institutions are; but it is the Christian family. And that institution has to a very large extent ceased to do its work."[3]

Christian families that assume that the education of their children is something that occurs exclusively outside the home are making a serious mistake. Christians must pay more attention to the essential, indispensable role of the family in the overall education of their children. Unfortunately, many families are not equipped to do a very good job in this regard. One way to see this is to approach parental responsibility in terms of what can be called the four levels of parental concern.

The first and most basic level of parental concern is *emotional*. This is usually where most normal parents begin. They love their children; they care what happens to them; they want the best for their children. There is nothing wrong with this level of parental concern. The problem arises when parents' concern for their children fails to rise above this level. It is important to recognize that parental concern must function on other levels as well.

A second and higher plateau is the level of *spiritual* concern. When a parent's concern is limited merely to the emotional level, that parent's vision of what is most important for the child will be lacking in important ways. Many parents seem incapable of seeing beyond the goal of temporal happiness and success for their children. For such parents, a college education is seen simply as a means to such an end.

The wise Christian parent recognizes that there is more to life than this. God calls His children to live their lives for Him and for others. Parents who reach the level of spiritual concern want more than earthly success and material prosperity for their children. They want their children to be faithful believers who love the Lord and His Word, and who sincerely want to do His will. Some of the important issues at the level of spiritual concern are conversion, Christian living, and Christian service. Of course, Christian service is not limited to "religious" (as opposed to "secular") vocations. God calls some people to be pastors and missionaries; he calls others to be bank tellers, auto mechanics, business people, and school teachers.

Level three is the level of *theological concern*. I have never met a genuine Christian who disparaged the importance of conversion, faith, commitment, sacrifice, Bible study, holy living, and the like. But I know lots of Christians who have not yet seen the importance of sound doctrine. It is important *that* we believe (spiritual concern); but it is also important *what* we believe (theological concern).

There are segments of Christianity that appear to stress *only* doctrines or creeds; they appear to say that the only important thing is believing the correct propositions. In the process of doing this, some of these churches fail to tell people that there is a personal and subjective side to the Christian faith. We must believe the right truths; but we must also believe *in* the right *Person*, Jesus Christ! What we know objectively must be combined with a genuine subjective commitment. But there are also elements of the Christian church that emphasize only the subjective or inner side of the Christian faith to the neglect of the objective, theological side. Whenever this happens, Christians are operating with something less than the full Gospel.

If Christian young people are to be properly prepared for the years ahead, they need to know the objective dimension of their faith; they should understand what they as Christians are supposed to believe. Moreover, they should also be introduced to the good and sound reasons *why* Christians believe these truths. The children of most Christian parents enter college with absolutely no preparation for the challenges to their faith that they will encounter. They have no idea why they believe that God exists or why Jesus is the Son of God or why the miracle of Christ's resurrection occurred. Suddenly, without warning, they are confronted by a professor who challenges their faith with a problem or question they didn't even know existed; consequently, they have no idea there are answers to these problems. And, even worse, if they dare to ask their parents what the answer is, the parents are even more uninformed than the students.[4]

Christian parents who have failed to rise to the level of theological concern cannot possibly be ready to provide help for their children in these matters. Some Christians don't know the Bible or Christian doctrine as well as they should; don't pay attention to what's going on in the world; don't read serious books; ignore the development of their minds (in spite of such biblical admonitions as Rom. 12:1–2). It is a tragedy that so many Christians possess such a weak understanding of their faith that they are unable to explain to others exactly *what* Christians are supposed to believe. The first step in getting children prepared theologically for what awaits them is for the parents of those children to prepare themselves.

The last level, that of *intellectual concern*, is undoubtedly the hardest rung of the ladder to get most Christian parents to climb. All normal parents are emotionally involved with their children, and it is relatively easy to get Christian parents to see that their parental love must be extended to include concern for their children's spiritual well-being. It is harder to get these same parents to recognize the importance of such studies as theology and apologetics. But, even at the level of theological concern, we are dealing with issues that have a clear relevance to the Christian faith. What makes this last level—what I call the level of intellectual concern—so much more difficult to achieve is its apparent irrelevance to typical religious concerns. What we are dealing with here is knowledge for its own sake; the study of history or mathematics or economics or philosophy or art, even when no direct relationship to Christianity is apparent (which is not to say there is no relationship between faith and the above disciplines).

One of the biggest obstacles in all this is getting Christian parents (and students) to appreciate the importance of their minds. How many Christians have ever noticed that the first and greatest commandment, according to Jesus, requires us to love God with all our heart and all our soul and all our *mind* (Matt. 22:37). The common Christian practice of compartmentalizing knowledge into sacred and secular is unbiblical and leads to the dangerous notion that secular knowledge is somehow less important, worldly, and hence unfit for the spiritual Christian. Although the truth God has revealed in Scripture is sufficient for faith and conduct, it is not exhaustive. The truth we can find outside the Bible is also important and worthy of our attention and careful study. Even revealed truth requires study and interpretation, tasks that can be aided by an education in such "secular" subjects as philosophy and history. We must reject the mistaken belief that faith somehow provides the Christian with a shortcut to the truth that eliminates any need for a grounding in so-called secular areas of learning.

In one of the better passages from *The Closing of the American Mind*, Allan Bloom speaks to this issue. He writes that many modern families "have nothing to give their children in the way of a vision of the world, of high models of action or profound sense of connection with others. . . . The family requires a certain authority and wisdom about the ways of the heavens and of men. The parents must have knowledge of what has happened in the past, and prescriptions for what ought to be, in order to resist the philistinism or the wickedness of the present."[5] In other words, few parents can be any real help to their children unless they also have acquired a foundation in certain important academic areas.

Bloom continues: "People sup together, play together, travel together, but they do not think together. Hardly any homes have any intellectual life whatsoever, let alone one that informs the vital interests of life."[6] Christians need to work at developing a Christian mind; and they should do this in partnership with every other member of their family. To seek knowledge is an important part of what it means to be a fully developed Christian.

If parental concern is functioning on all the proper levels, it will include a concern that children develop mentally as well as spiritually. In order for parents to have the same degree of input on the level of ideas as they might have, say, on the emotional and spiritual levels, the parents themselves have to work at keeping in touch with the contemporary world of ideas.

Student Motivation and Preparation

Another factor contributing to the dismal educational state of many students is the students themselves. Many students fail to learn, not because of incompetent or indifferent teachers, but because they lack motivation or commitment as well as a proper foundation for their present studies. For many students, the only thing that counts is getting by.

One reason high school and college students never reach their full potential is because they failed to reach a number of intermediary goals along the way. Picture a long-distance runner who wants to be close enough at the finish line to challenge for first place. This runner should know that in order to be in that position at the end of the race, he or she will have to meet certain goals all through the race. The runner may know, for example, that he or she must run the first half of the race within a certain time. Many high school and college students have fallen way behind in important areas of intellectual development. Sometimes, this is the fault of others; but often the student's family has contributed to the problem by failing to provide the proper help, motivation, and encouragement.

Every year, I teach about two hundred students in an Introduction to Philosophy course (about fifty students in each section of the course). Most of them are freshmen. In addition to teaching the students about philosophy, I use the course as a way of helping them to organize and express ideas in essay form. This is something that few contemporary students have been prepared to do by their high school courses. Recently, however, I have begun to realize that there is another reason why today's college students cannot write decent essays: they simply have not read enough. They spell poorly because they haven't seen most of these words in print; they cannot write decent sentences because the little they learned about grammar hasn't been reinforced by sufficient reading experience; their paragraphs cannot rise above the mundane because their exposure to the vocabulary and writing style of good authors is so limited. One of the most important things parents can do for their children is encourage them to read; and to read quality literature.

Allan Bloom points out that students today "have lost the practice of and the taste for reading. They have not learned how to read, nor do they have the expectation of delight or improvement from reading."[7] The rich, wonderful world of great books is as foreign to most modern students as the American continent was to the pilgrims when they first set foot on this land. They knew something was out there but could only guess as to what it was. The failure to read good books, Bloom continues, "enfeebles the vision and strengthens our most fatal tendency—the belief that the here and now is all there is."[8]

Parents should do everything possible to develop a love for reading in their children. As children reach appropriate levels in their development, they should be encouraged to read quality books suitable for young people with their ability. It is even better when at least one parent reads the book at the same time and is able to discuss it with the child. Any good reading program, of course, must include the Bible. Make sure a good, readable, modern version of the Bible is available.

Some parents might complain at this time that I'm confusing them with their children's teachers. Such a response only demonstrates one of the problems of the modern family. *Fathers and mothers* are the most important teachers their children will ever have. It is the failure of so many parents to fulfill this role that is at the root of many students' problems. It is a sacrificial role that parents must play if their children are to be good students. It may mean time, energy, or material wealth, or all three. But that sacrifice will be rewarded if carried out with the spirit of love that we are called to demonstrate as parents. Our children will be able to read, write, and communicate with greater skill.

Increasing Local Control of Schools

One of the best discussions of the subject of school control is found in a book published by The Heartland Institute of Illinois titled, *We Can Rescue Our Children: The Cure for Chicago's Public*

School Crisis. While the problems addressed in the book may appear most common in the public schools of our larger cities, the recommendations offered by the book make sense for any school district in America.[9]

People whose children must attend public schools in cities like New York, Philadelphia, Cleveland, Chicago, and Los Angeles don't need anyone to tell them how bad the schools are and how pitifully weak the educational experience is. Parents who live in smaller communities sometimes have difficulty appreciating how much worse the public schools in large urban areas are from their own. Once in a while, their level of consciousness may be raised by such things as the recent Hollywood movie, *Stand and Deliver.* This was the inspiring film about a Hispanic teacher in a Los Angeles barrio who brings his underprivileged students through a difficult calculus course with tear-jerking success, in spite of a bad environment. His success was a monument to dedication and care.

I will not burden the reader with another recitation of the depressing SAT scores of Chicago school students. They are every bit as bad or worse than one would expect. Other pieces of evidence speak just as eloquently about how low Chicago's public schools have sunk. One of them is the number of Chicago public school teachers who make sure their own children attend private schools. While only 22 percent of all school-age children within Chicago attend private schools, 46 percent of the children of people who teach in Chicago's public school system attend private schools. That reveals what the teachers themselves think of their own school system. The other piece of evidence I'll mention is the dropout rate in the Chicago school system. The average rate of high school dropouts across the entire state of Illinois is 24 percent. But the rate of high school dropouts in Chicago's public schools averages between 43 and 53 percent.

The Heartland Institute book takes note of the recommendations teachers' unions like the NEA always make in response to the depressing state of Chicago's public schools. "Pay teachers more money," they say, "and give them smaller classes." But the authors of the Heartland book produce evidence that shows that these recommendations are not the solution:

> Higher teacher salaries and smaller class sizes (except class sizes of less than ten) have been found repeatedly

to have no significant positive effect on learning. Similarly, total spending per pupil is unrelated to educational results, as are administrators' salaries and teacher
experience.... [I]ncreased expenditures go mainly into
administrative and auxiliary activities that have little
or no effect on educational outcomes.[10]

The Heartland authors focus their attention on the enormous
size of the Chicago public school bureaucracy. Even though
Chicago public schools serve two and a half times as many
students as Chicago's private Catholic schools, the public school
system has one hundred times the number of administrators.
This bloated bureaucracy provides jobs for thirty-three hundred
people who, it is claimed, have administrative tasks of one kind
or another. This bureaucracy is so out of proportion to what is
needed that it's easy to believe that many members of this
bureaucracy must think the major purpose of the Chicago public
school system is not teaching youngsters but providing well-
paying, cushy jobs for college of education graduates who don't
want to teach.

What troubles the Heartland authors is not simply the enormous
waste of money that this bloated bureaucracy takes from the taxpayer and diverts from teachers' salaries, classroom size, building
maintenance, and supplies. It is also the fact that this bureaucracy
insists on centering the control of individual schools in itself. Even
when a Chicago school is fortunate enough to have a good principal, her hands are often tied by constraints imposed on her by the
central office. The teacher or principal who recognizes that a change
here or there can result in improving the level of education is unable
to make that change on her own initiative. As Michael Dukakis said
during the 1988 presidential campaign, a fish always rots from the
head down. Had Dukakis really cared to find examples of his
proverb, he could have started with the bureaucracies that control
public education in our large urban areas.

According to the authors of our book, the cure for Chicago's
public schools "requires taking control of the schools from a
remote and too-powerful bureaucracy and returning it to principals, teachers, and local community representatives. It requires
giving the parents of students enrolled in each school a voice in
the selection of its principal and the establishment of school

policies. And it requires allowing parents to choose which schools their children will attend."[11]

Parents of children forced to attend public schools with problems similar to those in Chicago and other large cities should begin immediately to organize and act on behalf of these recommendations. They should demand that control of the schools be decentralized (as they were in Chicago in the fall of 1989), that the unnecessarily large and wasteful bureaucracy be dismantled, and that parents be given a greater voice in the running of their school. And of course such parents should do everything possible to gain the freedom to choose which schools their children attend. Now the question is, How to accomplish such lofty goals? I have several recommendations.

Reducing control of schools by a centralized bureaucracy is the crucial first step and can only be accomplished by deft political action. That includes good organization and a careful campaign to educate parents on their rights. Mine is not a book on political action, so I'll refer you to the book by Rockne McCarthy, et. al., mentioned previously and to some good books on political action for Christians. In addition, Dr. James Dobson's organization, Focus on the Family, has recently joined with the Washington-based Family Research Council run by former Reagan administration official Gary Bauer to begin a citizen's group that aims to inform Christians and help them organize for public policy action on important family issues like education.[12] The point is to inform yourself and then do it—seek out like-minded parents, get together with them, and organize for action!

Parents who succeed in gaining control, then, must inculcate the vision outlined by other parts of this book: (1) functional literacy, (2) cultural literacy, (3) moral literacy—it's imperative that good values can be taught in public schools. I recognize that the values question is difficult and is most easily solved by placing your children in private schools. However, I also know there are parents out there for whom this is impossible. For them, only two options are left: (1) home-schooling,[13] which is a legitimate option, though not as desirable as a Christian school in my judgment; or (2) fighting it out on the public school front.

For those who choose the last option, and do not want to give up on the public schools there are three "musts." (1) Consciousness raising: Parents must know that they have the right to speak on behalf of their children and to control their children's education. But they must also know they have allies! (2) Activist parents must lead the reform movement in the local district. By activist, please note, I do not mean left-wing radical activism; rather, I simply mean people who care to speak out for their right to control their children's education. Conservative parents can be activists, too. We may be pro-life on the abortion issue, but we ought to be pro-choice in education! (3) Coalition building is the final "must." Building a network of conservative Jewish, Catholic, and Protestant parents is the first step here. Then, an agreed-upon set of values must be established as the primary agenda. Finally, building upon these established educational goals and personal networks, we should strive for control of parent-teacher groups.

Outside certain geographic sections of the country (such as certain parts of the Northeast), many members of the NEA will lend support once they recognize what the parents are after. Some may feel a bit threatened at first. But once parents make it clear that they only want a voice in what is taught, and that jobs won't be jeopardized, support should build quickly. Some teacher's unions, such as the American Federation of Teachers (which is much less radical than the NEA), are already much more sympathetic to the value-concerns of parents.

But this road won't be an easy one. It will take a lot of hard work for parents who choose it.

Since I believe that the pro-choice position in education is so important, it will occupy me for the remainder of this chapter and for most of the chapter that follows.

Increasing Parental Choice

In a paper delivered at Florida State University in March, 1989, John E. Chubb (The Brookings Institution) and Terry M. Moe (Stanford University) drew attention to a new and hopeful sign for all who care about school reform. They wrote:

> A new wave of school reform is beginning to sweep the nation. From coast to coast school boards and state legislatures are looking at ways to use parental choice, an innovative concept in school organization, to improve education. . . . Properly implemented, parental choice would eliminate perhaps the most crucial source of

school failure in the United States today and create powerful new forces for school success in the years ahead.[14]

The authors go on to note the important role that parental choice can have in improving our nation's schools:

> A basic premise underlying the concept of parental choice is that America's educational systems are a large part of the reason that American education is mediocre. Organized as public monopolies, America's schools and school systems have come to exhibit many of the potentially serious problems—excessive regulation, inefficient operation, and ineffective service—that are inherent in this form of organization. If these problems are to be more than temporarily alleviated, America's educational systems will need to be reorganized fundamentally. Public school monopolies will need to be opened to competition, and social control over schools will need to be exercised less through politics and central regulation and more through markets and parental choice.[15]

In a September 1989 report, Herbert J. Walbert and Joseph L. Bast also attack the monopoly that public schools have attained and discuss the need for using the discipline of the marketplace as part of the cure for the problems of our schools. Walbert and Bast begin by describing how market discipline in the business world affects quality and cost:

> When a business—say a restaurant or even a private school—adopts policies that lead to poor quality products or unnecessarily high prices, the free choice of consumers eventually leads to fewer sales by this business. Consumers "vote with their dollars" against the inefficient business by favoring other businesses that charge less or deliver a better product. In order to avoid bankruptcy, businesses must adopt policies that produce goods or services that are at least as good as or less expensive that those of their competitors. Those that fail are forced to close, and their assets are passed on to persons who are able to use them more efficiently. This "market discipline" works well in other industries, in-

cluding restaurants, hotels, and car manufacturing, even though the typical consumer could not identify which policies in these industries lead to good results and which to bad. In short, market discipline produces efficiency and quality without requiring that consumers be experts in how these objectives are achieved.[16]

Most of the debate about the quality of public schools has ignored the importance of restoring a similar kind of market discipline to American schooling. Public schools are protected from the discipline of the marketplace and thus have little or no incentive to offer an improved product at a lower cost. Students who attend public schools are usually given no choice. They are forced to attend whatever public school the school system dictates. The monopoly protection of the public school is enhanced by the fact that parents who choose to send their children to private schools are still forced to pay for the public schools they don't want and that many other parents would opt out of, if given a choice.

Because their schools are protected from the discipline of market forces, public school administrators lack any incentive to improve quality or performance. The bureaucrats don't care that huge sums of money are diverted from the classrooms to support the bureaucracy; they are the bureaucracy, and the lack of any real competition minimizes the importance of cost-effectiveness. According to Walbert and Bast, "Pay scales and management policies become shaped by the organized interest groups within the school systems, not the desire to encourage excellence and responsiveness to student and parent interests. Parental input in such areas as curriculum, discipline, and teacher recruitment becomes increasingly limited because parents have no real clout in negotiations with teachers and bureaucrats."[17]

Pete du Pont, former governor of Delaware, has become another voice advocating greater parental choice in education. According to du Pont, it is time to realize that neither giving more money to public schools nor demanding closer monitoring of the use of this money is going to solve the educational crisis. What is needed, he maintains, is not more money or more regulation, but more *competition*. He writes:

> [W]here others pursue structure, we must pursue freedom; where others pursue regulation, we must pursue

entrepreneurship and innovation; where others pursue monopoly, we must pursue competition and diversity.

In short, I do not believe there is any single answer to improving American eduction, at least not in the sense most people today are looking for an answer. We must look for an answer in diversity and initiative, and government does a very poor job of encouraging those qualities. Rather, they are qualities associated with competition and the marketplace.[18]

It is ironic, du Pont points out, that public school teachers send their own children to private schools at a significantly higher rate (twice as often) as other parents. This seems to be pretty good evidence that private schools are doing a better job; at least it suggests that public school teachers believe they are.

We should never underestimate the power of competition. "Competition," writes du Pont, "will reward good schools, force bad schools to get better, and provide every family in the United States with choices it does not have today. I believe our goal should be to encourage universal educational choice—for all students, not just the poor or wealthy—by the year 2000. States and localities should be able to provide vouchers or other funding mechanisms so that all families can choose the education that best fits their children's needs."[19]

There has been some movement towards giving parents greater choice in cities like Boston, New York City, Milwaukee, and soon the entire state of Minnesota. But their choices are limited only to other public schools. The solution to our education crisis requires that parents have unlimited choice to select any school they believe is best for their children whether that school be public or private.[20]

U.S. Secretary of Education Lauro F. Cavazos has spoken publicly on behalf of greater parental choice. In an interview reported in *U.S.A. Today* (July 10, 1989), he said: "I believe in choice because it holds promise of giving children that one crucial ingredient—the opportunity for a quality education. When choices are offered to parents, students and educators, the results have been a renewed commitment by all and a revitalizing of our schools—and these, in turn, have led to higher achievement."

Cavazos went on to say that "choice offers all involved the opportunity to select alternatives when they believe their neighborhood schools fail to provide the best possible educational opportunities. No child, regardless of circumstances, should be compelled to attend a second-rate school or one that fails to meet the child's special needs." Cavazos made it clear that he disagrees strongly with the NEA's opposition to the parental right to choose which school their children attend. "By rejecting educational choices," Cavazos continues, "the NEA rejected the reform that has transformed schools in East Harlem and brought new opportunity to families and teachers in states where it has been adopted. East Harlem District 4 was once the worst in New York City. Then the district introduced choice. As a result, student performance, teacher satisfaction and parental involvement improved measurably."

We can welcome support for greater parental choice from the Secretary of Education. Unfortunately, the Bush administration has backed away from the promises it made about support for private schools in the 1988 presidential campaign. Supporters of private schools need to make known their displeasure with the President's violation of his word. This breach of trust is unconscionable, but probably not insurmountable; Mr. Bush may yet listen should there arise a groundswell of support for the pro-choice position in education.

If competition, slight as it is, among public schools has produced demonstrable improvements, even greater competition from private schools is bound to result in greater gains in quality education.

We especially need to remember that greater educational choice is probably most important for the poor since, as Stephen Arons points out, "it is the poor who suffer most from the present educational system." As Arons explains,

> They [the poor] get both biased and poorly taught classes. The rich can pay public school taxes and still manage to pay private school tuition. Others can move to suburbs with public schools that at least teach some skills effectively. But this, of course, means being able to buy a house and pay expensive property taxes to finance the local schools. As usual, the poor family has no such options. The local public school, especially in the inner cities, is often both an educational and a moral disaster, but poor parents have no choice but to

send their children there, often at the price of an inadequate education for their children.[21]

Conclusion

We've examined four additional elements in America's educational crisis. When a particular family falls down in its educational responsibility and when students are poorly motivated and ill-prepared, even the best schools and teachers can appear to have failed. Parents, especially in Christian families, dare not assume that the education of their children is the exclusive responsibility of the school. We've seen that another reason why schools are doing such a poor job is because control of the schools has been centralized in some bureaucracy too distant from the school to know or care about its particular problems. Control of schools must be returned to the teachers and administrators in the local school. And parents in the locality should be given an increased voice in the running of the school. And finally, the most important factor of all requires that parents be given greater choice in where their children attend school, with this increased choice including the option of private, religious schools. Christian parents need to become the vanguard in the fight for the pro-choice position in education.

CHAPTER

7

Before Americans, Christian and non-Christian alike, agree in principle to the complete severance of all affinities between the religious and the civil realms, between spiritual and political principles, it would be good to examine the consequences that the incipient divorce is already producing, and to ask ourselves what the long-range results are likely to be.
—Harold O. J. Brown, *The Reconstruction of the Republic*

The Separation of School and State

The monopoly control that public schools have over tax-supported education should be obvious by now. The last chapter drew attention to the growing recognition that ending this monopoly and creating educational alternatives that would give the public schools real competition for a change are important steps in easing the school crisis. In this chapter I want to explore related aspects of this topic. First, this chapter explains how public schools acquired their monopoly control. Was this the way things have always been since the settlement of this continent? If not, what were things like at first and when did they begin to change? And why? Is a public school monopoly over education mandated somehow in the U.S. Constitution? Or did it develop later? Is it possible to detect significant differences between the arguments that the earliest proponents of a public school monopoly used to win support for their cause and the real, hidden agenda of these people? These are a few of the questions worth asking about this matter.

The second thing this chapter considers is the case that can be made for a new understanding of education in this nation. Many of its advocates use the term "pluralism" to describe this model. One thing we'll learn is that a pluralistic approach to education is working successfully in all of the advanced nations of the Western world with one exception, the United States. And finally, given that educational pluralism is a practical and desirable goal, this chapter will explore ways in which pluralism can be realized.

The Evolution of the Public Monopoly in Education

While there is presently a clear line of separation between private and public schools in America, this was not always the case. The slow establishment of the line that now has most Americans believing there is something wrong when tax dollars support private schools is a relatively recent development in the history of American education. Barnard Bailyn comments:

> The modern conception of public education, the very idea of a clean line of separation between "private" and "public," was unknown before the end of the eighteenth century. Its origins are part of a complex story involving changes in the role of the state as well as in the general institutional character of society. It is elaborately woven into the fabric of early modern history.[1]

Before the American colonies' break with England, and indeed, for several decades after our birth as a nation, there was no such thing as a line that distinguished secular (or so-called "public") from religious or other private schools.

During the seventeenth and eighteenth centuries, people living in New England, for example, believed that the most important goal of any human being was to live and promote the Christian faith. Their view of education functioned within this context. As Rockne McCarthy and his co-authors explain, "Religious schools, therefore, were to play an important role in society. The notion that it is desirable and possible to separate religion from education, to make religion an entirely private matter by confining it to personal beliefs and to family and church matters, is a modern assumption that did not shape the educational theory of the early settlers."[2]

A careful study of colonial America reveals, therefore, little interest in setting up some sharp line of separation between private and public schools. To be sure, the words "public" and "private" were used then. But the terms never carried any meaning that turned public schools into secular institutions. More often than not, McCarthy indicates, "both public and private schools consciously taught from a religious perspective and both received public funds to support their academic work."[3] The justification for giving public funds to private schools was simple: such schools provided a service to the community and the communities believed that service had important public dimensions. The constitution of Massachusetts, adopted in 1780, clearly stated that the commonwealth should encourage both private and public schools in the teaching of such things as literature, the sciences, agriculture, trades, and the arts. "While the distinction between public and private schools was relevant in matters of ownership and management, it was irrelevant in such matters as funding. Thus 'public' implied the performance of broad social functions. It was not limited to public or private control or to distinctions between secular and religious education. In colonial America there was no clean line of separation between public and private schools."[4]

When then did things begin to change? The major impetus for change within the Commonwealth of Massachusetts came from the increasing influence and power of Unitarians in New England in the first half of the nineteenth century. Undoubtedly, the single most important person in the campaign to separate public and private education was the Massachusetts Unitarian, Horace Mann (1796–1859). As a result of Mann's efforts in the 1830s and 1840s, Massachusetts became the first state to abandon state support for private schools and adopt a governmental monopoly for funding schools. Mann argued that doing this would expand educational opportunities for everyone.

It is important to see that the establishment of this kind of public monopoly had no essential connection with the argument that persuaded so many to support such a policy. The idea was that you could justify the establishment of a public school monopoly on the grounds that it would expand educational opportunities to everyone. *This was and still is a specious argument.* Educational opportunity could have been expanded by continuing to include private schools in the orbit of public funding. The elimination of private schools from the sphere of public funding had nothing to do with the alleged logical superiority of Horace Mann's position. It was really the consequence of a particular ideology achieving majority status. The fact that Mann and many others who were early supporters of his cause were Unitarians is something that should not be ignored in all this. Their public agenda—the one that won the day—was humanitarian in the sense that it appeared to be a plea to help the masses by increas-

ing educational opportunity. The real and hidden agenda was
their hatred for orthodox Christianity and their desire to weaken
and even destroy its influence in American public life. As Richard
Baer explains:

> Horace Mann and other proponents of public educa-
> tion were intent on reforming society by changing the
> values of children. Mann had little sympathy for Cal-
> vinists or Catholics, and he was determined to use
> every legal means—including state coercion in school-
> ing—to ensure that other people's children were taught
> the truth as he understood it.[5]

By the 1950s, a century after Mann had won his crusade in
Massachusetts and other states followed New England's lead,
the private-public and secular-religious distinction had begun to
acquire the hallowed status of federal law. Various Supreme
Court decisions, each one more restrictive than those before,
have become stumbling blocks "to the development of a strong
pluralist elementary and secondary school system in the nation.
[The Supreme Court] has found constitutionally permissible
only those forms of aid that are peripheral to the main academic
task of the school as school."[6] These decisions of the Supreme
Court, McCarthy observes, exhibit an unmistakable "bias against
freedom of associations, particularly school associations, by
striking down legislative funding proposals favorable to family
choice."[7] The so-called Establishment Clause of the First Amendment has functioned as the Court's major club in all this. The
Establishment Clause says that "Congress shall make no law
respecting an establishment of religion, or prohibiting the free
exercise thereof." The courts have come to interpret this clause
in a way that sets up a wall between church and state.

In one of the more enlightened discussions of the Establishment Clause, Lutheran theologian Richard John Neuhaus
argues that the establishment of religion is not the real issue, as
is often claimed in debates over the First Amendment. The real
issue, Neuhaus contends, is *religious liberty*, the free exercise of
religion. Strict separationists treat the two clauses of our famous
statement as opposed to each other, as clauses that set up a
balance between two distinct and different actions. On this reading, the first clause prohibits the establishment of religion while
the second clause proscribes Congress from prohibiting the free

exercise of religion. Hence, we get the supposed wall between church and state.

Neuhaus argues for a different interpretation of the two clauses as follows:

> The two-part religion clause of the First Amendment stipulates that there must be no establishment of religion. The reason for this is to avoid any infringement of the free exercise of religion. Put differently, the free exercise of religion requires the non-establishment of religion. Non-establishment is not a good in itself. The positive good is free exercise, to which non-establishment is instrumental. Had one additional word been included in the First Amendment, we might possibly have been spared much of the grief over the religion clause in the last forty years. . . . With that added word, the religion clause would read this way: "Congress shall make no law respecting an establishment of religion, or otherwise prohibiting the free exercise thereof."[8]

In other words, Neuhaus adds, "Free exercise is the purpose of the religion clause, non-establishment is the means to that end."[9]

Of course, this is hardly the first time an activist Supreme Court has altered American society for the worse by reading something into the Constitution that was never intended by the Framers. McCarthy and his co-authors find it curious that a First Amendment clause that was originally intended to provide support for religious freedom and that would maximize choice "has become the prime stumbling block in the path of educational pluralism and the free choice of schools that pluralism makes possible."[10] The fact that church-related colleges continue to receive significant public funding makes it clear that nothing in the First Amendment proscribes in some ultimate or basic way public funding for private schools. (By significant public funding, I mean the fact that many students on Christian college campuses receive federal loans and faculty receive federal grants for important research.) The problem for private schooling on the elementary and secondary level results instead from a disjunction between the public and private or between the secular and religious "that is so deeply embedded in the American consciousness and the judicial reasoning of the Supreme Court that it is difficult to see our way clear of that false distinction."[11]

What makes all of this even worse is the fact that the public schools are not religiously neutral. There is a religion taught in and tacitly endorsed by our public schools (though certainly not by all public school teachers); it is the religion of secular humanism. But this fact is often difficult for many Americans to see. What is required is a stance that recognizes that religion cannot be equated simply with a belief in God plus such activities as prayer and worship along with an institutional framework within which these beliefs and activities occur. The approach to religion that is more relevant to the educational question views religion in the sense of ultimate commitment or world view. Understood in this more profound sense, "religion" may be manifested in the belief that God does not exist or even in the belief that the traditional content of religions like Christianity and Judaism has no proper place in the teaching of a public school.

Public schools do not achieve religious neutrality by eliminating things like prayer and the reading of the Bible from their institutions. They do not demonstrate religious neutrality by adopting textbooks that avoid any mention of the role that religious convictions have played in the history of our nation. Under the guise of religious neutrality, our schools have become propagandists for a different kind of religion. The secular humanists usually deny this but their denial is hypocritical; they know the claim is true and revel in the unlimited power they've achieved. If the Supreme Court would once acknowledge this fact, it would face an enormous problem. McCarthy explains: "If the Court has ruled consistently that public money may not aid religion, and if it can be shown that public schools teach a real and legally defined religion [secular humanism], then the courts must abandon the secular-religious distinction and decide either to fund no schools, or to fund all schools."[12] The time has come for this nation to move towards genuine pluralism in education that recognizes "that the secular-religious line is no longer tenable as a legally or educationally meaningful distinction for constitutionally deciding questions of educational funding."[13]

Pluralism: A New Educational Model for America

What does pluralism in education mean? How would it differ from the educational monopoly we have had for too long now? One of the better and more complete accounts of educational pluralism can be found in the book, *Society, State and Schools*, by Rockne McCarthy and several co-authors.[14] Their kind of pluralism recognizes that "the state has a legitimate role to play in education in ensuring that all citizens obtain an education." But they continue, the state "is not the single locus of educational authority, nor should its funding power be used to discriminate against those who hold that the church or the family is the locus of educational authority."[15] The foundation on which their model of pluralism rests is the conviction that "the choice of a school in the future must be made as free as the choice of a church or political party is now, with the state acting only with malice toward none and with charity for all."[16]

In the previous chapter, we noted how the argument for educational choice can be grounded on the issue of quality of education. When families have a choice and when schools are subject to market discipline, the quality of schools improves. McCarthy and his partners are arguing for choice on the basis of *justice*. Because the present secular-religious distinction cannot work, because public schools cannot eliminate religion, the courts simply end up siding with one set of religious beliefs and discriminating against all others. This is unfair; it is unjust when government aids one religion—in this case, secular humanism—and discriminates against the rest. Justice requires either that the state end all aid to all schools or that it find ways to help all schools, including private Christian schools.

The call for educational pluralism is not a request to establish an educational model in the United States that would be unique to our nation. With the exception of the United States, every major Western democracy provides public money to private (including religious) schools. In Canada, six of ten provinces provide funds for public and "separate" schools including Catholic and Protestant Christian schools. In Israel, Hebrew, Jewish, Arab, Moslem, and Christian schools all receive uniform help for almost all faculty and full financial support for non-religious, academic programs, regardless of religious affiliation. Significant funding for independent private schools of various stripes is also available in England, Belgium, and The Netherlands. The Dutch system is so successful that seventy-three percent of their students attend non-state schools, yet the public system is as efficient and well-funded as ever.[17]

The refusal of the United States to provide financial help to its private schools makes us an exception, not the rule, among nations in the West. The experience of other Western nations proves that pluralism is not an exercise in utopianism. Evidence from its adoption in other countries shows how realistic a model it is.

McCarthy and his co-authors answer several fears about pluralism. First, they point out, private schools are not divisive. They are in a position to make important contributions to society. The competition they offer to public schools is good for those schools and good for the parents who benefit from stronger and more diversified educational opportunities. Second, they reject the claim that private schools under the pluralistic model would somehow be undemocratic. "On the contrary," McCarthy replies, "they are more democratic than the present American unified and monopolistic education system. True freedom implies freedom of choice. Under the present American system this freedom cannot be realized by all, for there is only one real choice: state-run education. True democracy offers a variety of alternatives; this criterion is fulfilled only in a structurally pluralist society."[18]

Nor is it correct to think that governmental schools suffer or are weakened in a pluralistic system. As McCarthy explains, "In the countries we have examined the governmental schools have not been hindered, crippled, or deprived of their function in society. The purpose of educational pluralism is not to usurp the government schools, but to give all schools a fair chance in order that rich and poor alike may experience true justice and freedom in education."[19]

In recent years, we have heard many Americans call for the separation of church and state. Educational pluralism will bring about the separation of school and state. McCarthy explains:

> The state is the state, and a school is a school. Each has its own unique structure and task, its own rights and sovereignty; this clear distinction between the state and the schools must be observed. Society must be led to respect the proper structural distance between

them—each having its own office, social identity, and integrity. The growing state monopoly in education must be broken. Schools must be depoliticized. Ways must be found to reduce the "excessive entanglement" of government in education. Rather than acting as the national educator, the state must play a different role, a positive but more limited one, seeing to it that schools enjoy the rights and freedoms they need as academic institutions to do their work; seeing to it also that the needed resources and revenues are available, and that basic educational standards are honored. These and similar considerations grow out of the state's central task of shaping a just public policy in education that honors the normative social realities embedded in the idea of structural pluralism.[20]

McCarthy and his partners expand on this by identifying three specific ways in which the state and schools are related. First, the state will have the duty to protect each school's right to decide freely the nature of its religious commitments and its philosophies of education. The religious options are completely open-ended and range from evangelical to Roman Catholic to Jewish to Atheist or whatever system of belief the community running the school happens to choose. Second, the state will have the responsibility of seeing that such things as health, safety, fair treatment, and similar concerns are not neglected or abused among either students or teachers. Third and finally, academic decisions are not the proper business of the state but of the people in each school who have been given the responsibility over such matters by the community. This means that the school, and not the state, makes the decisions about such things as what is taught, how certification of teachers—if any—is handled, how student achievement is evaluated, how long the school is in session, and so on. With regard to internal operations, each school should be self-regulating.

In the pluralist system that McCarthy envisions,

all schools would become public schools, thus laying to rest the untenable public-private, secular-religious distinction. The state could still operate schools along the lines of the present public school system. But the privileged status and favored financial treatment of a single school system would make way for a multi-plicity of school systems, each enjoying the right and freedom to determine its own philosophy and to regulate its own internal academic affairs without financial penalty.[21]

This kind of pluralistic model insists that a truly just social policy would give each religious community in a society the legal right to develop its view of God and the world in its own educational program. This means, McCarthy points out, that

> no school community would be coerced, either overtly or subtly, to adopt another's view concerning the locus of educational authority. Views on this differ widely. Some locate it in the state, others in the home, or in the church, or in the school itself. This plurality of viewpoints could remain and should be respected. The principal matter of concern to the state in administering a just public policy in education is simply whether a school is really a school. That is, does it meet the basic structural standards of adequate educational achievement as defined by the demands of public justice in contemporary society? Once this legitimate concern of the state is met, confessional pluralism in education will be able to flourish.[22]

Advancing the Cause of Educational Choice

One of the first things that must be done is provide support for litigation that would reverse Supreme Court precedents with regard to the Establishment Clause of the First Amendment. And this must be done in ways that guarantee that the people handling such litigation are competent and know what they're doing. This litigation will have the objective of causing the courts to reevaluate their past prejudice against the rights of school associations. What is presently taken for granted as constitutionally permissible must be challenged and changed.

Other than litigation in the courts, the second battleground is the Congress and state legislatures, where a strong push on behalf of new legislation should be made. Parents who wish their children to attend private schools are forced to carry an unjust tax penalty. Academics, legislators, and parents should continue to urge the passage of laws that will give all American families relief from the burden of double taxation. Connaught Coyne Marshner explains:

> The fact remains; parents who send their children to nonpublic schools are punished by double taxation. They pay to support the public schools and they also pay to support the private school of their choice. A parent who cannot afford that double taxation is thus effectively denied the right freely to practice his religion, or to pass it on to his children. For parents who are financially able, the burden is nonetheless a discouragement to religion. Does not the 14th Amendment require equal protection of the law for all citizens, regardless of race, religion, or economic condition? How, then, constitutionally, can state laws force parents to sacrifice their religious freedom in order to obtain "free" education for their children?[23]

One form of legislation that has wide support is a voucher system. Connaught Coyne Marshner explains one way such vouchers might work. "Briefly, a voucher is an educational food stamp that parents can use like cash to purchase education for their children from the institution of the parents' choice. The institution would then be reimbursed (by the school district, say) in cash equal to the face value of vouchers collected."[24] The vouchers can be valued in several different ways, one being the expenditure for each pupil in a given locality. This policy would recognize that it costs more to educate a student in some areas than in others. On the other hand, the value of vouchers could be the same for each recipient.

Under this approach, McCarthy explains, "the state will not operate schools but will encourage them by appropriate legislation that gives grants to consumers to purchase the educational services of their choice. In this business model of education the present monopoly of governmental schools is broken. The present public schools compete with other forms of schooling on a equal basis. Thus, the voucher becomes the mechanism for reform of education through competition."[25]

The voucher system also makes sense to people who are influenced more by social than by religious concerns. As McCarthy notes, the present system of "public education funding perpetuates both racial and economic segregation, and therefore discriminates against the poor and minority groups."[26] The poor and minority groups would be major beneficiaries of educational pluralism. Greater educational choice would enhance their opportunities to move their children to better schools as well as to schools with less racial imbalance.

Many supporters of a voucher system, however, fail to see a potentially serious threat in this approach. Private colleges in the U.S. have already seen how far a power-hungry state will go in extending its control over schools that take public funds, no matter how indirectly the receipt of those funds may be. There is a very real danger in private elementary and secondary schools becoming recipients of public funds. As Ms. Marshner asks, "would not the state also be able to exert control over the private schools that might participate in the [voucher] program? Would not public money gradually turn the private schools into public schools? And would not this control be as undesirable as the other types of control that have caused problems already?"[27] Sooner or later, Marshner warns, "private schools will probably regret taking state or federal money.... The disenchantment with public money might come gradually: for instance, when the school can no longer bear the administrative burden of gathering the statistics and information required for participation in a hot-lunch program."[28] McCarthy and his co-authors also see problems ahead. For one thing, the voucher system still leaves, they say, "the power of the present monopoly of the state in education unquestioned. It will leave nonpublic schools defenseless against the increasing expansion of state power to dictate the details of non-public school operation. Such legislation may produce tax reform but not educational reform."[29]

All this leads Marshner to suggest: "Ideally the safest course for a private school to follow if it wishes to maintain its independence is simply that: independence. Do not accept any favors from any government body; do not try to curry favor with any either."[30] Once again, it seems, we are stuck with an age-old dilemma: *Those who live by the state, die by the state.*[31] Ironically, the best advice at this point comes from the same people who gave us the model of government outlined in the U.S. Constitution. Better than most members of the executive, legislative, and judicial branches of government we've had in recent days, the Founding Fathers warned of the dangers of a central government that was too strong. The genius of the system of government they left us insisted on decentralizing political power as widely within society as possible. It has been the liberals in our midst who have successfully transformed that model and created the Leviathan state. A voucher system that will expand educational opportunity to include private schools *is* an indispensable step in improving American education. But any legislation establishing a voucher system *must* include indisputably clear language that will prohibit the state from interfering with the internal and academic affairs of each school. And if such legislation should ever be passed, proponents of the Christian school movement will have to be on constant guard against the inevitable statist attempt to tear down the wall between school and state. But, as Baer observes, "the problems with a voucher system remain a matter of speculation; the problems associated with the coercive nature of our public school monopoly, on the other hand, are a present reality for dissenting minorities."[32]

America's level of consciousness about the importance of private schools must be raised. Everything possible should be done to help Americans realize how increased parental choice is necessary if there is to be any real hope of improving the quality of education. Parents, churches, academics, and legislators who support private schools are the vanguard of those working for better schools in America. It is a matter of the greatest urgency that we add our voices to this debate and that our efforts on behalf of greater educational choice succeed.

CHAPTER

8

There is an attempt to isolate us from the very culture which is pre-eminently ours as Christians by playing down the Christian content of a work of art or literature as something which, if emphasised, would somehow vulgarise response to that work by sullying the purity of a supposed aesthetic substance loftily superior to creed or ideology.

—Harry Blamires, *Recovering the Christian Mind*

The Christian School Movement

In the previous two chapters, I argued in support of the following three points: (1) If the education crisis in this country is to be addressed successfully, it is imperative that we increase the educational choices available to American families. (2) But it is not enough that we simply increase choice among public schools. The governmental monopoly over publicly funded schools is a large part of our educational problem. (3) It is imperative that educational choice include the option of attending without financial penalty, without the burden of double taxation, any private school that any family wishes. This includes the private school of any religious group, if that is the family's desire.

In this chapter I will take a closer look at Christian elementary and secondary schooling. This chapter will provide some general background information that will introduce unfamiliar readers to Christian schools operated by theologically-conservative Protestant communities. The pluralistic model of education defended thus far insists that any private school that is really a school has a right to support from public funds. Because I'm an evangelical Protestant and thus know more about evangelical Christian schools, my discussion will focus on such schools. People familiar with other traditions can write their own books to discuss Roman Catholic or Hebrew schools.

The Growth of the Christian School Movement

No segment of American private education is growing faster than the evangelical Christian school movement. One million children (20 percent of all private school students) presently attend evangelical Christian schools. According to respected estimates, two Christian schools on average have been established every day since 1960. According to Susan D. Rose, "Private school enrollment peaked at 6.25 million in 1964, according to the data of the Census Bureau. By 1979, it had declined to 4.23 million. While Christian and independent schools were growing, enrollments in Roman Catholic schools plummeted by 2.5 million. Between 1965–1975, Christian schools showed a 20% increase in enrollments; Hebrew schools showed a modest increase of 37%; Roman Catholic schools showed a decrease of 38%."[1] Roman Catholic schools presently enroll some 3.2 million students while evangelical schools come in second among private schools with their total of approximately one million. The Christian school movement's 20 percent share of America's total private school enrollment equals about 2 percent of America's total school population.

The Purpose of Christian Schools

Various writers have attempted to identify what they see as the major purpose of Christian schools. According to Kenneth Gangel, "The purpose of Christian schools is to present to our children, as clearly as possible, the truth about God, about life, about our world and everything in it, and to present the Word of God as the authoritative source upon which to build a life that has purpose and meaning."[2] Connaught Coyne Marshner explains that "Christian educators are set apart from secular educators by their concept of the purpose of education: to a religious educator, the education of a child cannot be separated from the child's eternal salvation. To a secular educationist, education is a nice process that provides social services and prepares future citizens."[3]

Gangel wants it understood that the people who run Christian schools do not oppose public education per se. As he explains,

> For the secular individual in a secular society, the American system of education may be the finest that has ever existed in the history of the world. But Christian children are not secular individuals. They are citizens of a different country with a different set of values, a different set of standards, and a different idea

of truth. When we [Christian] parents give our sons and daughters to the state for education, we invite the values, standards, and untruths of a godless cosmos to penetrate their spirits, and that is not healthy for any family, especially the Christian family.[4]

Several things trouble me about Gangel's last statement. I'm bothered first of all by what appears to be a ghetto-approach to the Christian's place in society. Ghettos used to be sections of European cities to which certain people were restricted. Unfortunately, many evangelical Christians in the last fifty years or so have developed a kind of ghetto-mentality. They have so emphasized their differences from the rest of American society that they have tended to lock themselves up in their own communities; they have surrounded those communities with invisible walls of their own making. Of course, this has thrilled the secularists in our society who are bent on taking over all aspects of American life. Millions of committed Christians who might otherwise be actively challenging the secular take-over have retreated into their private little ghettos.

I have no desire to criticize Christians who want to separate themselves from conduct and beliefs that are contrary to their religious and moral convictions. But this kind of separation must be practiced in a way that does not lessen or negate the otherwise powerful influence for good that they could have on society. Gangel seems to be saying that we Christians are different from the people who control secular society; therefore, we will continue to live our lives and educate our children in an environment (a ghetto, if you will) of our own making.

In my view, a more biblical approach to secular society is described in the Book of Joshua. When the Israelites reached the Jordan River, they didn't stop, wring their hands, sit down, and say, "We're different from those people on the other side. We'll just stay here and keep to ourselves." On the contrary, they followed the Lord's command and set out to take dominion over the land that the Lord had promised them.

It is not enough for Christians to have their own schools and be content with that. Christians have an obligation to do battle with the forces of secularism that have taken control of public schools and institutionalized a pagan religion in those schools.

But something else troubles me about Gangel's paragraph. Missing from it is an explicit statement about the *educational role* of the Christian school. Christian schools must be concerned about biblical truth and about the salvation and spiritual growth of their students. But Christian schools must also be concerned to offer the very best education possible. Many (perhaps most) Christian schools need no encouragement along this line. But, I fear, some do.

A Secularist Critique of Christian Schools

The appearance of a recent book provides valuable insights into the thinking of secular opponents of the Christian school movement. It helps us understand how Christian schools are presently viewed by one group of secular academicians. While it tells us what they see as the strengths and weaknesses of Christian schools, it also reveals how the evaluations of such people are seriously compromised by bias and misunderstanding. The book I'm referring to is *Keeping Them Out of the Hands of Satan: Evangelical Schooling in America* by Susan D. Rose, an assistant professor of sociology at Dickenson College.[5]

Rose sees the movement as an outgrowth of evangelical parents' desire to retain control over the socialization of their children. "Attempting to enclose their children within the trinity of family-church-school, evangelicals hope to win their children over to Christ before they are 'seduced' by the secular world."[6] The title of the book is obviously derived from this interpretation of the parents' motives.

Rose spent two years in upstate New York studying two such schools and their sponsoring churches. One school is an offshoot of a fundamentalist Baptist church that ministers largely to working-class parents. The second school is a ministry of an independent, charismatic congregation that serves largely middle-class parents, many of whom have had some education at the college level. The Baptist school uses a pre-packaged curriculum known as Accelerated Christian Education (A.C.E.) that is a special target of Rose's scorn throughout the book. The charismatic school has adopted a more traditional approach to education that encourages children to think for themselves, while still promoting Christian values.

The book begins with two chapters that (1) discuss how Americans have turned to religion in their search for coherence; and (2) give the author's understanding of the role that Christian schools are playing in contemporary evangelical culture. The long middle section (about 150 pages) details the philosophy, social organization, and demographic traits of the two schools and their associated religious communities. The book ends with a critique that is both surprising and disappointing in certain respects.

One reason the last chapter is surprising is because Rose completely ignores the important practical question, What do the students in such schools learn in comparison with public school students in the same locale? It would have been relatively easy for Rose to compare I.Q.'s and college board scores. This could have been extremely valuable information, yet Rose failed to look into the matter. Is it possible that she would have discovered that the Christian school students did better than their counterparts in the public schools? Would that kind of information have weakened what she was trying to do in her book? We'll never know. But it is interesting that Rose does not criticize the Christian schools on academic grounds. Of course, information on this matter is available from other sources. For example, we can compare the SAT scores of students who attend schools belonging to the Association of Christian Schools International with SAT scores nationwide. Kenneth Gangel did this research and reports that "Christian school students are performing approximately one year and four months ahead of the national norm."[7] Average SAT scores for 1989 graduates of private, religious schools were eleven points higher than for graduates of public schools.

Rose sometimes hints at racism as a partially hidden motive behind Christian schools. This is classic liberal pap. According to a highly regarded study published by the Ethics and Public Policy Center in Washington, D.C., the charge of racism is false. Christian schools, the report states, "were established primarily out of religious, not racial, convictions (parents were concerned about 'creeping humanism' and moral relativism in the public schools) and the quality of instruction they offer matches or exceeds that given in most public schools."[8] For people on the left like Rose, opposition to racism must include the support for reverse discrimination along racial lines that is such an important part of their political agenda. The last thing such liberals want is a genuinely color-blind society.

Rose's major objection to Christian schools concerns the effect she thinks the schools have on the socialization of the students. The heart of her critique concerns what she sees as the unintended consequences of Christian schooling. For example, she writes that "the two schools are doing more than preparing their students for a proper Christian life. They are both resisting and reinforcing the values of the secular world. While the schools provide alternative education, they also reinforce the social hierarchy of our society by socializing their children to adapt to certain class roles."[9]

What Christian schools do best, Rose thinks, is prepare their students for jobs in a factory, some automated office, or the army. Hence, while the parents may think the schools are helping to keep their children out of the hands of "Satan" (the godless humanism that presumably controls public education), the children are really being delivered into the hands of another "Satan," which for Rose is the materialistic god of corporate America and the military-industrial complex. By the time most readers reach this point in the book, they will realize that Rose has long since stopped gathering and reporting evidence; she is preaching. And more than that, her preaching is based on a number of question-begging neo-Marxist premises that she does not bother to defend.*

Rose's neo-Marxist picture of American society affects her discussion of the fundamentalist school in a special way. She sees a strong analogy between the way a corporation like McDonald's does business through effective packaging and marketing of junk food and the way fundamentalist pastors function as merchandisers of prepackaged educational curricula that also, in Rose's view, is "junk food." The long paragraph in which she draws this comparison is worth studying:

---

*I do not want to give the impression that I'm equating Christian faith with either conservatism or liberalism. I have defined those terms in an irenic way in my book *Social Justice and the Christian Church*. A lengthy repetition of that material should not be necessary here since most Americans can supply examples of the terms even when a definition escapes them. A look at chapter 9 should suffice to explain why I am so concerned here with Ms. Rose's neo-Marxist world view.

If we consider the Baptist school as a corporate franchise, the minister is the educational entrepreneur in the modern corporate sense; he brings [the Christian school curriculum—A.C.E.—and its prepackaged programs] to his community the way someone else brings a McDonald's or Wendy's fast food franchise. The minister may get some financial rewards for his efforts, but his major gain is his increased control over the spiritual and educational lives of his congregation. The owner of a McDonald's can feel like an independent businessman at the same time he is purveying the same low quality food that thousands of others are feeding to millions of Americans on behalf of the same corporation. So too, the independent Christian school can feel as if it is breaking free from the "secularist humanist" stranglehold on education—only to buy a repetitive, programmed meal of knowledge which fits the needs of corporate society (or the military-industrial complex) much more efficiently than do the public schools.[10]

It would be difficult to find a better paragraph to illustrate how donning the spectacles of a neo-Marxist world view can alter one's perception of reality. At the same time, I can sympathize with Rose's concern over pre-packaged teaching material that may not be up-to-date and that may also exemplify less than desirable teaching methods. This is one weakness that schools using this kind of material will have to address. But even this point has its counterpoint. It may well be that a "system of transmitting information through manuals under the direction of adults who are more like supervisors than teachers" provides less than an ideal education. But it is highly debatable whether such a system has either the direct or indirect consequence of preparing students primarily for jobs in factories, automated offices, or the army.

Rose herself admits that the problems she sees with the Accelerated Christian Education (A.C.E.) curriculum are not universal in scope. They do not, for example, apply to the other school she studied for two years. About this second school, she has this to say:

In contrast, the middle-class parents and educators [of the second school] challenge their students to think more critically. Like all parents, they want to instill their values and beliefs, but the process of instruction is more important than the specific content. Group work, discussions that examine a spectrum of values and beliefs, and various strategies for formulating and resolving problems characterize school life. Challenge and interpretation rather than conformity and security are stressed.[11]

Rose's socialization thesis clashes with the conclusions of James Coleman that grew out of research done under a contract from the National Center for Education Statistics. Coleman drew the following conclusions:

1. Private schools provide better character and personality development than public schools
2. Private schools provide a safer, more disciplined environment than public schools
3. Private schools are more successful in creating an interest in learning than public schools
4. Private schools encourage interest in higher education and lead more of their students to attend college than public schools with comparable students
5. Private schools are more efficient than public schools, accomplishing their educational task at lower cost
6. Private schools have smaller class sizes, and thus allow teachers and students to have greater contact[12]

While Rose does not speak directly to points (5) and (6), it is unlikely that she would disagree. The points seem pretty indisputable. With regard to the first four points, irreconcilable differences exist between the Coleman report and Rose's book. But Coleman's research was based on a much wider sampling. Rose's conflicting claims can be dismissed on the grounds that they're not supported by a sufficiently broad sampling and that they're due to highly subjective or biased readings of what little evidence she did have.

Many readers, not all of whom will necessarily be evangelicals, will be disappointed in the extent to which Rose's bias frequently gets the better of her. Some of her negative comments are more important for what they reveal about the workings of a contemporary Marxian sociologist's mind than for anything they reveal about the real deficiencies of evangelical schools. Her frequent disappointment with her subjects results from the fact that they are not as socially "enlightened" or "progressive" as she. This particular bias also shows up in the introduction to the book written by Michael Apple, a neo-Marxist sociologist at the University of Wisconsin-Madison. What bothers Mr. Apple most about Christian schools is the fact that these Christians dare to exercise their freedom to establish schools that defend *conservative beliefs*.

But there may be a far more serious weakness at the heart of Rose's book. We must remember that the subtitle to her book is *Evangelical Schooling in America*. Whoever gave the book this subtitle (Rose or her publisher) clearly wanted its potential purchasers to think that this book would give them the inside information on the *whole* evangelical school movement. If there is anything that Rose's work reveals, however, it is that she does not understand evangelicalism, a major fault in an author writing about the movement.

This confusion about evangelicalism is apparent in material from the publisher that accompanied my copy of the book. While it was a mistake made more by the publisher than the author, it suggests the depth of misunderstanding about evangelicalism in the secular world. This promotional material included the following question: "Why has evangelism [*sic*] become a way of life for so many Americans?" What the writer meant to ask, of course, is why has *evangelicalism* become a way of life? The brochure then went on: "What are the schools of evangelists [*sic*] like?" People who don't know the difference between an evangelical and an evangelist are hardly the people we want instructing others about Christian schools. While Rose herself presumably knows better than this, she makes other mistakes almost as bad.

Evangelicalism is an incredibly complex and diversified movement. This diversity is reflected in the existence of a number of evangelical subcultures.[13] But only two of these subcultures (fundamentalism and the charismatic movement) are represented in Rose's study. Ironically, the type of extreme fundamentalism that characterizes the Baptist school Rose investigated regards itself as separate from evangelicalism, which it views as insufficiently "biblical" in faith and practice. Even worse, the *center or main-stream* of the evangelical movement is nowhere represented in Rose's book. She says nothing even to indicate she is aware of its existence or of how it differs both from fundamentalism and the charismatic movement. This seriously compromises the scholarship of her work. This evangelical mainstream includes most of its educated, academic leadership. Representatives of the evangelical mainstream have published widely in the areas of elementary, secondary, and higher education.[14] Yet nowhere in her book does Rose quote any of these sources. On the rare occasions when she does quote, her sources are fundamentalist or pentecostal preachers and evangelists whose lack of expertise on educational matters is well-known to mainstream evangelicals.

In spite of its subtitle, then, Rose's book is not really about *evangelical* schooling at all. In order to have written *that* book, she would have had to spend at least an equal amount of time investigating schools affiliated, let us say, with the Christian Reformed Church, the Presbyterian Church in America, or the Southern Baptist Church. The two schools she did study are simply *not* representative of the broader evangelical movement.

An Expanded Vision for Christian Schools

In some respects, large pockets of evangelical Christianity have been slow to respond to the educational crisis. Millions of evangelicals in company with millions of non-evangelicals have little grasp of the extent of America's educational crisis. They continue to send their children to public schools that offer an inferior education at the same time that the schools undermine important Christian values and beliefs.

But, some might ask, Is not the founding of thousands of Christian schools evidence that large numbers of Christians are responding to the crisis by offering an alternative to the public schools? It is true that many Christian schools do evidence a clear vision of the fact that alternative education must be provided, that it is a responsibility of Christian churches to make this alternative available, and that the Christian school must give its students a solid educational experience in addition to its expected emphasis on biblical truth and Christian living. Unfortunately, it is also true that a large number of Christian schools (and the people who operate them) lack the vision to see that the mission of their school must be to do more than provide a safe haven for Christian students for six hours a day.

Many Christian schools have been formed for reasons that have little to do with improving the quality of education; the reasons for establishing them were primarily religious and moral. In more than a few instances, such schools came into existence because a fundamentalist or pentecostal pastor believed the school could expand the evangelistic ministry of the church. Concerns like this are legitimate, in their place. But it is now a matter of great urgency that schools that may have been started from such a motive now achieve an expanded vision. Many such schools and the churches that operate them still function with the unbiblical assumption that there is a wall between the sacred and the secular. They regard such secular subjects as mathematics, science, and literature as necessary evils to be endured as part of the price that must be paid to operate a "school." The pastors of the sponsoring churches and the faculty and administration of schools like this need a more adequate vision of the Christian world view and the cultural implications of that world view. They need to see the importance of giving the students in their schools the best possible education. They need to realize that they and their schools have an essential role to play in raising the level of education in this nation, in helping to combat the academic crisis in our public schools.

Ironically, many Christian schools are still providing an education superior to what's available in regional public schools, without fully understanding what's going on. They are doing this with much less money and often with teachers whose credentials are scorned by the very educationist bureaucrats who control teacher certification and who have helped create the disaster we call public education.

If there is one major weakness in some elements of the Christian school movement, it is related to the seemingly unlimited evangelical propensity for superspirituality and anti-intellectualism. There is absolutely nothing wrong with a proper emphasis on spirituality. But what must be abandoned is a thoughtless, mindless type of otherworldliness that denigrates the importance of truth.

Too many Christian schools still offer a curriculum that stresses simple memorization of information presented in less than adequate teaching material. The Christian church needs young people who have been exposed to the best of Western culture and who are able to interact thoughtfully and reflectively with the literature, history, philosophy, and science of that culture. In short, we need Christians who have broad minds that have been sharpened to the point of usefulness.

Christian schools need to begin remedying whatever weaknesses they may have tolerated to this point. The various organizations to which Christian schools belong should do everything possible to raise standards and improve the quality of teaching material. Such schools should take advantage of the growing number of competent advisors who can improve the quality of their faculty and curriculum. Or they might read some of the books recommended in the For Further Reading list provided in the back of this book.

One important concern held by many in middle-class evangelical schools is in the area of curriculum. Concerns vary from the need for high quality education to the need for practicality in the curriculum. Appendix 1 offers an overview of a curriculum used in one of the finer Christian schools in this country, an independent school in Addison, Texas, just north of Dallas, called Trinity Christian Academy. This curriculum is not elitist or utopian in nature; it is a curriculum that is in practice daily at Trinity and is designed to be used in any school. It is a well-designed program that requires both Christian materials and classical material from the great books of the Western world. I recognize that many Christian schools operate on a very tight budget; but we must not sacrifice the quality of our children's reading matter. Moreover, they must be afforded the opportunity to read the original thoughts and writings of the greatest thinkers in history, rather than what someone else wrote about them. As C. S. Lewis said, "read Plato, not books about Plato." I think you will find the curriculum in Appendix 1 helpful and affordable for nearly any Christian school's budget.

Fortunately, there are thousands of Christian schools that are doing an outstanding job. Their racially integrated student bodies attend classes in clean, safe, and well-designed facilities. The teachers all hold degrees from fine colleges. In many cases, these teachers hold state teaching certificates. Even when they don't, it is not a sign of inferior preparation or ability; it is instead a sign that they spent their undergraduate years taking content courses that would give them something to teach. The administrators of these better Christian schools are equal in training, competence, compassion, and vision to their peers in the public schools. In the case of these finer Christian schools, no parent need worry about her child suffering academically or socially.

Conclusion

In this chapter, I have not hesitated to point out some of the weaknesses of the Christian school movement. But the weaknesses are not universal; they do not affect the broad sweep of the Christian school movement. If one is fortunate enough to live in a community where a really fine Christian school is functioning (and there are thousands of schools that qualify), one should take the time to visit the school, talk to the administration and faculty, sit in on some classes, watch one of its athletic teams perform, observe the character of the teachers and students, and recognize the concern about providing a quality education in an environment that honors God and His Word. These better schools are places that one can be proud to be associated with. And then, in case one hasn't done so in a while, visit the local public school and compare what it does with its significantly larger budget.

Nothing authentic is known or taught in Soviet universities about Christianity; whereas practically everything is known or taught in Western universities about communist doctrine and practice. And as we shall see, this blunting, inhibiting virus has infected Western universities themselves with respect to the knowledge of Christianity. The non-West is gradually overpowering the West!

—Charles H. Malik, *Christian Critique of the University*

American Higher Education and the Radical Left

Many people think that little survives from the radical Left's rejection of American society that we remember so well from the 1960s and early 1970s. Paul Hollander, a professor of sociology at the University of Massachusetts (Amherst), disagrees.[1] It is true, he admits, that many of the older radical movements and organizations seemed to have disappeared for several years. But, while they were publicly less visible, they continued to survive and grow below the surface. By the late 1980s, the adversary culture (Hollander's name for the radical Left) had resurfaced with a vengeance. While in its earlier incarnations the adversary culture was part of the counterculture, many of its beliefs, values, and attitudes have become part of mainstream America. During the 1968 Democratic convention, the representatives of the adversary culture were outside the convention rioting in the streets. During the 1988 Democratic convention, they were inside helping to run the show.

Without question, Hollander points out, the place where this radicalism is most evident is the college campus, where large numbers of the faculty go about the task of politicizing their disciplines and their campuses. The college campus is one place where the dispositions of the old adversary culture (the mindset of the radicals of the 1960s and 1970s) still thrive. The survival of the adversary culture is also apparent in the statements and actions of the liberals who control the hierarchies of America's so-called mainline Christian denominations. Surprisingly, its influence continues to grow in many pockets of American evangelicalism, especially on the campuses of respected and trusted evangelical colleges and seminaries.

According to reliable sources, some ten thousand American college and university professors freely identify themselves as Marxists. To this number can be added thousands of others who strongly sympathize with left-wing political and social values. According to one source, the percentage of the faculty at a number of American universities who identify with Marxism ranges as high as 90 percent.[2] This army of radical professors has more than a dozen Marxist journals at its disposal, which it uses to repeat familiar diatribes against America, capitalism, economic freedom, and whatever else the Left happens to despise at the moment.

According to Paul Hollander, the single major resource of left-wing culture in America is the college campus. He writes: "Even if the majority of the students in the nation today do not subscribe to [this] mentality, large and vocal portions of their teachers do, especially in the humanities and social sciences. My own discipline, sociology, has, for example been quite thoroughly politicized and probably a majority of its practitioners take [this way of thinking] for granted."[3] His book cites many other examples of the inroads that Marxist thinking has made into other academic areas.

William Simon, a former secretary of the Treasury and current president of the John M. Olin Foundation, describes the effect a core of radical Leftists has had at Stanford University in California:

> Stanford's pattern of scholastic bias and academic double standards is, by now, well-established. In 1983, the school expelled a scholar from the Ph.D. program for documenting the Chinese policy of massive, coerced abortions. Earlier this year [1988], it removed several books from its core Western civilization reading list because of the sex or race of their authors.[4]

Simon goes on to provide numerous examples to support his claim that "colleges are, once again, becoming a battleground . . . with the radicals trampling the right of free expression and bullying those who do not share their zealotry to place ideology over the pursuit of truth."

Stanford University's decision to water-down the quality and radicalize the content of its Western civilization course in deference to the radical element on its campus is without question a victory for the Left. What is even more incredible is the way in which the administration of Stanford has attempted to portray this decision as a triumph of open-minded tolerance over narrow-mindedness. William Anderson, writing in *World* magazine, is correct when he warns that what happened at Stanford is really "the victory of single-minded zealotry over what has been recognized for centuries as the academic process. Because radicals have control on so many university faculties, they are able to determine who and who will not receive tenure, who and who will not be permitted to speak on campus. Most left-wing faculty members are not judicious with their selections (most tend to favor like-minded cronies, as can be expected at the academy)."[5]

One nationally syndicated columnist notes a special irony in all this. "When American students return to U.S. colleges and universities [in the fall of 1989]," she writes, "they will make an extraordinary voyage—from a summer where the whole world was denouncing and renouncing Marxism to just about the only place where self-righteous Marxists still exist and thrive."[6] Where is that place? The campuses of American colleges and universities.

While students and governments all over Eastern Europe are denouncing (indeed, overthrowing!) Marxism, American students will return to schools "where Marxist academics do not deign to take notice of the real world." Georgie Anne Geyer quotes Arnold Beichman of the Hoover Institute who has stated: "The Marxist academics are today's power elite in the universities and [because of] the magic of the tenure system they have become self-perpetuating. . . . It has successfully substituted Marxist social change as the goal of learning, instead of a search for objective truth." Later in this book, I'll provide an example of how the search for objective truth has been replaced by a quest for Marxist-style social change even on the campuses of so-called evangelical Christian colleges.

"Despite the dramatic death of Marxism throughout a world suddenly freeing itself," Geyer continues, "utopian Marxist thinking is infecting American education on virtually every level." Geyer finds the explanation for this "in the rarefied utopianism of so many

American academics." This Marxism neutralizes "the legitimacy, the genuine intellectuality, and the mission of America and its newest generation." We dare not misunderstand, Geyer warns. These Marxists are not interested in an education that opens the American mind or heart. Their objective is to subvert the truth in an effort to capture the minds and hearts of their students for their radical cause. "While Eastern Europeans are finally freeing themselves from horrendous falsehoods, such as the Russian denial of the Stalin-Hitler pact that divided up Eastern Europe, most of our unhampered, pampered professors are avidly embracing that pact's philosophy." According to Geyer, these men and women "are intellectual disgraces to a free society."

Similar warnings can be found in the writings of many academicians. Gregory Wolfe, for example, has written:

> The ideologies which gained entry into the academy in the Sixties claim that the fundamental intellectual principles of Western culture are illegitimate and must be overthrown. Indeed, the campus revolutionaries of the Sixties are now members of the Establishment— tenured professors, heads of professional organizations, and directors of institutes. Perhaps the most significant aspect of the assault on the humanities is that it is now an ongoing revolution from within.[7]

One of the best accounts of the Left-wing revolution within the universities has been provided by Lee Congdon, a professor of history at James Madison University. Congdon relates that when he was doing graduate work in history during the late sixties and early seventies, the teachers and students in the circles he traveled in took Marxism very seriously. "Most history courses," he writes, "were taught from a Marxist, or a 'radical,' perspective and discussions in and out of class were punctuated with buzz words such as 'fascists,' 'ruling class,' 'liberation,' and that old stand-by 'the People.'"[8]

> For many, to be sure, Marxism meant little more than a festering discontent and a rage that seemed to be greatest when it was least explicable. Only a handful of the more intelligent, and earnest, radicals ever bothered to read Marx and it is important to note at the outset that almost all of them rejected the rigidly deter-

ministic doctrine that Engels had formulated.... These impatient people favored the Neo-Marxism of Herbert Marcuse, Theodor W. Adorno, Ernst Block, George Lukacs, and Karl Korsch, Wiemar theorists in whose opaque texts they believed they had discovered a warrant for their own brand of revolutionary helter-skelter.[9]

Congdon reports that a helpful key to unlocking what really goes on in the minds of Marxist academicians can be found in the work of the Italian communist, Antonio Gramsci. In Gramsci's view of the world, Marxists should not expect the final victory of socialism in the short-term. If the radicals

> could not have apocalypse at once, radical intellectuals could console themselves with the thought that they might have it little by little. In the latter event, they had important work to do, for according to Gramsci the workers could not win political power before they achieved cultural "hegemony," or control of society's intellectual life. Here, at last, was a Marxism that moved intellectuals from the wings to the center of the revolutionary stage. If Gramsci was right, it was intellectuals, not proletarians, who constituted history's messianic class. It was the cultural, not the economic, struggle that mattered most.[10]

Later in this book, I will draw attention to similar views presently emerging on Christian college campuses. Leftist radicals on these campuses are engaged in a similar attempt to tilt the cultural balance to the left.

But back to Gramsci about whom Congdon says the following:

> Thanks to Gramsci, then, radical intellectuals could have their cake and eat it. With a clear conscience, they could accept academic appointments at bourgeois institutions and still perform revolutionary acts, namely teaching, writing, and the making of a Marxist culture. That, certainly, is how Frederick Jameson, the extravagantly praised literary theorist sees it: "To create a Marxist culture in this country," he has written, "to make Marxism an unavoidable presence and a distinct, original, and unmistakable voice in American

social, cultural and intellectual life, in short to form a
Marxist intelligentsia for the struggles for the future—
this seems to me the supreme mission of a Marxist
pedagogy and a radical intellectual life today."[11]

Jameson's words should be read carefully since they admit for
the whole world to see what Marxist academicians are really
about, how they view their own work in the college classroom.
The new Marxist culture which these radicals seek to bring about
is the adversary culture that was discussed earlier in this chapter.
It is to be "a culture of critical discourse," which means that it
will be "negative through and through, at war with a culture that
places a premium on received truths and hence . . . on a class
authority hostile to nonconforming intellectuals."[12] The adversary culture is bent on obliterating the past from our memory,
bent on destroying the past, bent on rewriting history.

What Congdon makes clear is that the radical Left sees the
function of education to be the nihilistic rejection of truth. Its
purpose is to make students dissatisfied, to subvert, to deny any
value to anything (except Marxism).

The title of Congdon's article is "The Marxist Chameleon."
What he is suggesting here is the ease with which Marxists change
the referent of the word "Marxism." Contemporary Marxists in
the West have abandoned some of the more obvious nonsense
found in the writings of such Neo-Marxists as Herbert Marcuse
while retaining and even strengthening its negativism. The radicals of today have

redefined Marxism as a compound of egalitarianism
and anti-Americanism. In this new and simplified
form, the doctrine commands a far wider allegiance
than it did when it defined itself more rigorously. As
matters presently stand, one may elect to be an existen-
tial Marxist, a phenomenological Marxist, a Freudian
Marxist, a Hegelian Marxist, a feminist Marxist, or a
deconstructionist Marxist.[13] No doubt I have left out
some other alternatives. What matters, though, is that
one struggle against cultural, and hence social, "elit-
ism." Contemporary Marxists therefore understand
the purpose of the humanities to be the destruction of
every distinction, between and within cultures. The
extent of their success may be suggested by the fact

that many Americans honestly believe Andy Warhol to have been an artist—and a great one at that.[14]

Congdon then turns his attention to the conviction of Marxist professors that they must find a way to take control of history. Radicals reason, he explains, that if "they are to control the future, they must first take possession of the past by inducing selective amnesia and reinterpreting events in such a way as to promote contemporary political ambitions. Should they ever have it in their power to silence opposing views, we may be certain that they would look for instruction to the Soviet Union and the communist states of East Central Europe."[15]

The ambition of all Marxist regimes is to possess and control human memory. Since our past helps to define who and what we are, control of what people remember of the past produces control of those people. This is why, Congdon states, radical historians are so interesting in rewriting the past in Marxist categories. "In this way they hope to compel us to understand the present in Marxist categories and thus to make the destruction of every order of rank seem to be the logical consequence of forces long at work in our history."[16]

Why, Congdon asks, do so many college-educated people now believe that anti-communism is simplistic, just another hangover of the Cold War? Why do so many view the United States and the Soviet Union as morally equivalent nations? Why are many Americans so much more critical of their own nation? It is difficult to ignore the indoctrination on behalf of these views that has become such an important message of the media and of left-wing academics. Congdon summarizes one of the important elements of this message:

> The Russians, you may have heard by now, "feel threat-ened" as a result of past experiences, such as World War II. The U.S., on the other hand, does not have a ready excuse for protecting its interests, much less for going against history's grain by supporting anti-communist, but undemocratic, regimes. It should be lending sup-port to revolutionary movements in the Third World, as penance for its sins as chief imperialist exploiter.[17]

As the leftist influence on university communities has grown, it has become increasingly more difficult to keep education separated from ideological, political considerations. The reason, of course, is because the Left sees the propagation of its ideology as the primary objective of its educational activity.

> In view of Marxism's influence and increasingly nihil-istic character, the guardianship and development of our tradition that are the humanities' principal respon-sibilities have taken on a fresh urgency. Those tasks are, in fact, far more consequential than efforts to promote public policy initiatives, however worthy they might be. If the tradition that bears our values is destroyed, we will lose hold of our very identity as individuals and as a people. If we allow the nihilistic impulse to go unchecked, we will put civilization itself at risk, with what consequences we ought by now to know.[18]

Once we understand Congdon's point, we will also see that defending the integrity of history and the other humanities as well as defending our traditions means challenging the gains of the Marxists on our campuses. They are truly the enemies of the permanent things.

Evangelical Marxists

Many people are only now becoming aware of the strong Marxist presence within American Christendom. In one sense, there is nothing new about this. During the heyday of Josef Stalin, many liberal churchmen in America acted as though the king-dom of God was being established in the Soviet Union. Even while Stalin's secret police were murdering millions of people within the Soviet Union, alleged spokesmen for Christ were praising his efforts to bring about a just social order.[19]

Much more recently, of course, a Marxist influence has ap-peared in the writings of people who call themselves liberation theologians.[20] But many Christians have yet to grasp the growing Marxist influence within pockets of American Christendom that have been theologically conservative. I am referring especially to those American Protestants known as evangelicals. It is dif-ficult to think of one Marxist idea mentioned earlier in this chapter that has not been propagated in radical left-wing but self-styled evangelical journals like *Sojourners* and *The Other Side*. Such magazines exhibit a double standard. Their standards for the United States are strict and severe. Their standards for every-one else, including the Soviets, Cubans, Vietnamese, and San-dinistas, are quite lenient.

Varieties of Marxist thought have become deeply entrenched on several major evangelical campuses. Some evangelical soci-ologists criticize their society from a Marxist perspective, while some evangelical economics departments present socialism as the only option for "thinking Christians." This pro-Marxist bias is also evident in other departments in these colleges and semi-naries.

One book that illustrates the growing Christian fascination with Marxism is Jose Miguez-Bonino's *Christians and Marxists*.[21] Not only was this book published by an evangelical publishing company, its contents were first delivered to an evangelical audience in London, England, under the auspices of John Stott, noted British evangelical and former rector of All Souls Church. In his book, Bonino discusses Communists like Lenin, Mao Tse-tung, and Fidel Castro in the same reverent tones he uses to describe Christian saints and martyrs. Bonino reports how he is moved by "their deep compassion for human suffering and their fierce hatred of oppression and exploitation."[22] Such words clearly reflect a mind that has, in good Marxist fashion, been severed from history. His observation would have surprised the millions of people who were oppressed, exploited, and murdered at the command of the tyrants Bonino admires.

In one of his more surprising claims, Bonino writes: "Indeed, when we observe the process of building a Socialist society in China . . . we see a significant, even preponderant, importance given to the creation of a new man, a solidary human being who places the common good before his own individual interest."[23] The reader must remember that the China Bonino thinks so highly of is the China of Mao Tse-tung, a China that the Chinese themselves repudiated—at least until the massacre of the sum-mer of 1989. Sociologist Peter Berger provides a healthy antidote to Bonino's ethical short-sightedness when he writes: "*Even if* it were true that Maoism had vanquished hunger among China's poor (and it is not), this achievement could not morally justify the horrors inflicted by the regime—horrors that entailed the killing of millions of human beings and the imposition of a merciless totalitarian rule on the survivors."[24]

But Bonino is not through praising Marxist dictatorships. He writes:

> The political and economic quality and the human value of Socialist revolutions has consistently increased as we move from the USSR to China and Cuba. [It is interesting to note the convenient omission of Cambodia where the Communist rulers murdered at least one-third of the populace.] The social cost has been reduced, the measure of compulsion and repression, particularly in the last case, has been minimised, the welfare of the people has been given at least as much priority as economic development, the disruptive consequences of a blind drive towards industrialization have been avoided. The Chinese and Cuban revolutions have created a sense of participation and achievement on the part of the people and have stimulated a feeling of dignity and moral termination.[25]

Such words would not be surprising if uttered by paid propagandists of Mao or Castro. But they come from a self-professed evangelical who was speaking to other evangelicals—*who believed him*! One must wonder why Bonino was so silent about the millions who died under Communist rule in China, the U.S.S.R., and Cambodia. Why did he fail to mention the persecution of the Christian church (and other religions) by these dictators he finds so admirable?

Many evangelical Christians refuse to believe that leftist views of the kind described in this chapter are really being propagated on evangelical college campuses. If there were one place where the radical Left would want to be sure it was doing its work unobserved, this would be the place. But once in a while, the tensions at this or that evangelical college rise to the surface in the form of some publication that draws public attention to the matter. Something like this happened during the summer of 1985 when Edward Ericson, Jr., an English professor at Calvin College in Grand Rapids, Michigan, found he could no longer keep silent about things occurring on his campus. His remarks appeared as an editorial in the August 1985 issue of *The Reformed Journal*.[26]

Ericson's subject was the sudden surfacing of political radicalism on campuses of evangelical colleges and seminaries, including his own school, Calvin College. He expressed amazement

at the ease with which evangelicals can now mouth the
platitudes of the far-Left "as if it were a new and viable intellectual alternative." For these new evangelical leftists, three major
tenets are paramount: "the self-aggrandizing romance with corrupt Third Worldism . . . the casual indulgence of Soviet totalitarianism . . . [and] the hypocritical and self-dramatizing
anti-Americanism which is the New Left's bequest to mainstream politics." Evangelical Leftists, Ericson observed, have
nothing to say about what communism has done to Ethiopia,
Cambodia, Afghanistan, or Nicaragua. "I see no indication," he
wrote,

> that those who want to internationalize the curriculum
> are panting for our students to know that 66,000,000
> human beings died in the [Soviet Union's] Gulag Archi-
> pelago or that Communists killed a third of all Cambo-
> dians in just a few years (a number estimated at two
> and a half million). . . . No, I think that they will want
> to tell our students that the United States is an aggressor
> state which patronizes such unbearable client states as
> South Africa and Israel, and they will want us to leave
> the Communist rulers of the Nicaraguans to their own
> devices. And all of this agenda they will justify by
> observing that Christ was on the side of the poor and
> the oppressed (*their* chosen poor and oppressed). There
> is a special moral urgency, they will say, to the causes
> which they espouse. The justifications offered will be
> always spiritual ones, never political ones.

Ericson is only one of many evangelicals who regard this
left-wing radicalism as a serious threat to evangelicalism in general and to the integrity of the education available in evangelical
colleges. One of his colleagues in this regard is Bill Anderson who
has expressed his concern that many evangelicals "have a strong
desire to be accepted and respected by their secular peers . . . and
nowhere is this wish stronger than on the evangelical college
campus." Also, he adds, "there has been a strong movement in
evangelical circles for the past 20 years to accept many of the
arguments of the left, especially arguments on socialism and
economics, as to what the Bible teaches. The popularity of the
works of Ron Sider and Jim Wallis [of the aforementioned

Sojourners] at Christian colleges (especially among faculty members) is proof of that."[27]

Anderson tells about an evangelical college that "held a symposium on Marxism several years ago. Many of the delegates concluded that Marx's dogma, while viciously atheistic, nonetheless described the current world condition and had many salvageable points that could be co-opted by Christian scholars. Indeed, they held that the real enemy was capitalism." One irony of all this, Anderson states, is that "the monopoly of the left at secular colleges and universities . . . presents Christian institutions with an unparalleled opportunity to offer an education that promotes objective analysis and tolerates contrary points of view (without having to resort to right-wing propaganda). A curriculum that encourages students to conduct research and examine the world through absolute standards will help educate the mind in ways that the murky, relativistic Stanford model cannot. At the present time, however, it looks as though many Christian colleges are either preparing to or are already following the path set by Stanford and the counterculture left."

Some Thoughts About Karl Marx

The obsession that many Western intellectuals demonstrate regarding the thought and writings of Karl Marx is a phenomenon that deserves more attention than it has received. By any objective reckoning, there is nothing in the content of these writings to merit this attention and devotion. In his recent book, *Intellectuals*, historian Paul Johnson documents Marx's propensity to distort the truth in his writings. Marx did not simply misquote his sources; it is obvious that he did so knowingly and intentionally in an effort to give his untenable claims an appearance of support. "The truth is," Johnson writes, "even the most superficial inquiry into Marx's use of evidence forces one to treat with scepticism everything he wrote which relies on factual data. He can never be trusted. The whole of the key Chapter Eight of *Capital* is a deliberate and systematic falsification to prove a thesis which an objective examination of the facts showed was untenable."[28]

This is not the place to discuss all of Marx's writings, the variations of Marxism offered by later thinkers like Lenin, or the innumerable interpretations and theories set forth by the army of Marxists running around American colleges.[29] It is ironic that there are few, if any, serious Marxists left in nations like the Soviet Union, mainland China, East Germany, and other nations once held captive by the power of the Red Army and the caprice of their non-elected rulers. The real game in such countries—apart from all the old rhetoric about things like the proletariat and the class struggle—has been how these nonelected rulers were able to retain their power. The recent revelations about Nicolae Ceausescu in Romania and his subsequent execution for crimes against the people of Romania serves as one example. Ceausescu maintained power by tryannical means. According to his tribunal, he ordered the deaths of some sixty-thousand-plus people during his twenty-three year dictatorship. Now perhaps another game will emerge: how the *new* rulers can stop the economic bleeding caused by the repeated failures of their socialist systems. The people unfortunate enough to live east of the Iron Curtain know that Marxism is intellectually and economically bankrupt. That's why so many now have rejected it. The "intellectuals" who choose to live west of the Iron Curtain find it easier to ignore the real world as they continue to propagate their master's falsified theories. While the oppressed and suffering citizens of Marxist nations have so longed for the freedom of the West that they have seized the new opportunities to overthrow Marxist tyranny, numerous western academicians continue to tell their students how evil the United States is in comparision with the Soviet Union. And while Marxist states like mainland China and the U.S.S.R. finally acknowledge the failure of socialism and turn increasingly in the direction of capitalist incentives,[30] Western intellectuals continue to urge their nations to abandon capitalism for the kind of socialism that has brought Marxist states to the brink of economic ruin.

For many of these individuals, Karl Marx has become the prophet of a new religion whose writings must be scrutinized with all the devotion and passion that Christians used to bring to their study of the Bible. The semi-religious faith of these Marxists has no essential link to reality. It is difficult to think of one nontrivial claim made by Marx that has not been falsified.

Paul Hollander observes that "The appeals and values associated with socialism . . . have provided the most powerful incentive for the suspension of critical thinking among large contingents of Western intellectuals.... The word 'socialism' has retained, despite all historical disappointments associated with regimes calling themselves socialist, a certain magic which rarely fails to disarm or charm these intellectuals and which inspires renewed hope that its most recent incarnation will be *the* authentic one, or at least more authentic than previous ones had been."[31] Of course, Hollander continues, "There is little evidence that intellectuals, or for that matter nonintellectuals, living in countries considered socialist are similarly charmed or disarmed by the idea of socialism."[32]

After examining the course of socialism in the Soviet Union, Eastern Europe, China, Cuba, Nicaragua, and in the so-called Third World, sociologist Peter Berger is led to conclude: "Even in the early 1970's it should not have been news that socialism is not good for economic growth and also that it shows a disturbing propensity toward totalitarianism (with its customary accompaniment of terror)."[33] Claims by the leaders of such nations that their adoption of socialism reflects their commitment to justice and equality is not simply empty rhetoric; it is hypocritical deceit. "Put simply," Berger declares, "Socialist equality is shared poverty by serfs, coupled with the monopolization of both privilege and power by a small (increasingly hereditary) aristocracy." While the world largely accepted the inevitability of this elitist aristocracy in the Soviet Union, the same phenomenon arose in every socialist state. "It seems to be the intrinsic genius of socialism to produce these modern facsimiles of feudalism." Gradually people are beginning to notice the absence of one single example of a socialist state that has succeeded economically and has not become totalitarian. "We know or should know, that socialism is a mirage that leads nowhere except to economic stagnation, collective poverty, and various degrees of tyranny."

At the time this chapter is being written (winter, 1989), the remarkable situation in Eastern Europe is unfolding. In Poland, for example, most of the political control has passed into the hands of the Solidarity movement. Much is being said about the elimination of socialist controls over the bankrupt economy and the gradual movement toward an economic system resembling more the free enterprise system than socialism. Given Poland's enormous debt, the scarcity of food, and other problems created by its socialist overlords, it is impossible to say at this time what

Poland's future holds; nor for that matter, is it possible to predict what will happen in the Soviet Union and such areas as the Baltic states. What is clear is that, for the moment at least, the failures of Marxism are on public display for the entire world to see: Poland, Hungary, East Germany, Bulgaria, Czechoslovakia, and Romania are all throwing off Marxist shackles.

One of the more ironic features of the Polish situation is a suggestion regarding the only way Solidarity will ever totally get the communists (who it must be remembered still control all the guns) out of the way. The suggestion is that Solidarity buy them off by allowing them to be first in line to become owners (through ownership of shares of stock) of privately held businesses and industries. These will constitute Poland's route to economic recovery—an economic recovery made necessary because of the economic insanity of these very same communists. It will be interesting to see what Marxist intellectuals in the West will tell their students when this happens.

Even more ironic is the fact that at the same time these nations are declaring their break with the Marxism of the past, so many Western intellectuals, including many professors on Christian college and seminary campuses (the next chapter will cover this trend in more depth), are embracing the very system that leads to slavery and poverty. This while the people who have been under such systems are throwing off the shackles and declaring themselves free!

Deconstructionism

Any complete account of the contemporary enemies of the permanent things must include a discussion of the movement known as deconstructionism. According to Allan Bloom, deconstructionism "is the last, predictable, stage in the suppression of reason and the denial of the possibility of truth in the name of philosophy."[34]

One of the best discussions and critiques of deconstructionism was authored by American economist Murrary Rothbard, and appeared in the 1989 volume of *The Review of Austrian Economics*. Rothbard begins by noting how quickly deconstructionism has spread throughout academic fields: "Discipline after discipline, from literature to political theory to philosophy to history, have been invaded by an arrogant band of hermeneuticians, and now even economics is under assault."[35] Since the word "hermeneutics" is not exactly a household word for many Americans, some explanation of the field and its relationship to deconstructionism is necessary. Hermeneutics used to be the discipline that studied the interpretation of the Bible. But this rather straightforward mission of hermeneutics changed with the murky metaphysics of the German philosopher Martin Heidegger and the subsequent work of his student, Hans-Georg Gadamer. Deconstructionism is closely related to hermeneutics. The leaders of the deconstructionist movement include Michel Foucault, Jacques Derrida, and Paul Ricoeur.

Rothbard sums up the essential message of deconstructionism in three words: nihilism, relativism, and solipsism. He explains:

> [E]ither there is no objective truth or, if there is, we can never discover it. With each person being bound to his own subjective views, feelings, history, and so on, there is no method of discovering objective truth. In literature, the most elemental procedure of literary criticism (that is, trying to figure out what a given author meant to say) becomes impossible. Communication between writer and reader similarly becomes hopeless; furthermore, not only can no reader ever figure out what an author meant to say, but even the author does not know or understand what he himself meant to say, so fragmented, confused, and driven is each particular individual. So, since it is impossible to figure out what Shakespeare, Conrad, Plato, Aristotle, or Machiavelli meant, what becomes the point of either reading or writing literary or philosophical criticism?[36]

Deconstructionists believe the activity of the interpreter is more important than the text being interpreted. In effect, the text becomes nothing and the interpretation becomes everything. Of course, there is no such thing as a correct interpretation. Not even the person who wrote the text knew what she meant; how can any interpreter hope to do better? "Thus," as Bloom says, "the one thing most necessary for us, the knowledge of what these texts have to tell us, is turned over to the subjective creative selves of these interpreters, who say that there is both no text and no reality to which the texts refer."[37] This explains what Rothbard means when he sums up deconstructionism as a form of nihilism and relativism.

The term *solipsism*, which is less familiar to many readers, refers to the fact that in deconstructionism the only thing that counts is the single, solitary interpreter who in effect creates meaning instead of drawing it from the world around her or from her texts.

Deconstructionism reduces to the claim that no one, not even deconstructionists, can understand literary texts—not even their *own* literary texts. What this means is that all writings of deconstructionists in which they analyze the writings of other authors are only "subjective musings."[38] But why should anyone care? And even if we did care about this or that author, the deconstructionists' own principles would prevent us from understanding those musings. If the deconstructionist is right, we can never understand *any* text, *including* the texts in which deconstructionists describe the principles of their own position. Deconstructionism turns out to be a self-refuting theory.

Rothbard finds it significant that Karl Marx is regarded as a forerunner of this movement:

> This century has seen a series of devastating setbacks to Marxism, to its pretentions to "scientific truth," and to its theoretical propositons as well as to its empirical assertions and predictions. If Marxism has been riddled both in theory and in practice, then what can Marxian cultists fall back on? It seems to me that hermeneutics fits very well into an era that we might . . . call "late Marxism" or Marxism-in-decline. Marxism is not true and is not science, but so what? The hermeneuticians tell us that nothing is objectively true, and therefore that all views and propositions are subjective, relative to the whims and feelings of each individual. So why should Marxian yearnings not be equally as valid as anyone else's? By the way of hermeneutics, these yearnings cannot be subject to refutation. And since there is no objective reality, and since reality is created by every man's subjective interpretations, then all social problems reduce to personal and nonrational tastes.[39]

It would be a serious error in judgment to think of deconstructionism as nothing more than a self-refuting exercise in interpretation or non-interpretation. What deconstructionists teach is intellectual permissiveness, to be sure. But it is much more than that. They also preach *practical* permissiveness. Those who insist that truth is relative always end up saying that ethics is relative too. Deconstructionism means the end of human learning. The catch is, of course, that there is absolutely no reason to take it seriously. Rothbard argues that advocates of such a nihilistic and self-refuting position are not worthy participants in any dialogue or conversation. Instead of a respectful point by point analysis and refutation of their writings which, by their own principles, can never be interpreted correctly, what they deserve instead, Rothbard argues, "is scorn and dismissal. Unfortunately, they do not often receive such treatment in a world in which all too many intellectuals seem to have lost their built-in ability to detect pretentious claptrap."[40]

It is nothing short of amazing that it is the pragmatists, the relativists, the deconstructionists, and other twentieth-century sophists who have the temerity to dismiss Christianity as a house of unreason. One sure sign of a rational human is her ability to recognize an intellectual charlatan when she sees one. What better candidates for this title can there be than people who claim that truth and meaning are relative and presume to tell us this by means of statements they assume to be both true and meaningful. What must we think of a society and of academicians who regard this sort of thing as serious scholarship?

Conclusion

Each succeeding chapter of this book is intended to peel away successive layers of our educational crisis. There is no simple solution because there is no single cause. The purpose of this chapter has been to reveal the role that the radical Left is playing, especially at the level of higher education. The relativism that is so central to the crisis in our public schools and the nihilistic relativism that dominates so much of higher education flow from different sources. But they complement each other perfectly. Nothing enhances the likelihood of their continued success more than the ignorance, apathy, and indifference of parents, educators, and legislators.

CHAPTER

10

If Aristotle, who was a pagan and a philosopher too, painted such a picture among men who were not holy and learned in the Scriptures, how much more is it fit for one who moves in the place of Christ to fulfill the task?

—Erasmus

Strengths and Weaknesses of the Evangelical College

With my discussion of Christian elementary and secondary education behind us, it is now time to turn to the subject of Christian higher education. The United States has a large number of private colleges that are strongly evangelical in their commitment. There are roughly one hundred or so colleges that fall into this group. Unfortunately, the total enrollment at all of these colleges combined is less than ninety thousand. This is fewer students than you could find at two large state universities.*

The evangelical colleges I'll be discussing in this chapter differ from theologically liberal colleges affiliated with America's large, mainline denominations in several ways. First, the evangelical college makes no apology for its commitment to Jesus Christ, to the inspired and authoritative Word of God, and to the essential doctrinal beliefs that have defined the nature of historic Christianity. This is evident in the doctrinal statement that most of these colleges place prominently in their catalogs. The evangelical college is not simply Christian in name. It is self-consciously Christian. Therefore, it works hard to see that every member of its administration and faculty is a committed Christian believer. Moreover, it checks continually to see that its faculty accept unreservedly its doctrinal statement. The good evangelical college sees no inconsistency between its Christian mission and its

---

* My comments omit several dozen non-accredited Bible colleges that often pay little attention to the liberal arts.

role as an academic institution. Many evangelical colleges evidence a greater commitment to academic excellence than one can find at many secular schools that have (undeservedly) somewhat better reputations.

Some Strengths of the Christian College

A number of evangelical colleges are excellent academic institutions, among the very best colleges in the country. In a recent study of graduates of American colleges between 1968 and 1973 who went on to earn Ph.D. degrees, Wheaton College (Illinois) ranked fifth nationwide while Calvin College made it into the top twenty-five. That is select company, and these schools can be justly proud of this recognition. Other evangelical colleges that ranked relatively high include Houghton, Geneva, Asbury, and Greenville.

The evangelical college's support for the beliefs and values of the Christian family is another positive consideration. Of course, it is also important to note that not every college that claims to be evangelical still supports these beliefs and values as they should. Still another strength of most evangelical colleges is summed up in a recent publication of the Christian College Coalition. According to that publication, "What sets Christian colleges apart from other institutions—more than size or academic offerings or denominational ties—is the educational environment: the culture of living and learning, sharing and caring."[1] One of the most important and frequently overlooked aspects of a college education is the role that being part of a small, learning and caring community for four years plays in the development of the student.

On other kinds of campuses, learning and faith are divorced from each other. If the Christian student wants to integrate her personal faith with what she's learning in the classroom, she has to do it herself. But, "at Christian liberal arts colleges," the Christian College Coalition correctly notes: "the integration of faith and learning is an ongoing quest."[2] When Christian professors on Christian campuses are doing their job properly (and sometimes they don't), the student will be helped to see how Christian beliefs and the Bible relate to what is being learned in history, literature, the natural sciences, and the social sciences.

Finally, the best Christian colleges offer their students something they cannot find in private colleges and state-supported universities that may have more money to play around with. The evangelical college can offer an approach to education that helps the student become a whole person, that enables the student to tie all the important aspects of her intellectual, moral, spiritual, and religious life together.

Wheaton College philosopher Arthur Holmes describes the kind of student better evangelical colleges are interested in producing. Not surprisingly, a solid grounding in what are called the liberal arts is a necessary element in this task. Holmes writes:

> [T]he educated person shows independence and creativity of mind to fashion new skills and techniques, new patterns of thought. She has acquired research ability, the power to gather, sift, and manipulate new facts and materials, and to handle altogether novel situations. The educated Christian exercises critical judgment and manifests the ability to interpret and to evaluate information, particularly in the light of the Christian revelation. In a word, if she is to act creatively and to speak with cogency and clarity to the minds of her fellows, the educated Christian must be at home in the world of ideas and people.[3]

This is a fine statement. It is disappointing, however, to find Holmes suggesting in the same book that this ideal of Christian education is somehow incompatible with another concern, that of propagating and defending the Christian faith. Holmes ridicules people who still think of the Christian college in terms of its role as Defender of the Faith. He seems to think that once one steps on the campus of a Christian college, other values and objectives must take priority over "the old-fashioned," outdated notion of defending the faith. I find this thinking odd. Holmes seems to believe that education and apologetics are incompatible. When a Christian college is busy defending the faith, he says, "the idea . . . is not so much to educate as to indoctrinate, to provide a safe environment plus all the answers to all the problems posed by all the critics of orthodoxy and virtue."[4] Fortunately, many Christian academics do not see things this way. It is hard to see why grounding students in the basics of the Christian faith and teaching them how to defend that faith necessarily turns education into indoctrination. Perhaps Holmes did not mean to suggest that Wheaton College has abandoned its own former role as Defender of the Faith. Possibly, he was thinking of academically weaker institutions with a less adequate philosophy of education. Most of us in the academic world know of schools that do a better job of indoctrinating than of educating students. Such schools need help. But let us hope that the better Christian colleges do not take Holmes' words too literally and surrender the important tasks of grounding students in the faith and helping them learn how to defend that faith.

The liberal arts are important and must be given a central place in the curriculum of the Christian college. As Holmes explains, "[T]he liberal arts are those which are appropriate to persons as persons, rather than to the specific function of a worker or a professional or even a scholar. . . . If one is to be anything more than a specialist or technician, if one is to feel life whole and to live it whole rather than piecemeal, if one is to think for himself rather than live secondhand, the liberal arts are needed to educate the person."[5]

And so evangelical colleges have many strengths. The value of the education they offer is enhanced when the college provides a strong emphasis on the liberal arts. As Holmes states, the distinctive of a Christian college "should be an education that cultivates the creative and active integration of faith and learning, of faith and culture."[6]

Some Weaknesses of the Christian College

Christian colleges also have their weaknesses. Some of these schools are long on spirituality but short on academics. The people running the show at some of the weaker evangelical colleges have yet to see that Christianity has nothing to fear from any area of human knowledge. Some of these colleges have dragged their feet in upgrading their faculty. There are thousands of unemployed Ph.D.'s representing many academic fields; some of them are evangelicals. And yet, some evangelical colleges still have many faculty members without earned doctorates. That situation is impossible to justify. I have already stated that some of the strongest colleges in the nation are evangelical schools; I must now admit that some of the weakest institutions are evangelical as well.

It is also true that some evangelical schools evidence a noticeable wobbling on important theological matters. Some schools that are evangelical by reputation do not take their doctrinal statements seriously any more. Some of these schools still want the public to think they're theologically sound, when, in fact, they are rapidly moving away from the evangelical camp. I have talked to many bitter and disillusioned parents who sent their children to this or that evangelical college, believing that it was as sound as when they went there twenty years ago. In the cases I am thinking about, the children now have a weaker faith or no faith at all.

The growth of liberal theological tendencies at a number of evangelical colleges was discussed more than ten years ago by author Richard Quebedeaux in a book titled *The Worldly Evangelicals*. Quebedeaux began by drawing attention to the influence of liberalism in schools associated with the Southern Baptist Convention.[7] Carl F. H. Henry, himself a Southern Baptist, has issued a similar warning. Several Southern Baptist seminaries, Henry writes, espouse "a murky neoorthodoxy; [and] some of its colleges, no longer unapologetically Christian, even hire faculty members who make no profession of faith whatever."[8] Author Bill Anderson quotes one knowledgeable academic who says, "It would be easier for a 'sun worshiper' to be hired on the faculty at a well-known [Southern Baptist] university . . . than it would be for a Bible believing Christian."[9]

According to Quebedeaux, the governing boards of several evangelical colleges are aware of liberal tendencies at their schools. "They know that many of their faculty sign the required statement of faith tongue in cheek."[10] But this never seems to bother these board members. What does concern them, Quebedeaux states "is that the infringement of doctrinal standards and rules of conduct remain a local, 'in house' matter. As long as professors do not publish their liberal views in widely circulated popular magazines read by conservative financial backers of these institutions, much can be tolerated."[11] Quebedeaux also wrote of an increasingly large number of evangelical professors "who really *have* moved beyond evangelical belief toward liberalism. In other words, they have rejected the evangelical position intellectually (though they may not admit or even recognize it), but they still have an *emotional* attachment to the [evangelical] movement in which they were converted and nurtured."[12]

Carl F. H. Henry is one of the most respected evangelical thinkers of the twentieth century. He rightly criticizes professedly evangelical colleges that promise "to expose students to the control beliefs of biblical Christianity" and then proceed "to dilute those beliefs in the classroom by concessions to the secular philosophies that [they profess] to critique." Henry asks, "Is it not both an academic and spiritual tragedy if students, parents, and donors are encouraged to think that an institution is firmly committed to the evangelical faith when students in one or another department of that school are presented instead with neoorthodoxy[13] or some other distortion of an authentic scriptural stance? Slowly but surely the inherited commitments are put under pressure, are spared suffocation only by a thousand qualifications, until finally they collapse under the weight of alien compromises and logical inconsistency."[14]

At a small meeting of evangelical educators convened in 1989 by the Washington-based Ethics and Public Policy Institute, I warned that a number of evangelical institutions, which many Christians uncritically assume are still solidly evangelical, have begun to show cracks in their theological foundations. It is important to remember that almost every theologically liberal, church-related college in the U.S. began as an evangelical school. Is it possible, I asked, that such stalwart evangelical institutions as Wheaton College, perhaps, could be lost to evangelicalism in two or three generations? Is it possible that the important educational role that evangelicals presently assign to outstanding schools like Wheaton will pass to younger institutions like Liberty University? Such a thing admittedly seems unlikely. But many Christians a century ago would have found similar comments about such colleges as Oberlin equally fanciful. Today, of course, Oberlin, which was founded by evangelist Charles Finney, is one of the most liberal schools in the country.

My comments at the Washington conference were followed by a response from Dr. George Marsden. Marsden is a well-known and highly respected evangelical historian who taught for many years at Calvin College and who is now a professor at Duke Divinity School. He is also the author of the critically acclaimed

book about the history of Fuller Theological Seminary titled
Reforming Fundamentalism which, incidentally, traces (or so many
of its readers think) the ways in which Fuller abandoned some
of the strongly evangelical convictions of its founding faculty.
Marsden agreed with my statement that a number of evangelical
colleges are drifting theologically; he admitted that their theological vacillating has become so dramatic that it is now possible
to question whether they'll still qualify as evangelical schools in
a decade or two. But, he then added, this is the way things have
always been in American evangelicalism. We evangelicals found
the schools; the schools serve our communities for a while; and
then they fall away. And their apostasy makes necessary the
establishment of still newer schools that will, in their own time,
also fall away. And so it goes.

It is impossible to disagree with Marsden's picture of what has
happened to evangelical colleges in the past or to what is occurring to some of them in the present. What I found disappointing
was his rather laissez-faire attitude to this on-going disaster, an
attitude that produces only a shrug of the shoulders and an air
of resignation. Once an evangelical school begins to fall away,
can nothing be done to turn the tide? Obviously, there is a line
which once crossed means a school has gone too far to be saved.
But just as obviously, there is a long period of time during which
the school's movement toward that line can be slowed and
possibly turned in the other direction. Whether that recovery is
possible depends on many things, including trustees, administrators, faculty, students, and alumni who see the danger and
who care enough to act.

Early in 1989, Carl Henry followed the lead of Dr. Walter
Kaiser, dean of Trinity Evangelical Divinity School, and asked
"whether the time may not have come for the formation of an
Evangelical Council for Academic Accountability which would
function in educational matters much as the Evangelical Council
for Financial Accountability functions in respect to promotional
and fund-raising practices."[15] Henry thinks it would be best if
such an agency were independent of existing agencies such as
the Christian College Coalition and the Christian College Con-
sortium. What Henry implies but does not say here is that the
two agencies may be part of the problem of evangelical higher
education; they often seem more interested in promoting a far-

left political agenda than dealing with any theological wobbling in member schools. The kind of agency Henry and Kaiser have in mind might, Henry says, "be coordinated with the commission of Higher Education of the National Association of Evangelicals. It would require an annual audit of academic fulfillment or nonfulfillment of publicly announced institutional principles and objectives, and stipulate the availability to the constituency of relevant records."[16] If anyone thought it was difficult to get television evangelists to submit to an examination of their financial accountability, wait until some effort is made to get evangelical colleges to submit to a test of their educational and theological accountability.

Evangelical Colleges and the Political Left

Evangelical colleges also manifest an incredibly rapid spread of left-wing ideology on their campuses. Some unintended support for this claim is provided in an essay by evangelical scholar Timothy Smith, who has never been shy about admitting his own commitment to political liberalism. Smith states that evangelical liberal arts colleges "are almost as estranged from right-wing religious publicists and politicians as religious and political liberals profess to be."[17] What Smith is really saying is that political liberals no longer need to fear evangelical colleges as bastions of conservative political views. From Smith's perspective, evangelical colleges are often as "enlightened" as schools in which the ideology of the Left has been king for years. Smith leaves no doubt as to the fact that he's delighted with this new situation. These evangelical colleges, Smith continues,

> find stridency on conservative political positions a threat to both evangelical culture and democratic ideals. The unpublicized influence of faculty members of these various institutions upon the merging political attitudes and ideals of their tens of thousands of students is a chief explanation of why such organizations as Evangelicals for Social Action, World Vision, and Young Life, as well as many of the smaller evangelical denominations themselves, oppose the right-wing militancy of the so-called 'moral majority.'[18]

Smith is clearly delighted to be able to say that evangelical colleges are graduating tens of thousands of students who have been turned into political liberals through the efforts of their Christian college professors. But his paragraph also provides unintended evidence of how simplistic the evangelical Left is when it comes to understanding and explaining conservatism. No informed conservative would ever confuse the Moral Majority (now defunct) in any way with a well-grounded conservatism. In some ways, the Moral Majority represented the worst of the old uninformed, naive, frequently mindless conservatism that used to characterize many elements of evangelicalism. But perhaps the most troubling aspect of Smith's equally naive, mindless, and uninformed endorsement of liberalism is that it evidences absolutely no awareness of that movement's enormous problems. If anything, his comments illustrate how shallow the evangelical Left really is in its understanding of political theory, of economics, and of the conservative alternative they consistently misrepresent.

Another representative of the evangelical Left sees the situation on Christian campuses rather differently. What bothers Dr. Richard Perkins of Houghton College is his belief that evangelical colleges typically are populated by "wall-to-wall" conservatives. The situation is so bad, Perkins declares, that he thinks he and other political liberals are justified in going overboard in propagating their liberal ideology, in attempting to convert their conservative students to their more enlightened political position.[19]

Perkins' position drew a response from James L. Sauer of Eastern College. Sauer thinks that Perkins' description of an organized conservative conspiracy on Christian campuses is simplistic and uninformed. This is not to say that one cannot find conservatives on such campuses. But Sauer insists "that most evangelical Christians are habitual, unthinking conservatives [who] would be hard pressed to define a thoughtful ideological conservative worldview. I think our Christian colleges are much more liberal than Mr. Perkins would admit."[20]

While many of the freshmen who enter evangelical colleges may come from conservative homes and may begin college with conservative instincts, neither they nor their parents come close to being informed conservatives. Most often, neither they nor their parents have ever read a book defending the political or economic views of conservatives. In fact, it is this widespread political and economic illiteracy of evangelical undergraduates that makes them such an easy target for professors whose major goal in life is getting students to think that the Bible obliges us to become good liberals.[21]

While there is little hard data, Sauer offers several observations to support his claim that Christian colleges are more liberal than Perkins allows:

> First, there is a clear emphasis in most Christian colleges for "social activism." Liberal organizations like Evangelicals for Social Action flourish; while there are no similar conservative organizations. The culture of the Christian collegiate feeds off a number of "social activist" journals: *The Other Side, Sojourners, Christianity and Crisis, Daughters of Sarah,* and *The Wittenburg Door.*[22] Again, no Christian conservative journal exists in this category [unless Dr. James Dobson's recent entry into the general Christian citizen field, called *Citizen,* emerges with a youthful, activist following]. Couple this with growth of leftward theologies—liberation theology, process theology, biblical feminism, antinomianism, pro-homosexuality, pro-choice abortionism, and socialist solidarity—which one encounters here and there on the Christian college campus and the notion that conservatives are a dominant force in Christian higher education comes into question. If conservatives are in a majority, they are an apathetic, inarticulate majority. Mr. Perkins sets up the strawman of a conservative establishment in order to have an ideology to use his "ideological analysis" against. The only problem is, the conservatives aren't in charge.[23]

Sauer's comments suggest an explanation for how political liberalism became entrenched on evangelical college campuses. While most evangelical families tended in the past to be socially conservative, their "conservatism" was more a product of instinct and habit than of informed judgment. These evangelicals never read a book about economics or political theory; consequently, most of them had no idea what conservatives believed or why. While the students who entered evangelical colleges in the 1960s and 1970s may have started college with the conservative instincts of their parents, they were easy prey for the first liberal ideologue who crossed their path. Sometimes encounters like this took place while they were still undergraduates in their Christian college. More often, their first serious exposure to liberal dogma occurred in graduate school.

Totally uninformed about conservatism, they simply accepted the caricature of conservatism that came from liberal professors they admired and wished to emulate. Since no one had ever told them what was correct about conservatism and what was wrong about liberalism, it became easy for them to question the unthinking "conservatism" their parents seemed to hold. But something else was taking place at the same time.

The values of political liberalism could easily be presented to unsophisticated and poorly read students as *Christian* values. After all, they were taught, conservatives are materialistic, self-centered individualists who do not and cannot care for the poor and oppressed. If one is genuinely compassionate, he or she will support such things as the liberal welfare state, the redistribution of wealth, and other standard liberal programs. Once started down this path, it was only a matter of time before many of these graduates of evangelical colleges absorbed the full liberal or radical agenda.

But while all this was taking place, someone forgot to tell these people that the conservative stereotype that they were rejecting as anti-Christian was just that—a misrepresentation. Had they or their families ever taken the time to find out what an informed conservatism stood for and about its strong Judeo-Christian heritage, they would have had no trouble recognizing the deception. Had they or their families ever taken the time to study some elementary economics, they would have realized that while the liberals *talked* compassion, their programs and policies did enormous injury and harm to the poor. What a growing number of recently published books are now making clear is this: if Christians really care about the poor and oppressed, they will reject the tired old policies of the Left and begin to support the kinds of economic and political programs that informed conservatives have been promoting for years.[24]

And so, many graduates of evangelical colleges who were soon to become professors or administrators in such schools went through a process in their graduate studies in which they became receptive to alien, even radical ideologies. They were deceived into thinking that they were tapping into legitimate Christian concerns. In some cases their understanding of the Bible also underwent subtle changes. What resulted was not an adaptation of the non-Christian ideology to Scripture but an *accommodation* of Scripture to the non-Christian ideology. A number of people who fit the description of the last few paragraphs are now tenured professors at evangelical colleges. They see their major mission in life to be a passing on of their liberal ideology to succeeding generations of evangelical students.

In an article mentioned in an earlier chapter, Edward Ericson, Jr., expresses concern about the extent to which the traditional curriculum of Christian colleges is being radicalized by some left-wing professors.[25] This radical assault on the curriculum is not all that different from what leftists have done to the curriculum at secular institutions like Stanford University. For a growing number of radicalized professors at Christian colleges, the end or goal of education is not knowledge or truth, but what Marxists call *praxis*. Until recently, it's been rather difficult to find published evidence to back up Ericson's concerns. The same Richard Perkins we noted earlier in the chapter has revealed that one of the ways liberals like himself want to change the Christian college is to use its curriculum for propaganda purposes.

Perkins begins by criticizing history courses that teach only history. What Perkins wants to see are history courses used in the service of his approved ideology.[26] What about art and music? Perkins states: "We need less information on how to frame pictures and how to play flutes, and more on the ideological significance of the arts. Exploration of the connections between artistic expression and social stratification, for example, should run throughout our lectures in arts." Aside from the fact that Perkins totally distorts the content of art and music courses, it is obvious that he wants such courses turned into instruments of the left-wing message he thinks Christian students need to hear. His approach to art is unquestionably Marxist in orientation. I, for one, would rather see students learning to develop their literary and musical talents in ways that express a desire to glorify God and live a life honoring to Him. I think most Christian parents would agree.

What about theology? What we need, Perkins says, is "less on early Anabaptist supralapsarianism, and more on the connections between theodicy and social class." It is impossible to figure out what this last sentence means. "Anabaptist supralapsarianism" is a contradiction in terms, something along the order of warmongering pacifist. I have even less idea what Perkins means by *"early* Anabaptist supralapsarianism." Theodicy is the branch of theology that deals with the problem of evil and attempts to justify the ways of God in the face of all the evil that exists in God's creation. Only a Marxist, I suppose, could see some connection between the notions of theodicy and social class.

What does Perkins think Christian colleges should say about the Bible? They should provide "less information on the particular order of towns visited by Christ, or where he performed his first seventeen miracles, and more on what a truly marginal character Jesus was, and how he responded to contemporary ideologies concerning women, the rich, the political rulers, and the poor." I guess what Perkins means is that Christian colleges should turn the Bible into a manual on liberation theology and use it, as liberationist thinkers do, as a way of converting the uninformed into activists for their leftist views about feminism and Marxism.[27]

As for literature, Perkins sounds precisely like the leftist professors at Stanford when they argue that the readings for the core course in Western civilization should include fewer selections from dead, white, Anglo-Saxon males like Plato, Aristotle, Shakespeare, and Milton. Here are Perkins' own words: "We need fewer reading assignments from the top—from affluent and educated [sic] authors, and more from revolutionary leaders, from the vanquished, the powerless, the poor; more from those people who do not ordinarily get much of a chance to write at all, much less be heard." To be sure, one does not often hear a college professor argue that students in literature courses should be given more opportunity to read the writings of *uneducated* writers. All that would be necessary to fulfill this condition, one supposes, is that the students substitute their own writings for those of Dante or Aquinas.

Perkins goes on to present his opinions about education and psychology, but I think we've covered enough to get the picture.[28] Perkins thinks Christian colleges are spending too much time dealing with content. He wants that content reduced, watered-down, or eliminated so that more emphasis can be given to ideology, *his* ideology. Sauer describes Perkins' philosophy of education as "a mechanism for subverting the transmission of revealed, rational, and empirical truth through a theological sociology of permanent agnosticism."[29] What Perkins has done, Sauer explains, is advocate an approach to education that turns every academic subject into a tool for his own ideology. Perkins' "doctrine of 'ideological analysis', when it is translated into other academic areas empties them of traditional value and content, and fills them with relative value and ideological meaning. Not being content to teach sociology in sociology classes, he now suggests that we teach sociology in everyone else's classes as well."[30] In Perkins' view of education, Sauer continues:

> Art and music stop being about art and music, and become lectures in "ideological significance" and "social stratification." Biology becomes a gab fest concerning the effects of technology on "the democratic process." Theology becomes a tool for studying "social class," and biblical study is turned into an apology for social relevance as we see how Jesus responded to "women, the rich, the political rulers, and the poor." My favorite plan of Mr. Perkins is to purge classicist counter-revolutionaries like Shakespeare, Milton, Swift, Johnson, [C. S.] Lewis, and Chesterton from our literature, and to replace them with "revolutionary leaders . . . the vanquished, the powerless, the poor; more from those people who do not ordinarily get much of a chance to write at all."[31]

Given half a chance, it is obvious that evangelicals like Perkins will attempt to change Christian college curricula as radically as the Stanford faculty changed theirs. What is clear is that if they have their way, Christian colleges will cease being educational institutions in any traditional sense and will become propaganda centers for the leftists' favorite causes.

Evangelical Sociology

Earlier we noted how Richard Perkins would like to see Christian colleges change the way they teach such subjects as history, literature, and art. The recent publication of a book by Perkins aids us in discovering what he thinks about his own field of sociology. The title of his book is *Looking Both Ways: Exploring the Interface Between Christianity and Sociology*.[32]

Perkins' book is an examination of the relationship between his academic discipline of sociology and the Christian faith. His title, *Looking Both Ways*, is meant to suggest two things. First, alluding to the way that wise people about to cross a busy street look both ways before proceeding, his book exhorts both Christians and sociologists to approach each other with caution. His second purpose is to encourage both Christians and sociologists that there is much that they can learn from each other. Because so many Christians distrust sociology and so many sociologists have a low regard for Christianity, this advice seems necessary. Sociology is a discipline that often seems at odds with important Christian convictions. However, Perkins advises, much of this Christian suspicion is due to conflicts, not with essential Christian beliefs, but with some excess ideological baggage that many Christian students carry with them into the sociology classroom. Of course, sociologists also have their own excess baggage, a fact that accounts for some of their supposed problems with the Christian faith.

Part One of the Perkins's book is a brief and often clear introduction to sociology from a Christian perspective. Its greatest value lies in its helpful analysis of sociological relativism. There is plenty of empirical support for the claim that different people understand their social reality differently. But there is no evidence for the far stronger claim that reality itself varies. This second kind of assertion is an example of metaphysics, not sociology.

One of Perkins's major concerns in Part Two of his book is structuralism, the belief that human problems are caused by such structural features of society as social roles, institutions, and so on. People who have trouble seeing the point to structuralism counter that social problems have their causes in the traits, dispositions, and behavior of individual persons. While Perkins is careful to avoid turning structuralism into an all-or-nothing proposition (he admits that structuralism cannot account for all social problems), he does treat opponents of structuralism in this simplistic way. In case the point remains a bit obscure, sociologists like Perkins think that all conservatives—his counterpart to the wicked witch of the West—are opponents of structuralism. I'll say more about the unfair way he handles non-structuralists shortly.

According to Perkins, good sociologists will try to help their students recognize that they have but two options: (1) the moderate structuralism that Perkins defends or (2) the simplistic, all-or-nothing individualism that he sets up as the complement of his own enlightened structuralism, an individualism that he equates with conservatism. When a social problem does have a structural cause, it is obvious that individualist solutions for that problem will be inadequate.

At this point in his argument, Perkins picks out some of his own students whom he thinks function as prototypes of a certain class of evangelical believer. According to Perkins, these evangelical, "middle-class" (his term) students have been conditioned to think of social problems in an individualist way. This is due, Perkins is sure, to their having been corrupted by "conservativism" (his word). The most significant fault of what Perkins calls conservatism and individualism lies in making Perkins' students unable or unwilling to recognize the wisdom of Perkins' structuralism. Clearly, he sees this as a problem he must deal with. As it turns out, this problem appears to have been his major motivation for writing Part Two.

The fact that Perkins's middle-class students have difficulty seeing structural causes for certain social problems hardly seems to warrant the attention he gives to the matter. Many people have trouble seeing truths until something is explained to them. When I run across students who appear unable to understand the role that social institutions play in creating social problems, I try to correct their misunderstanding. Any conservative individualist (the boogey-person that Perkins keeps bouncing his own views off of) can and should acknowledge that some social problems have structural causes. In my books, *Poverty and Wealth* and *Social Justice and the Christian Church*, I point out how often various social problems are either caused by or made worse by governmental actions. Over the past twenty years, incredibly dumb welfare policies have created a social structure that encourages poverty and illegitimacy. This kind of problem *is* structural. Of course, it is also the kind of structure that many left-leaning evangelicals like Perkins want the rest of us to support.

Perkins' problem is that he just doesn't understand individualism and conservatism. I have already pointed out how an individualist can recognize how structuralist features of society help cause social problems. Perkins slanders individualism when he claims that individualists must be opposed to voluntary communities, a claim I explicitly reject in my two aforementioned books. The proper way to understand Christian individualism is to see it as an opposition to societal models that subordinate the individual to the coercive state. What makes some of us individualists is not our opposition to voluntary communal societies but rather our resistance to coercive states (including our own) that violate the rights of individual people *and* the voluntary societies to which we belong. A true individualism supports the kinds of communal relationships that Perkins professes to endorse. Ironically, many evangelicals with whom Perkins sides end up supporting politicians and policies that undermine voluntarism and communalism. What Perkins fails to recognize is that the position he offers as an alternative to individualism is really what individualism is all about.

Two other topics—reflexivity and parochialism—keep popping up in Part Two of Perkins' book. *Reflexivity* refers to a cognitive detachment from conventional social reality; it enables the reflexive person to attain a self-critical stance that helps her recognize the limitations of her own point of view and thus become more open to (and tolerant of) competing points of view. Perkins seems to think that reflexivity is one of the more important benefits students can acquire through taking a sociology course. Perkins also seems to think that reflexivity is one trait he has in abundance.

People who have not yet attained Perkins' lofty level of reflexivity lack the trained capacity to see in other ways. The word he uses to describe such people is *parochial*. Parochialism is a kind of narrow-minded or bigoted mind-set that leads people to absolutize their own culture or point of view. Perkins thinks his middle-class students are afflicted with parochialism. Not surprisingly, he thinks their conservatism and individualism is largely responsible for their deficiency. Perkins wants his students to exchange their parochialism for his reflexivity. But a careful reading of his book suggests that Perkins might need to scrutinize his own presumed reflexivity with a bit more care. It is puzzling why a scholar with Perkins' training seems unable to recognize the misrepresentations and distortions of conservatism that show up throughout the second half of his book. Is it because he hasn't read the right books, none of which incidentally appear in his notably left-of-center bibliography? Or is it because he cannot free himself from his own ideological bias when reading such books? Is it because his own culture-bound, parochial thinking prevents him from achieving the cognitive detachment—the reflexivity—necessary to understand this literature? And is it possible then that Perkins is just as afflicted with parochialism as the students he feels so qualified to help?

In the United States, looking both ways (the title of Perkins's book) usually means looking first to the left. The car that poses the immediate threat to the U.S. pedestrian is the one coming from the left. But whenever I take groups of students to Great Britain, I warn them that the different traffic pattern there should lead them to look first to the right. Richard Perkins gives every appearance of having been conditioned to look only to the Left for his answers. It might be good if he would heed the advice of his own title and recognize that sometimes it is wise also to look to the right. Perkins himself fails to look both ways. And in that failing lies perhaps the major weakness of his book, of his political ideology, and of many professors at Christian colleges whom he represents.

The term "democracy," as I have said again and again, does not contain enough positive content to stand alone against the forces that you dislike—it can easily be transformed by them.

—T. S. Eliot, *Christianity and Culture*

Renewing Christianity's Links to Its Past

There are at least two reasons why this chapter has a place in this book. One of the earlier chapters referred to the importance of theological literacy for the Christian church. Many Christians do not understand the importance of what I called the level of theological concern. Consequently, they fail to get grounded on such crucial matters as theology, apologetics, and church history; seldom, if ever, do they bother to read serious books about such subjects. Since, I trust, some people who fit the description have read this far, this chapter is my chance to offer a way to improve their theological literacy.

But there's another problem that makes a chapter like this necessary. Theological illiteracy is one issue; theological apostasy is another. The chapter deals with a number of central Christian beliefs that are no longer discussed on some Christian campuses. The reason they are no longer discussed may be that some faculty on those campuses no longer believe them. The major challenge facing Christianity on the eve of its third millennium is the crisis of unbelief rapidly spreading within the church. Such unbelief, of course, is hardly new. Christianity has always had those within its gates who have sought to use Christian language, symbols, and institutions while engaged in the task of altering the essential nature of the faith. While pretending to be Christianity's prophets, priests, and gatekeepers, they have been busy subverting the nature of the faith, turning it into a totally different religion that is more acceptable to their tastes. In a day when honesty meant more than civility, such people were called heretics. They were also asked to peddle their new versions of the historic faith outside the city walls. However, a major change took place beginning about the middle of the nineteenth century.

Up to that point in the history of Christianity, Roman Catholics and Protestants continued to share a common world view that taught that this world was the creation of a personal, almighty God whose providence was manifested in history. They also agreed about the general historical reliability of the teachings and miracles that the Gospels attributed to Jesus. They agreed that Jesus' death was a sacrifice for human sin that was followed by His miraculous resurrection from the dead. This Catholic-Protestant consensus (otherwise known as orthodoxy) continued to be the dominant expression of Christian thought well into the nineteenth century.

But then a century and a half ago, a process began that was to remove Christian orthodoxy from its central place as the unifying force in Western life and culture. Doctrinal non-conformists and heretics, who formerly would have left the church or been expelled, began to teach their views *within* the church. To an increasing degree, unbelief began to set up residence within the church. The Catholic-Protestant consensus on such things as the Trinity, the deity of Christ, the Incarnation, the Resurrection, Jesus' death as a sacrifice for human sin, the human need for redemption—all this came under attack not only from the people outside of Christianity who had always rejected it but increasingly from individuals who now insisted on being denominational leaders or seminary professors. This anti-supernaturalist, anti-revelational, anti-Trinitarian, and frequently anti-theistic new religion dominated much of American and European Protestantism for the first half of the twentieth century.

Richard John Neuhaus describes the kind of unbelief that passes for theology in present-day Catholic and Protestant liberalism:

> The new class of the diffuse denomination that is Catholic-Protestant Liberalism is . . . supremely confident about the implausibility of what millions of Americans believe. "A Christian in the modern world can no longer believe such and such," they authoritatively declare. But of course there are all kinds of Christians in the modern world who believe precisely

such and such. The new class ploy in response to this embarrassing reality is that such Christians are simply stupid. Or, if such Christians are indisputably very smart, it is said that they are living in the nineteenth century.[1]

The new class of liberals that pretends to speak for contemporary Catholicism and Protestantism is not interested in reaffirming the historic Christian faith. As Neuhaus explains,

> Between reaffirming the faith and reconceptualizing the faith, reconceptualizing wins hands down. It is the very stuff of the academic and publishing industries. If there were no need for thorough reconceptualizations, fundamental reexaminations, moral transvaluations, hermeneutical revolutions, and historicocritical transformations, there would be no need for all the people who are very expensively trained to engage in just such things. Those who resist the efforts of such talented people are perceived to be anti-intellectual because most of the people who are paid to be intellectuals are on the other side.[2]

One shocking example of a Roman Catholic order that has lost its bearings is the Maryknoll Order. Neuhaus paints the picture:

> The Maryknollers were established many years ago to win the world to Christ and his Church. Many remember Maryknollers chiefly for their heroic mission work in China. Aficionados of irony will appreciate that years later, during the rule of Chairman Mao, the Maryknollers would be promoting the view that China was the most Christian nation in the world, albeit without Christ and his Church. Carrying Karl Rahner's notion of "anonymous Christians" to an extreme, it is the triumph of the missionary enterprise by fiat. Certainly it is much more convenient than the heroic but apparently misguided course of Maryknollers of old who gave their lives to winning unbelievers for the Gospel one by one.[3]

There is a seemingly endless stream of books about liberation theology issuing from the Maryknoller's Orbis Press.[4] This illustrates the extent to which radical representatives of the movement are willing to abandon the Christian faith's historic beliefs about the nature and mission of Jesus, the radical nature of sin, and the atonement for that sin on the Cross.

Also worth noticing is the large number of Catholic and Protestant thinkers who have begun reshaping Christian thought in the categories of what is called process thought. The result is process theology, which is often proclaimed as the most important development in Christian thought since the first century. It is significant, proponents claim, because the movement gives sophisticated moderns an intellectually and emotionally satisfying reinterpretation of Christianity that is compatible with late-twentieth century ways of thinking. Moreover, they add, process thought finally removes from Christianity the dominating influence of Greek and Hellenistic notions that have, in their view, distorted the essence of Christianity for almost two millennia.[5] A proper reply to this nonsense begins by pointing out that process theology does not eliminate pagan ideas from the Christian faith. Rather, *process theology is a total capitulation to paganism*. Take any essential Christian belief and one will find that process theologians supplant it with an alien belief.[6] Is God the sovereign, personal, omnipotent, and all-knowing creator of the universe? Is Jesus Christ the eternal and divine Son of God whose incarnation, death, and resurrection were necessary to effect the redemption of human beings? Is faith in Christ the only ground for human forgiveness? To these and other questions that touch the very heart of Christianity, the official answer of process theology is, "No." Process theology teaches that God is finite and ever-changing. Also, the god of process thought is a being to whom the future is totally hidden. This is a big change from the orthodox view of God as infinite, all-powerful, and all-knowing. This god for whom ultimate victory over evil is but wishful thinking is more akin to the god of Buddhism than to the God of Abraham, Moses, and the New Testament.

It is the battle over this kind of unbelief that is the real issue in the dispute between liberal Roman Catholics and the Pope. Neuhaus is correct when he states that Pope John Paul II "is exercised *not about dissent but about apostasy*. He is attempting to chart a Christian course that is not so much against modernity as it is beyond modernity. The only modernity to be discarded is the *debased modernity of unbelief* that results in a prideful and premature closure of the world against its promised destiny."[7] Once one realizes that what is at stake is nothing less than the integrity of the historic Christian faith, there is nothing ironic about a twentieth-century Lutheran applauding the efforts of a twentieth-century Pope to steer Catholicism away from apostasy.

> It conveys a feeling of relief that at last somebody, John Paul, is calling the church to order, is seizing a few unruly adolescents by the scruffs of their necks and knocking some sense into their heads. In short, there is a sense of being fed up, of having had enough, of refusing to take it anymore. No doubt many Catholics, along with church authorities, feel they have been subjected to extreme provocations. When, for example, at the end of the 1970's the Vatican finally withdrew from the European theologian Hans Kung the license to represent himself as a Roman Catholic theologian, the response of many Roman Catholics was to wonder why it took so long.[8]

To the extent that American evangelicals understand what is going on, they will join in the applause.

There is little value in discussing how Christianity will cope with the challenges of the twenty-first century if that "Christianity" is one of the essentially new religions that now masquerades under the old label. The dishonesty inherent in such a practice and the confusion it generates among the uninformed leave the orthodox Catholic and Protestant no alternative: they must take the steps necessary to counter the illegitimate takeover of Christian language and institutions for the propagation of new and anti-Christian forms of faith.

One required step in this task is obvious. If the Christian church is to move responsibly towards the future, it must restore or renew its ties with its past. Contemporary Catholic and Protestant radicals want to claim that Christianity means whatever "Christians" today happen to believe and practice, be it pantheism, unitarianism, or sodomy. The Christian faith has suffered immeasurable harm because of the tendency of people to use the word "Christian" in a careless and non-historical way. Nothing in this argument would preclude liberal Protestants and Catholics from developing and practicing any religion they like. But when a person promotes a religion in total conflict with the historic Christian faith, he ought to give it a new name that will indicate to the uninitiated that he is promoting a new product. What honorable purpose can be served by allowing the Christian name to be extended to beliefs that *contradict* the founding documents of the faith?

Of course, many have broken with Christianity's past precisely because they have come to believe that no one can know the truth about that past. The grounds thought to support this break with the past are specious, resting more in the presuppositions biblical critics have brought to their study than in any scientific methodology.[9]

Christianity's past defines its essence; it helps us distinguish between proper and improper uses of the word "Christian." Historian Herbert Butterfield explains that Christianity is a historical religion because "it presents us with religious doctrines which are at the same time historical events" or interpretations of such events.[10] Butterfield goes on to note: "Certain historical events are held to be part of the [Christian] religion itself—they are considered to have a spiritual content and to represent the divine breaking in upon history."[11] Christians believe that in Jesus Christ God actually entered into human history. Christianity is also a historical religion in the sense that the actual occurrence of certain events like the crucifixion and the resurrection are necessary conditions for its truth. If there are good reasons to believe that an event like the resurrection of Christ really happened in history, important Christian claims will be vindicated.[12] From its inception, Christianity has been a religion with a past. Without that past, Christians can have no grounded or reasonable hope for the future.

If contemporary Christians are to restore their faith's ties to its past, three steps must be taken. First, *the Christian church needs to recover an understanding of the essential role that truth plays in the Christian faith.* Christianity offers a faith to the world that it regards as *true.* As Christopher Derrick states,

> This might seem too obvious to need saying. But in our skeptical time, there is such a widespread dislike of dogmatism—of certainty and final conclusions in any ultimate matter at all—that the Church's central claim is constantly being evaded or watered down. Some

maintain that no question of truth or falsity arises in connection with doctrinal statements: these (they say) are merely verbalizations of religious experience, valid for those concerned, interesting for others, but equally misinterpreted by the man who asserts them as truth and the man who denies them as falsehood. Others, certain Catholics included, want the Faith to be a suggestion, a point of view, a process of enquiry, anything rather than a blunt assertion: they want it to be offered to mankind as being congenial, or comforting, or relevant to modern problems of the political and social kind, or "meaningful" in some sense which implies a strong appeal to twentieth-century imaginations. Such people are right in what they assert but wrong in what they deny, and they confuse the issue.[13]

Almost a century ago, about the time when the liberal Protestant assault on the central place of truth in the Christian faith was just getting under way, Scottish theologian James Orr pointed out: "If there is a religion in the world which exalts the office of teaching, it is safe to say that it is the religion of Jesus Christ." While doctrine is unimportant in most non-Christian religions, Orr continued, "this is precisely where Christianity distinguished itself from other religions—it does contain doctrine. It comes to men with definite, positive teaching; it claims to be the truth; it bases religion on knowledge, through a knowledge which is only attainable under moral conditions."[14]

The last two centuries of Christian theology are the record of an evolving attack on the role of knowledge and truth in the Christian faith.[15] We may call this emerging trend *theological agnosticism*. Typifying this new theological agnosticism is Gordon Kaufman of Harvard's Divinity School. "The real reference for 'God,'" Kaufman writes, "is never accessible to us or in any way open to our observation or experience. It must remain always an unknown X, a mere limiting idea with no content. It stands for the fact that God transcends our knowledge in modes and ways of which we can never be aware and of which we have no inkling."[16] Kaufman goes on to add: "God is ultimately profound Mystery and utterly escapes our every effort to grasp or comprehend him. Our concepts are at best metaphors and symbols of his being, not literally applicable."[17] Theological skeptics like

Kaufman always seem unaware of the contradiction inherent in their position. If absolutely no knowledge about God is possible, where do they obtain their knowledge that God is unknowable?

When theologians begin to think that knowledge about God is impossible and that religious truth is unimportant, it is only a matter of time until doctrines and creeds lose their relevance. Why worry about denials of Christian creeds if doctrine and truth are unimportant? Neuhaus shows how this gives additional impetus to the movement away from historic Christian beliefs:

> Liberation theologians such as Juan Luis Segundo or liberationist-cum-feminist theologians such as Rosemary Radford Ruether have no patience with the noble lie. They are eager to bring the masses in on the secret about traditional religion, namely, that it is not about what people have thought it was about. It is not about God and angels and heaven and hell 'out there' or in the distant future but about radical change here and now.[18]

"When theology becomes anthropology, when talk about God is just another way of talking about ourselves," Neuhaus continues,

> then the question of authority in the church takes center stage. The reason this happens is not hard to discover. As a consequence of the aforementioned "geological shift," Christian doctrine and ritual become mere "symbols" that, like Silly Putty, are marvelously plastic in response to what we human beings think about ourselves, how we are and how we ought to be. First we make our decisions—political, ideological, social, cultural, psychological—and then, *mirabile dictu*, we discover that Christianity is in wondrous agreement with what we decided, thus once again demonstrating the "relevance" of the faith. . . . the most touted of today's new ideas are, with few exceptions, time-tattered items in the list of the refuted and repudiated.[19]

Because of their refusal to be moved with regard to truth's central role in Christianity, orthodox Catholics and Protestants will repudiate liberal claims that: (a) correct belief is unimportant; (b) the beliefs that earlier generations of Christians deemed essential are no longer indispensable; and (c) the liberal Christian of today is free to believe anything he wishes.

As for the second step, *the Christian church needs to recover an understanding of the essential role that REVEALED truth plays in the Christian faith.* The church's access to truth is not a consequence of the greater wisdom of its apostles. It results from the fact that God Himself has graciously revealed Himself and truth about Himself to select individuals who have given the church an inscripturation of that revealed truth in the Holy Scriptures. Many who today teach in Christian seminaries and colleges do not believe and perhaps do not understand the time-honored notion of revealed truth. To a great extent, much non-orthodox theology over the past two hundred years is a chronicle of futile attempts to retain respectability for religious faith while denying Christianity any access to revealed truth. About the only thing such thinkers can agree on is that God has not spoken and, indeed, cannot speak. And even if God could speak, this view teaches, humans are incapable of understanding whatever God might attempt to say. The human relationship to God, therefore, must be understood according to some model other than that of receiving information or truth. Instead, it must be understood as an inward personal experience with God that is totally cut off from any objective, cognitive tests of that experience's validity.

Influenced by such views, many theologians and members of the clergy trivialize or repudiate the *central role* that revealed truth has played in the Christian religion. Knowledge about God is simply declared impossible and replaced by personal encounter, religious feeling, trust, or obedience.[20] This relatively new teaching clashes with the traditional view that divine special revelation is a communication of truth and that human knowledge of this revealed truth is an essential component of any personal relationship with God.

A study of the literature reveals that religious thinkers who reject the possibility of revealed truth seldom bother to support their position with arguments. They advocate a theory that has simply become part of the theological mind-set in many departments of religion. Moreover, the doctrine of revealed truth that is so widely rejected today is a straw man. And finally, the most serious problems with their noncognitive view of revelation are simply ignored.[21]

Nothing in this position is inconsistent with an equally important stress on the human need to respond in faith to God's revealed truth. A proper view of divine special revelation will see it as *both* propositional *and* personal. Personal knowledge of God is not in competition with propositional knowledge about God. After all, what kind of encounter could occur between two people who had absolutely no information about each other? God does not treat humankind in this impersonal way. Scripture declares that people require information about God that He has taken the initiative to supply. As the writer of the Epistle to the Hebrews put it, "Without faith it impossible to please God, because anyone who comes to him must believe that he exists and that he rewards those who earnestly seek him" (Heb. 11:6). The writer of the Fourth Gospel admitted that many things Jesus did were not recorded in his book. But those that *are* were written "that you may believe that Jesus is the Christ the Son of God, and that by believing you may have life in his name (John 20:30). Personal encounter cannot take place in a cognitive vacuum. Saving faith presupposes some genuine knowledge about God (Rom. 10:9–10; 1 Cor. 15:1–4).

The theological agnosticism that is such an important feature of contemporary nonorthodox theology marks a dramatic break with a major tradition of historic Christianity, a tradition that affirmed both an intelligible revelation from God along with a divinely given human ability to know the transcendent God through the medium of true propositions. Once this theological agnosticism is adopted, New Testament Christianity, with its proclamation of a divine Christ whose death and resurrection secured redemption from sin and gave hope beyond the grave, can be replaced by almost anything. The contemporary eclipse of God can be seen in Sartre's "silence of God," in Heidegger's "absence of God," in Jaspers' "concealment of God," in Bultmann's "hiddenness of God," in Tillich's "non-being of God," and finally in radical theology's assertion of "the death of God." In Tillich's version of theological agnosticism, all that is left of Christianity is a "religion" that is neither objective, rational, miraculous, supernatural, nor even personal. Why should anyone be surprised that this vacuum has been filled by systems that deny everything that the New Testament stands for?

A third step that must be taken if contemporary Christianity is to restore its ties to the past is this: *the Christian church needs to recover an understanding of the essential role that SUPERNATURAL truth plays in the Christian faith.* In this last sentence, the adjective *supernatural* refers to an essential component of the reality witnessed to by the Christian revelation.

Use of the term *supernatural* in our generation has some disadvantages, due largely to its frequent association with the fantastic novels and movies of such authors as Stephen King. It is important therefore that Christians make it clear that they use *supernaturalism* as the antonym of *naturalism*.

Since naturalism has already been discussed in an earlier chapter, there is no need to repeat that material here. What is relevant for the present discussion is this: It is their prior commitment to naturalism that grounds that historical skepticism of modern radical biblical critics.[22] It is their prior acceptance of naturalistic presuppositions that leads Catholic and Protestant radicals to reject the miraculous and supernatural elements of traditional Christianity. Their opposition to miracles is not a function of their superior education or intellect; it is a function of their naturalistic world view.

While it is not necessary to provide a detailed, critical evaluation of naturalism here, the interested reader can find those arguments presented elsewhere (see chapter 2).[23] The contemporary church needs to recognize the extent to which the rejection of essential Christian beliefs by radicals within the church is a reflection, not of their greater openness to truth or evidence, but of their religious commitment to an alien conceptual system (for example, an ideology such as that discussed in the chapter on Marxism) which influences how they see reality. The contemporary church needs to know that Christian supernaturalism is neither dead nor irrelevant.

We all know the story of Aladdin's lamp. While old and apparently less valuable than the shiny new lamps that the slick peddler offered in exchange, it was really invaluable and irreplaceable to those who understood its power and worth. Assorted theological hucksters are trying to persuade Christians to exchange the historic Christian faith for new style religions more in tune with modernity. Wise Christians will reject all such offers. As the Christian church faces the new challenges that it is bound to encounter in the twenty-first century, these Christians will know that the only faith capable of meeting those challenges, the only faith worthy of their continuing commitment, is historic Christian orthodoxy.

So long as we consider "education" as a good in itself of which everyone has a right to the utmost, without any ideal of the good life for society or for the individual, we shall move from one uneasy compromise to another.

—T. S. Eliot, *Christianity and Culture*

Reopening the American Heart and Mind

I began this book by talking about the closing of the American heart, which was my way of referring to the systematic elimination of moral and religious values from American public education through the second half of the twentieth century. As I've explained, there are many other things that are wrong with American education. Our educational system has turned out millions of people who are functionally illiterate. As we have seen, some of those functional illiterates are now being paid to teach. Our educational system has allowed millions of students to graduate who are culturally illiterate. A much larger number of these people are now teachers. All this, we are told, is due to glitches in the system. But those who control the system are not shy in admitting that it is their intended goal to turn out students who are *morally* illiterate. Under the guise of running a value-neutral system of education, they are acting as traitors to our culture and to their profession. To repeat a claim made earlier in the book, if teachers are doing their job properly, they "form the great link in the chain of civilization without which it cannot hold. They are both the conservators and the transmitters of culture. It is from them that future generations come to appreciate the ideals of their country and the wider civilization of which it is a part."[1] There is much that needs to be done to rectify the educational crisis in America, but without question one necessary action is recovering the belief that "the development of the intellect and moral character are intimately related."[2]

Throughout this book, I have refused to isolate the issue of moral and spiritual literacy from functional and cultural literacy. My approach has been holistic in the sense that a proper education takes proper account of both mind and heart, both intellectual virtue and moral virtue, as necessary. But in this, the last chapter of the book, I want to explore what we can do to reopen the American heart, that is, to restore moral and religious values to the central place they once had in American education.

William J. Bennett and "The Three C's of Education"

While he was still U.S. Secretary of Education during the Reagan presidency, William J. Bennett said more in one sentence about curing our educational crisis than many writers have said in entire books. Bennett suggested that the remedy for our educational problems can be found in what he called "the three C's of education." Those three C's, Bennett went on to explain, are Content, Character, and Choice.[3]

The word *content* suggests a number of things already covered in this book. For one thing, it states the obvious point that one reason why our public schools and colleges are turning out so many poorly educated students is because those students are not being given anything to learn. Students in college can slip through four years of courses with only a small number of liberal arts courses and with even a smaller number of courses that have any significant writing requirement. Traditional high school courses in history have been replaced in many schools with watered-down social science courses. Some of the weakest college programs—those with the least academic courses—happen to be the ones that are supposed to prepare prospective teachers to meet certification requirements. College majors like Black Studies and Women Studies are too often disgraceful refuges for the academically impaired. As Charles Colson observes, "Higher education is better funded and more accessible than ever before, [but] it has nothing left worth teaching. Our educational establishment seeks to instill a passion for intellectual curiosity and openness, but allows for the existence of no truth worth pursuing."[4] Educators in such a system can find only one justification for their existence: they are preparing people for a career. "As a result, our colleges and universities have become merely expensive job-training centers—steps on the ladder to material success."[5] In the meantime, educationally impoverished students in the lower grades are being "taught" by people whose training in professional education has indoctrinated them in the position that content (what children learn) is unimportant. One way of assuring the teaching of content in grades one through twelve is the establishment of competency tests both for promotion to a higher grade and for graduation.

Bennett's second "C" word is *character*. The formation of character and the attainment of moral literacy are essential corollaries of a good education. Bennett states: "If we want our children to possess the traits of character we most admire, we need to *teach* what those traits are. They must learn to identify the forms and content of those traits. They must achieve at least a minimal level of moral literacy that will enable them to make sense of what they will see in life and, we may hope, that will help them live it well."[6]

Of course, as soon as anyone these days begins to suggest that public schools should get back into the business of teaching character, the voices of protest can be heard all over the land. The implication in all these protests is that there is and can be no consensus on which values are to be presented in the classroom. Bennett's answer to this academic amoralism is both simple and sufficient. Responsible people, he replies, have no difficulty recognizing the basic traits of character that are relevant. "In defining good character," he writes, "we should include specific traits such as thoughtfulness, fidelity, kindness, diligence, honesty, fairness, self-discipline, respect for law, and taking one's guidance by accepted and tested standards of right and wrong rather than by, for example, one's personal preferences."[7] Does anyone seriously wish to suggest that we want a society where people are praised for acts of cowardice and dishonesty?

Bennett readily acknowledges that life often confronts us with difficult choices and ambiguous situations. But these tough issues can be handled later. We should not allow the relatively few ambiguous situations in life to deceive us into thinking that we cannot know, most of the time, what actions and virtues are required of us. While we should certainly exercise caution and prudence with regard to any complex moral issue, there is no justification for allowing our children to function in a moral vacuum. "There is no reason," Bennett insists, "for excessive timidity, and the kind of virtually paralyzing caution that responds to any reminder of the importance of schools' role in the formation of character."[8]

Just because we cannot agree on everything, it does not follow that we cannot agree on *anything*. We certainly ought to be able to agree, Bennett argues, on "the basic traits of character we want our children to have, and that we want our schools to develop."[9] Bennett continues:

> Not only is there a consensus among the American people on the elements that constitute good character, most Americans want their schools to help form the character of their children. According to a recent Gallup Poll, Americans in overwhelming numbers say they want schools to do two things: first, teach our children to read, speak, think, write, and count correctly; and second, help our children develop reliable standards of right and wrong to guide them through life.[10]

Later in this chapter, we'll notice some of Bennett's specific recommendations about how schools can help students attain higher degrees of moral literacy.

In addition to content and character, Bennett's third requirement for improving American education is *choice*. Given the present state of affairs, the best way—perhaps the only way—to improve our schools is to increase people's educational choices. Even if our public schools don't get worse (how could they?), the likelihood of turning such schools around is slim indeed. Here and there perhaps, possibly in rural areas or small towns where local control of the schools might pass into the hands of competent, dedicated people, something worthwhile might be achieved. But with thousands of radicals, misfits, and incompetents entrenched in public school systems across the land, our best hope is to initiate policies that will give families the right and the power to choose schools other than the one dictated by the system.

Increasing parental choice is important for at least two reasons. First, increased choice is a matter of simple justice. As Paul Vitz argues:

> [T]ens of millions of Americans are paying school taxes—each taxpayer is providing hundreds or even thousands of dollars a year—to support a system that

fails to represent their beliefs, values, history, and heritage. Indeed, the present public schools are actively supporting anti-religious positions and pushing liberal permissive values and politics. This is a serious injustice. Quite simply, it is a classic case of "taxation without representation." We are being taxed to support schools that are systematically liquidating our most cherished beliefs.[11]

The injustice of the public school monopoly is also apparent in the double tax burden families are forced to bear when they wish to send their children to private Hebrew, Roman Catholic, or Protestant schools. This situation deprives poorer families of an opportunity presently available only to wealthier families. Wealthier families have the means to pay for their children to attend private schools that not only provide a better education but that also support the religious and moral values of the family. Or in the case of public schools, wealthier families can afford to live in more exclusive neighborhoods that usually mean better schools than the ones that serve poorer neighborhoods.

The second argument for increasing parental choice is the undeniable effect that market discipline has on the quality of schools. One reason why America's public schools are such a disaster is because they do not have to worry about competition. Good or bad, public school #81—wherever it is—is assured of the same number of students and the same amount of funding. But if things suddenly were to change and competition from other schools resulted in the school's losing students and funding, market discipline would mean that unless the school became competitive by improving the quality of its programs, it would go out of business and its teachers would be out of a job. Consider how such a prospect might alter the behavior of teachers and administrators alike.

If we're serious about improving the quality of education in America, we must increase parental choice. If we care about justice in educational opportunity, we must increase parental choice. Nothing has the potential to turn our present educational mess around more quickly than increasing the educational choices available to American families. And, as I've made clear, this expanded choice must include private religious schools.

I've said all that I can in this book about Bennett's first and last topics, content and choice. For the rest of this chapter, I want to examine more carefully Bennett's second topic, the role that schools ought to play with regard to character. What can be done to bring about greater moral literacy among our youth?

I will explore two apparently different approaches to this problem. The first approach is articulated by Charles Colson who seems to recommend that we turn away from the schools and emphasize exclusively the essential role that the family and church have in this matter. In the second approach, William Bennett not only argues that the schools have a legitimate, indeed a necessary educational role regarding moral literacy, but also suggests how this duty can be met.

Charles Colson's Approach: The Family and the Church

Colson begins his discussion with an explanation of his understanding of one of the ways moral virtue is related to intellectual virtue. He writes: "Moral virtue without intellectual virtue may be inarticulate, unable to produce a systematic justification for its convictions. But moral virtue remains the prop that holds up the social order by controlling passions that would otherwise require a repressive apparatus of law enforcement."[12] Let no one be foolish enough to think that all a society needs are people who are functionally and culturally literate. Let us never forget what one such society—Adolf Hitler's Germany—did to the world.

Colson believes it is a mistake to think that moral virtue can arise solely from education. If this were all he meant to say, I doubt that many people would disagree. However, some of what Colson has written seems to go further and suggest that the school cannot play any role in enhancing the moral literacy of the young. Two statements from his book, *Against the Night*, seem to point in this direction. In the first, Colson states the following:

No social institution is more captive to culture's relativism than today's value neutral education. Even in a best-case scenario—even in the context of a belief in absolutes—education is no provider of moral virtue. It can inculcate a passion for truth, informed by history and tradition. It can communicate a faith that the universe is so constituted that it yields truth to those who seek it with tenacity. But colleges and universities, as Russell Kirk has noted, "cannot make vicious students virtuous or stupid students wise, but they can endeavor to prove to their students that intellectual power is not hostile to moral worth, and they can aspire to chasten intellectual presumption with humility.[13]

Colson's paragraph makes it clear that even schools that still recognize the existence of absolutes cannot provide students with moral value. As if to emphasize this point, Colson goes on to say that "we cannot pin our hopes for the future of moral education on the classroom. . . ."[14] "No," he says, "I believe there are only two institutions that can cultivate moral virtue: the family and the church . . . where traditions, history, and discipline provide a context for understanding the world. The enduring strength of our society lies in strengthening these two communities."[15]

I have no quarrel with Colson's claim that "the family is the primary and most important source of moral instruction."[16] Character and moral literacy begin in the home. The family is the arena in which moral literacy takes shape and matures. Colson is surely right when he states that the family is the most important factor in any child's education. Unfortunately, he is also correct when he observes that the American family is in a state of disarray and decline.

In former generations, books, imaginative play, and dialogue with members of the extended family were major influences in the moral development of children. Today, many children belong to one-parent families or to families where both parents work. The most significant influence on the lives of many American children is the ever-present television set. This device not only keeps children from reading and imaginative play and from special times with the family, it keeps them exposed to the worst features of a corrupt and mindless culture.

The family is indeed the most important factor in any child's education. But the family is failing in its educational and moral task and thus must bear the blame for much that is wrong with today's youth. When the family fails, Colson argues, "it fragments the transmission of manners and morals from one generation to the next, breaking the fragile chain of instruction that upholds society by instilling moral virtue. No matter how we try to compensate, it is nearly impossible for those left drifting at this stage to catch up later. (There is no makeup exam in moral instruction.) Unable to hand down our moral heritage, we raise generation after generation of increasingly rude, lawless, and culturally retarded children."[17]

It is clear then what needs to be done. "We must," he writes, "strengthen our commitment to model strong families ourselves, to live by godly priorities in a culture where self so often super-cedes commitment to others. And as we not only model but assertively reach out to help others, we must realize that even huge societal problems are solved one person at a time."[18]

The second element in Colson's remedy is the church. The darkness of our present age can best be illumined, he writes, "by character and hope transmitted through those structures God ordained long ago: the family, the first school of human instruc-tion and the best building block of society; and the church, the community called by God to love him and to express that love in service to others. If we are faithful, these will light the way back to eternal things."[19]

While Colson's point is correct, his words unfortunately only point to another problem. Just as many American families are failing to do their God-appointed task, so too are many churches. I am not just talking about the thousands of liberal Protestant churches in the land where one can hear practically anything taught—except the Gospel.[20] I also have in mind thousands of supposedly conservative, "Bible-believing" churches. Such churches tend to adopt such nice-sounding names as "Bethel Baptist Church" ("Bethel" means "House of God") or "Grace Presbyterian Church." Some of these churches ought to change their name to something like "Ichabod Methodist Church"[21] or "Laodicean Baptist Church."[22]

Many fundamentalist pastors are proud of their unrelenting allegiance to the Bible and their opposition to worldly living. But the poor people in many of their churches are starving for messages that will take them into the deeper things of God's word and that will relate God's truth to the urgent issues of the day. Many pentecostal and charismatic preachers are proud of the emotional excitement generated in their services but fail to do anything that touches the *minds* of their church members. It's as though such pastors have forgotten what Jesus called the first and greatest commandment: "Thou shalt love the Lord thy God with all thy heart, and soul, and *mind*" (Matt. 22:37).

Much of the problem with these otherwise dedicated church leaders lies in such factors as a culture-denying otherworldliness, an unbiblical superspirituality, and a weak educational background that leaves many of them tottering on the brink of cultural illiteracy. Regrettably, all too many of them are woefully weak in such areas as theology, church history, theological ethics, and apologetics. When preachers like this happen to pastor churches that sponsor Christian schools, they are often more a part of America's educational problem than its solution.

If Christian churches are going to operate private schools, we need pastors and leaders in those institutions whose own academic preparation surpasses the barely adequate. We need teachers in those schools who recognize that one of their responsibilities is broadening the horizons of their students and helping them achieve functional, cultural, and moral literacy. Christian leaders, teachers, and parents have a duty to improve their own education, along with their understanding of the Christian world view. They have an obligation to read serious books about the important issues of the time, instead of some of the psychological and biographical pap often sold in the typical Christian bookstore. It is a matter of the greatest urgency therefore that the people who operate these Christian schools realize that they exist to do more than simply add Bible teaching and Christian values to the rest of a normal curriculum. The curriculum in many Christian schools needs upgrading. Teaching materials that reduce the educational experience of students simply to rote memorization need to be changed.

When Charles Colson affirms the unsurpassable importance of the family and the church in the education of our youth, I agree. But when Colson argues, as he seems to, that there is no role for the school—public or private—in the task of increasing moral literacy, I have to disagree. If I've read Colson correctly, he seems to be urging the re-establishment of a kind of Christian ghetto mentality. (If he's not I hope he says so soon!) While the formation of character certainly begins in the home, wise Christian families will not ignore a possible ally in this important matter. As William Bennett sees it, this potentially powerful ally is the school.

Bennett's Approach: The Family, the Church, and the School

Bennett believes that education can play a role in forming character and helping students achieve moral literacy. It is nothing short of madness that we should have reached the point in our society that some people believe that public schools are somehow prohibited from including moral literacy among their objectives. As Russell Kirk states, "the great end of education is ethical. In the college, as at all other levels of the educational process, the student comes to apprehend the differences between good and evil. It is this humane tradition and discipline which makes us true human persons and sustains a decent civil social order."[23]

But how does Bennett propose that our schools fulfill this ethical objective? He answers: "It is now the case, as it has always been the case, that it is by exposing our children to good character and inviting its imitation that we will help them develop good character for themselves. This means our schools must have what the ancient Greeks would have called an 'ethos'—that is, our schools themselves must have good character."[24] Bennett believes there are two ways in which this can be done.

First, he says, "teachers and principals must be willing to articulate ideals and convictions to students."[25] Bennett is not talking about indoctrinating students or browbeating them. He is talking about ethical candor. "To put students in the presence of a morally mature adult who speaks honestly and candidly to them is not to violate their rights. On the contrary, it is essential to students' moral growth."[26] As the second condition, he writes: "We must have teachers and principals who not only state the difference between right and wrong, but who make an effort to *live that difference in front of students*. In this business of character, there has never been anything as important as the quiet power of moral example."[27]

Bennett then turns his attention to the important matter of curriculum. While the teacher can model good character, what the teacher teaches is also important. Bennett is hardly alone in recognizing this. In fact, it is an emphasis one can find in many critics of modern education. Christian philosopher Gary Weaver has noted how many of these writers' proposed method for restoring moral truth, vision and virtue to our educational system "involves restoring the humanities, especially literature and history, to the center of the educational endeavor."[28] After all, Weaver explains, the purpose

> of the humanities is to strengthen one's grasp of a transcendent moral order, and to counteract self-interest and provincialism. This is a purpose, however which . . . has been forsaken in the humanities today, largely because humanities scholars and teachers no longer believe in such a moral order. But if the humanists deny that a moral order is revealed in their disciplines, the humanities have nothing left to do but provide entertainment for the masses and employment for the professors, in which case they deserve to be marginalized or replaced by the vocational studies offered by [so many colleges of today].[29]

Without question, the humanities have lost their sense of direction. Ultimately, Weaver concludes, this will beget "a drifting, meaningless life, a life with no commitments and no sense of place or identity, and a citizenry ill-prepared for participation in democratic political institutions."[30]

What the views expressed in the last paragraph lead to is the recognition that the teaching of literature and history can and should have a *moral* function. As Russell Kirk puts it, "The aim of great books is ethical: to teach what it means to be a man. Every major form of literary art has taken for its deeper themes what T. S. Eliot called 'the permanent things'—the norms of human action."[31]

Bennett takes this viewpoint and applies it to elementary and secondary schools. When it comes to finding material that can be used to teach moral literacy, he says, "we don't have to reinvent the wheel. And we don't have to add new courses. We have a wealth of material to draw on—material that virtually all schools once taught to students for the sake of shaping character. And this is material that we can teach in our regular courses, in our English and history courses."[32] Bennett suggests that we invite students "to discern the moral of stories and the moral or morals of events and lives."[33]

If we want to teach the importance of honesty, we could, for example, tell about the time when Abraham Lincoln walked three miles to return a few pennies. Literature and history abound with impressive examples of the virtue of courage. Such literature as Dickens's *Christmas Carol* and *The Diary of Anne Frank* can be used to illustrate the importance of kindness, compassion, as well as the vices that serve as their complements. The importance of human rights can be introduced through the reading of the *Declaration of Independence*, or Lincoln's *Gettysburg Address*, or Martin Luther King, Jr.'s, "Letter from Birmingham Jail."

And certainly, Bennett insists, no quality education will ignore the Bible, from which Bennett draws just a few examples: "Ruth's loyalty to Naomi, Joseph's forgiveness of his brothers, Jonathan's friendship with David, the Good Samaritan's kindness toward a stranger, Cain's treatment of his brother Abel, David's cleverness and courage in facing Goliath."[34] Bennett makes it clear that the Bible has a legitimate place in the curriculum of every public school. Why? "Because," he says, it teaches "moral values we all share. And [its stories] shouldn't be thrown out just because they are in the Bible."[35]

Bennett offers three reasons why literature like this can and should be used in our schools' approach to moral character. The first reason is that children find such stories interesting; and this makes the stories effective attention-grabbers and teaching tools. "Second, we should be teaching these stories because, unlike courses in 'moral reasoning,' they give children some specific common reference points. Our literature and history are a rich quarry of moral literacy. We should mine that quarry. Children must have at their disposal a stock of examples illustrating what we believe to be right and wrong, and good and bad—examples illustrating that, in many instances, what is morally right and wrong can indeed be known. We offer them knowledge of these stories as reliable moral reference points."[36]

Bennett has a third reason that supports the important place these stories and works of literature deserve in our curriculum. "They give children a mooring," he states. This mooring is necessary, "because individual morality, of course, is inexplicably bound to the conscience and the memory of society. Our traditions are a source of knowing the ideals by which we wish to live our lives. We should teach these accounts of character to our children so that we may welcome them into a common world, and in that common world to the continuing and common task of preserving the principles, the ideals, and the notions of greatness we hold dear."[37]

Part One of this book's bibliography identifies well over one hundred pieces of literature by almost fifty authors that illustrate how easily great literature can be adapted to the cause of moral literacy. History also abounds with countless examples of events and lives that can be used in helping children attain a moral anchor in the conscience and memory of human society.

Bennett is too cautious a scholar to recommend that teachers rush in where angels fear to tread. Earlier in this chapter, I noted his distinction between the many simple and obvious moral points one can make and the much smaller number of ambiguous and difficult issues in life. Because of this, Bennett says, "We should 'teach values' the same way we teach other things: one step at a time. We should not use the fact that there are indeed many difficult and controversial moral questions as an argument against the basic instruction in the enterprise. . . . Every field has its complexities and controversies and every field has its basics."[38]

Only fools, therefore, would fail to notice that the matter of helping students to attain moral literacy also has its complexities and its basics. "You have to walk before you can run, and you ought to be able to run straight before you are asked to run an obstacle course or a mine field. So the moral basics should be taught in school, first. The tough issues can, if teachers and parents wish, be taken up later."[39] What America's schools have stopped doing in recent years is teaching our children how to walk. It's time that we recognized that this view of education is not only inconsistent with moral common sense; it is also a repudiation of our heritage and good education.

Conclusion

It is time to bring this book to an end. I cannot think of a more fitting way to do this than to draw attention to some recent remarks by Charles Colson. I may have found it necessary to disagree with Colson's approach to moral literacy earlier in this chapter. But he is completely on target in this matter.

Colson is unsure if it's wise to speak simply of America's education crisis. Such talk risks creating a serious misunderstanding. Oh, the education crisis exists, all right. Indeed, it is far more serious than most of us realize. But what we call the education crisis is only the tip of the iceberg. According to Colson, "the crisis that threatens us, the force that could topple our monuments and destroy our very foundations, is within ourselves. The crisis is in the character of our culture, where the values that restrain inner vices and develop inner virtues are eroding. Unprincipled men and women, disdainful of their moral heritage and skeptical of Truth itself, are destroying our civilization by weakening the very pillars upon which it rests."[40]

Colson believes that sometime during the twentieth century, the West, including America, has passed through the door into a new Dark Ages. His book reinforces this conviction with chapter titles like "Barbarians in the Parlor" (the home), "Barbarians in the Classroom" (the school), "Barbarians in Power" (government), and "Barbarians in the Pews" (the church).

To ignore the education crisis, then, is to commit a mistake that could well prove fatal to Western and Christian civilization.

One final word: we dare not forget the most important person in all of this—the young man or woman who has the potential to become a Christian leader of tomorrow. These young people are the church's most precious treasure. Whether it is through teaching or modeling, whether it is in the church, the home or the school, let us do everything possible to love them, to motivate them, to challenge them, and *to educate them.*

Appendix 1:
Curriculum Proposal

One important concern held by many in middle-class evangelical schools is in the area of curriculum. Concerns vary from the need for high quality education to the need for practicality. This appendix contains a suggested curriculum that Christian schools can use from middle school through twelfth grade. This particular curriculum is used in one of the finer Christian schools in this country, an independent school in Addison, Texas, just north of Dallas, called Trinity Christian Academy.

This curriculum is not elitist or utopian in nature; it is a curriculum that is in practice daily at Trinity and is designed to be used in any school. It is a well-designed program that requires both Christian materials and classical material from the great books of the Western world. I recognize that many Christian schools operate on a very tight budget; but we must not sacrifice the quality of our children's reading matter. Moreover, they must be afforded the opportunity to read the original thoughts and writings of the greatest thinkers in history, rather than what someone else wrote about them. As C. S. Lewis said, "read Plato, not books about Plato." I think you will find this curriculum helpful and affordable for nearly any Christian school's budget.

Appendix 1: Curriculum for Middle School

	Fifth	Sixth	Seventh	Eighth
Knowledge	Old World history and geography Ancient myths and legend Christian heroism; Events, people, and places of the Bible; Grammar/spelling Art and music history	New World history and geography New World myths and legend Christianity in the New World (missions and pioneers) Grammar/spelling Art and music history	American Studies (colonies to pre-Civil War) Key people, events, ideas, and writings of the U.S. State history Grammar/spelling Art and music history	American Studies (Civil War to present) Key people, events, ideas, and writings of the U.S. Grammar/spelling Art and music history
Skills	Writing (paragraphs, poetry, term paper) Reading (character, plot, moral) Map reading Outlining as thinking Speaking (informational) Listening (for main ideas and characters)	Writing (paragraphs, stories, essays) Reading (major/minor ideas, events) Map reading Outlining as thinking Speaking (informational) Listening (for key themes and ideas)	Writing (paragraph essay) Reading (history vs. fiction) Map reading Outlining as thinking Speaking (oral interpretation) Listening (for fact and interpretation)	Writing (one- and five-paragraph essays) Reading (ambiguities, values) Map reading Outlining as thinking Speaking (argumentative) Listening (for both sides of an issue)
Wisdom	Appreciation of wisdom and beauty of works of the Old World Understanding roots Distinguishing pagan from Christian views	Appreciation of the influence of the Old World on the New Appreciation of the people and values that shaped the U.S.	Appreciation of the principles that founded the U.S. Basis and cost of freedom Appreciation of the richness of your state's history	Meaning of the Civil War and human equality Personal and universal impact of war Individual and group progress and wealth
Readings	*Language for Daily Use; A Dog Named Kitty; Old World Geography & History; The Bronze Bow; Aesop's Fables; Be a Better Reader; The Wind in the Willows; The Boy's King Arthur; Tales from Shakespeare; The Lion, the Witch, and the Wardrobe*	*Be a Better Reader; Sign of the Beaver; The Incredible Journey; Adventures of Tom Sawyer; Across Five Aprils; Where the Red Fern Grows;* Selected short stories of J. F. Dobie	*Our Land Our Time* (text); *Light in the Forest; The Witch of Blackbird Pond; The Crucible; Sarah Bishop; My Brother Sam is Dead; Thirteen Days to Glory;* Selected writings of Paine, Thoreau, Poe, Longfellow, Twain, Whittier, J. F. Dobie, etc.	*Our Land Our Time; The Red Badge of Courage; Huckleberry Finn; The Jungle; My Antonia; Cheaper by the Dozen; The Hiding Place; To Kill a Mockingbird; Profiles in Courage; In the Presence of Mine Enemies*

Appendix 1: Curriculum for Upper School

Ninth	Tenth	Eleventh	Twelfth	
Western history, culture, and geography of Greece's Golden Age and Judah's exile Art and music history Great writings of the ancient world	Western history, culture, and geography of Hellenistic Greece, post-exilic Judah, Rome, the early Church, and Middle Ages Art and music history Great writings	History, culture, and geography of the Renaissance, Reformation, and Enlightenment Art and music history Great writings	History, culture, and geography of the nineteenth and twentieth centuries Art and music history Great writings	**Knowledge**
Writing (historical research paper and the five-paragraph essay) Reading (following arguments and drawing inferences) Speaking (formal seminars and persuasive speech) Listening (seminars)	Writing (critical essay which analyzes and explains a work of literature) Reading (ways to read the various genres of literature) Speaking (style and persuasion) Listening (debate and seminars)	Writing (creative; eight- to ten-page historical research paper) Reading (levels of interpretation and theological reading) Speaking (debate and seminars) Listening (debate and seminars)	Writing (fifteen- to twenty-page critical essay analyzing a work) Reading (reading a text for relative significance of information) Speaking (students lead class) Listening (college lectures)	**Skills**
How world view shapes cultures and individuals Appreciation of biblical world view Shaping a personal world view	Gentile vs. Jewish world view Our Judeo-Christian and Greco-Roman heritage How the people of God can influence whole cultures	Influence of certain virtues and vices on human character Priority of faith and the place of works Possibilities and limits of human greatness	Link between national consciousness and a people's faith Justice and righteousness toward poor and oppressed Creative responses to human problems	**Wisdom**
Mainstreams: Ancient Civilizations; Gilgamesh Epic; Exodus; Theogony; Job; Prometheus Bound; J. B.; Oedipus Rex; The Odyssey; The Oresteia; The Clouds; Plato's Apology; Samuel and Kings (excerpts); Jonah; Esther	*Mainstreams: Ancient Civilizations and Medieval and Modern Times; Crito; Trojan Women; Ezra; Nehemiah; Maccabees (excerpts); Julius Caesar; I, Claudius; Selections from Roman poets and historians; Macbeth; Confessions; Koran (excerpts); Beowulf; Morte D'Arthur (excerpts); Sir Gawain; The Inferno*	*Mainstreams: Medieval and Early Modern Times; Hamlet; Elements of Style; The Prince; Dr. Faustus; Henry IV; Pilgrim's Progress; The Age of Reformation; Robinson Crusoe; Candide; Rasselas; Selected poetry, essays, and sermons*	*Mainstreams: Modern Times; War and Peace; Hard Times; Communist Manifesto; A Passage to India; Things Fall Apart; Farewell to Arms; Sound and Sense; MLA Handbook; Night; One Day in the Life of Ivan Denisovich; The Plague; Cry the Beloved Country; Selected essays and excerpts*	**Readings**

Appendix 1: Sample Curriculum for One Year

Seventh	Eighth	Ninth	Tenth	Eleventh	Twelfth
American Humane Letters I*	American Humane Letters II	Humane Letters: Ancient to Classical Greece	Humane Letters: Hellenism to Middle Ages	Humane Letters: Renaissance, Reformation, and Enlightenment	Humane Letters: 19th/20th Century American Citizenship
Bible: Old Testament Survey	Bible: New Testament Survey	Bible: John and Genesis	Bible: Luke, Acts, and Church History	Bible: Select History, Poetry, and Prophets	Bible: Romans and Apologetics
Life Science	Earth Science	Physical Science	Biology	Chemistry	Physics or Independent Studies
Mathematics	Pre-Algebra and Algebra I	Algebra I and Geometry	Geometry and Algebra II	Algebra II and Trigonometry	Trigonometry and Calculus Elective
Physical Education and Athletics	Physical Education and Athletics	Physical Education and Health	Physical Education	Typing	Accounting Elective
Fine Arts	Fine Arts	Fine Arts Elective†	Fine Arts Elective	Fine Arts Elective	Fine Arts Elective
Foreign Language	Foreign Language	Foreign Language	Foreign Language	Foreign Language	Foreign Language Independent Study

*Humane Letters combines English and History and meets twice daily.
†High School students must take one year of elective Fine Arts.

Notes

Preface

[1] If any reader needs help understanding this branch of American Christendom, she can consult the following book: Ronald Nash, *Evangelicals in America* (Nashville, Tenn.: Abingdon, 1987).

[2] According to Chester E. Finn, Jr., "[T]he average per-pupil expenditure in American public education this year (1988-89) is about $4,800, some $1500 higher than when *A Nation At Risk* was released (in 1983). Today we are spending roughly twice as much per student in real terms as in the mid-60's, and nearly three times the level of the mid-50's." Chester E. Finn, Jr., "A Nation Still At Risk," *Commentary*, May 1989, p. 17. This expenditure per pupil in public schools is approximately twice what it costs to educate a student in a Catholic school and as much as three times the tuition cost for students in evangelical Protestant schools. Most of this huge increase in public spending has gone into higher teacher's salaries and fringe benefits with the balance going mostly to fund increased school bureaucracies. As Samuel Blumenfeld states, "If money were the answer, our problems would have been solved long ago, for no nation in history has pumped more of its wealth into education than this one, and no people has been more generous to and trusting of its educators." Samuel Blumenfeld, *NEA: Trojan Horse in American Education* (Boise, Idaho: Paradigm, 1984), p. 242.

Chapter 1 *The Closing of the American Heart*

[1] Samuel Blumenfeld, *NEA: Trojan Horse in American Education* (Boise, Idaho: The Paradigm Co., 1984), p. xiv.

[2] Charles J. Sykes, *Profscam: Professors and the Demise of Higher Education* (Washington, D.C.: Regnery-Gateway, 1988), p. 4.

[3] Ralph Kinney Bennett, Review of *The Closing of the American Mind*, *Reader's Digest*, October 1987, p. 81.

[4] Joseph Baldacchino, *Educating for Virtue* (Washington, D.C.: National Humanities Institute, 1988), p. 9.

[5] Ibid.

[6] Allan Bloom, *The Closing of the American Mind* (New York: Simon and Schuster, 1987), p. 346.

[7] David Gress, "Diagnosis of a *Kulturkampf*," *The New Criterion*, May 1987, p. 24.

[8] Russell Kirk, *Decadence and Renewal in the Higher Learning* (South Bend, Ind.: Gateway, 1978), p. xii.

[9] Ibid.

[10] Ibid., p. xiii.

[11] Ibid., p. 312.
[12] Bloom, op. cit., p. 25.
[13] Ibid, pp. 25–26.
[14] Ibid, p. 26.
[15] Ibid.
[16] Ibid, p. 34.
[17] Ibid.
[18] Ibid, p. 41.
[19] Ibid.
[20] Donald J. Devine, "The Opening of the Socratic Mind," *Modern Age* 32 (1988-89), p. 14. This entire issue of *Modern Age* consists of criticisms of Bloom.
[21] Charles R. Kesler, "The Closing of Allan Bloom's Mind," *The American Spectator*, August 1987, p. 14.
[22] Baldacchino, op. cit., p. 6.
[23] Ibid., p. 7.
[24] Ibid.
[25] Ibid.
[26] Bloom, p. 344.
[27] Kesler, "The Closing of Allan Bloom's Mind," op. cit., p. 14.
[28] Gordon H. Clark, *A Christian Philosophy of Education*, revised edition (Jefferson, Md.: The Trinity Foundation, 1988), p. 21.
[29] Ibid.
[30] John W. Robbins, Foreword to Clark's *Christian Philosophy of Education*, p. x.
[31] Ibid., p. xxi.
[32] For a discussion of the individual who may have been responsible for recent attention to this matter, see Ronald Nash, *Dooyeweerd and the Amsterdam Philosophy* (Grand Rapids, Mich.: Zondervan, 1962). I apply this notion to philosophical thinking about God in the early chapters of my book, *Faith and Reason* (Grand Rapids, Mich: Zondervan, 1988).
[33] Paul Johnson's chapter on Ernest Hemingway in his book, *Intellectuals* (New York: Harper and Row, 1988) is an excellent example of this point.
[34] I am certainly not claiming this is always the case, simply that it happens far more often than people realize.
[35] Baldacchino, op. cit., p. 10.

Chapter 2 *Reason and Virtue*

[1] Joseph Baldacchino, *Educating for Virtue* (Washington, D.C.: National Humanities Institute, 1988), p. 11.
[2] Joseph Baldacchino, Foreword to *Literature and the American College* by Irving Babbitt (Washington, D.C.: National Humanities Institute, 1986), p. x.
[3] Ibid.

[4] Russell Kirk, the Introduction to Babbitt's *Literature and the American College*, p. 7.

[5] Russell Kirk, *Decadence and Renewal in the Higher Learning* (South Bend, Ind.: Gateway, 1978), p. 125.

[6] Baldacchino, *Educating for Virtue*, pp. 10–11.

[7] For a classic statement of this claim, see Augustine's *City of God*, Book 19. For a discussion of Augustine's view, see Ronald Nash, *Faith and Reason*, op. cit., chapter 20. A modern classic advocating this position is C. S. Lewis' *The Abolition of Man* (New York: Macmillan, 1947). Lewis reminds us that, for Aristotle, "the aim of education is to make the pupil like and dislike what he ought" (p. 26). The relevant text is Aristotle's *Nichomachean Ethics* 1104 B.

[8] (Berkeley, Calif.: University of California Press, 1985).

[9] Wilfred McClay, Review of *Habits of the Heart*, in *The Intercollegiate Review*, vol. 21 (1986), p. 50.

[10] Ibid.

[11] Ibid.

[12] Ibid.

[13] Ibid.

[14] Rockne McCarthy, Ronald Oppewal, Walfred Peterson, and Gordon Spykman (Coordinator), *Society, State and Schools* (Grand Rapids, Mich.: Eerdmans, 1981), p. 148.

[15] Henry Zylstra, *Testament of Vision* (Grand Rapids, Mich.: Eerdmans, 1958), p. 145.

[16] Ibid, p. 147.

[17] For an important study that documents the extent to which public school textbooks have eliminated religion from American history, see Paul C. Vitz, *Educational Choice*, Vol. 2 (May 1986).

[18] Francis A. Schaeffer, *A Christian Manifesto, The Complete Works of Francis A. Schaeffer*, second edition (Westchester, Ill.: Crossway, 1985) 5:423.

[19] Ibid.

[20] Michael L. Peterson, *Philosophy of Education* (Downers Grove, Ill.: InterVarsity Press, 1986), p. 87.

[21] Ibid., p. 82. For more on this important point, see Ronald Nash, *The Word of God and the Mind of Man* (Grand Rapids, Mich.: Zondervan, 1982).

[22] Ibid., p. 83.

[23] Ibid., pp. 83–84.

[24] Several paragraphs in this chapter appeared first in my article, "Christian Liberal Arts Education," *Christian Educators Journal*, January 1971.

Chapter 3 *Three Kinds of Illiteracy*

[1] Samuel L. Blumenfeld, *NEA: Trojan Horse in American Education* (Boise, Idaho: The Paradigm Co., 1984), p. xii.

2 See *Time*, 14 August 1989.

3 Chester E. Finn, Jr., "A Nation Still At Risk," *Commentary* 87 (May 1989) p. 18.

4 Ibid.

5 Karl Shapiro, Presentation to the California Library Association; quoted by Blumenfeld, op. cit., p. 95.

6 Blumenfeld, p. 127.

7 Ibid.

8 See Reginald G. Damerell, *Education's Smoking Gun: How Teacher's Colleges Have Destroyed Education in America* (New York: Freundlich, 1985).

9 E. D. Hirsch, Jr., *Cultural Literacy: What Every American Needs to Know* (Boston: Houghton Mifflin, 1987), p. xiii.

10 William J. Bennett, "Moral Literacy and the Formation of Character," *Faculty Dialogue*, Number Eight (Spring/Summer 1987), p. 24.

11 See the appendix to Hirsch's book, cited in note 9.

12 Diane Ravitch and Chester E. Finn, Jr., *What Do Our 17-Year-Olds Know?* (New York: Harper and Row, 1987), p. 1.

13 Hirsch, op. cit., pp. xiv–xv.

14 Ibid., p. xv.

15 Ibid.

16 Ravitch and Finn, op. cit., p. 17.

17 Ibid., p. 17.

18 Paul C. Vitz, *Censorship: Evidence of Bias in our Children's Textbooks* (Ann Arbor, Mich.: Servant Books, 1986), p. 89.

19 Ibid., pp. 89–90.

20 Russell Kirk, *Decadence and Renewal in the Higher Learning* (South Bend, Ind.: Gateway, 1978), p. 192.

21 Will Herberg, "Modern Man in a Metaphysical Wasteland," *The Intercollegiate Review*, 5 (Winter 1968–69), p. 79.

22 John Silber, *Shooting Straight* (New York, Harper and Row: 1989), p. xiv.

23 Christina Hoff Sommers, "Ethics Without Virtue: Moral Education in America," *American Scholar* (Summer 1984), p. 381.

24 Ibid., p. 382.

25 Ibid., p. 383.

26 Ibid.

27 Kenneth Gangel, *Schooling Choices*, H. Wayne House, ed. (Portland, Oreg.: Multnomah, 1988), pp. 126–27.

28 Ibid., p. 127.

29 Ibid.

Chapter 4 *Three Enemies of "The Permanent Things"*

1 Will Herberg, "Modern Man in a Metaphysical Wasteland," *The Intercollegiate Review*, vol. 5 (1968–69), p. 79.

2 Ibid.

[3] Allan Bloom, *The Closing of the American Mind*, p. 25.

[4] The reader may wish to refer back to Herberg's explanation of what he means by "a creeping conviction" (See p. 61).

[5] Will Herberg, "Modern Man in a Metaphysical Wasteland," op. cit., p. 79.

[6] Mortimer J. Adler, *Six Great Ideas* (New York: Collier Books, 1981), p. 41.

[7] Ibid.

[8] Ed L. Miller, *God and Reason* (New York: Macmillan, 1972), p. 87.

[9] Ibid., p. 90.

[10] W. T. Stace, "The Concept of Morals," In *Problems of Ethics*, ed. R. E. Dewey, F. W. Gramlich, D. Loftsgordon (New York: Macmillan, 1961), p. 42.

[11] Herberg, op. cit., p. 79.

[12] Ibid.

[13] Some of the arguments responsible for the demise of Logical Positivism are reviewed in Ronald Nash, *The Concept of God* (Grand Rapids, Mich.: Zondervan, 1983), chapter 9.

[14] J. P. Moreland, *Scaling the Secular City* (Grand Rapids, Mich.: Baker, 1987), p. 197.

[15] Del Ratzsch, *Philosophy of Science* (Downers Grove, Ill.: InterVarsity Press, 1986), pp. 98–99.

[16] Herberg, op. cit., p. 79.

[17] Ibid., p. 80.

[18] For example, see my *Faith and Reason*, op. cit., chapter 19.

[19] The quotations are taken from the *Humanist Manifesto* of 1933 as printed in *Humanist Manifestoes I and II* (Buffalo, N.Y.: Prometheus Books, 1973) pp. 7–11.

[20] For helpful summaries of humanism, see McCarthy, et al, *Society, State and Schools* (Grand Rapids, Mich.: Eerdmans, 1981), pp. 116–20; and John Whitehead and John Conlan, "The Establishment of the Religion of Secular Humanism and its First Amendment Implications," *Texas Tech Law Review*, 10 (1978).

[21] Richard John Neuhaus, "No More Bootleg Religion," in *Controversies in Education*, Dwight Allen, ed. (Philadelphia: W. B. Saunders, 1974), p. 77.

[22] Rockne McCarthy, et. al., *Society, State and Schools* (Grand Rapids, Mich.: Eerdmans, 1981), pp. 125ff.

[23] See Paul C. Vitz, *Censorship and Our Schools* (Ann Arbor, Mich.: Servant Books, 1986).

[24] McCarthy, op. cit., p. 133.

[25] Quoted by Kenneth Gangel in the book, *Schooling Choices*, op. cit., (Portland, Oreg.: Multnomah, 1988), p. 131.

[26] Friedrich Nietzsche, *The Genealogy of Morals*, III, 26 (New York: Doubleday Anchor Edition, 1956), p. 288.

[27] The full text from which I quote can be found on pages 95–96 of *The Portable Nietzsche*, ed. Walter Kaufmann (New York: Viking Press, 1954).

[28] Nietzsche, *Thus Spoke Zarathustra: First Part*, in *The Portable Nietzsche*, p. 171.

[29] Nietzsche, *The Antichrist* in *The Portable Nietzsche*, p. 570.

[30] *Thus Spoke Zarathustra*, p. 124.

[31] *Thus Spoke Zarathustra*, pp. 126–127.

[32] Herberg, op. cit., p. 81.

Chapter 5 *The Educational Establishment*

[1] Samuel Blumenfeld, *NEA: Trojan Horse in American Education*, p. 211.

[2] John Silber, *Shooting Straight*, (New York: Harper and Row, 1989), pp. 20–21.

[3] Richard M. Weaver, *Visions of Order* (Baton Rouge, La.: LSU Press, 1964), p. 114.

[4] Ibid., p. 115.

[5] Samuel L. Blumenfeld, *Is Public Education Necessary?* (Old Greenwich, Conn.: Devin-Adair, 1981), p. 5.

[6] Gordon H. Clark, *A Christian Philosophy of Education*, revised edition (Jefferson, Md.: The Trinity Foundation, 1988), p. 1.

[7] Reginald G. Damerell, *Education's Smoking Gun: How Teachers' Colleges Have Destroyed Education in America* (New York: Freundlich, 1985).

[8] Chester E. Finn, Jr., "The Campus: 'An Island of Repression in a Sea of Freedom,'" *Commentary*, Sept. 1989, p. 23.

[9] Damerell, op. cit., p. 13.

[10] Thomas Sowell, *Black Education: Myths and Tragedies* (New York: David McKay, 1972), p. 221.

[11] James B. Koerner, *The Miseducation of American Teachers* (Boston: Houghton-Mifflin, 1963), p. 17.

[12] J. Gresham Machen, *Education, Christianity and the State*, ed. John W. Robbins (Jefferson, Md.: The Trinity Foundation, 1987), p. 14.

[13] Damerell, op. cit., p. 34.

[14] John Silber, *Shooting Straight*, (New York: Harper and Row, 1989), p. 19.

[15] Ibid., p. 20.

[16] Reginald Damerell cites a number of authorities who call for the elimination of all colleges of education. See his *Education's Smoking Gun*, p. 287.

[17] See Damerell, p. 270.

[18] Damerell, p. 280.

[19] To be more precise, 1.6 million members of the NEA are public school teachers. The rest are support people, retirees, students, and college professors. The second largest teachers' union, the American Federation of Teachers (AFT) has a membership of 715,000. It has tended to be more supportive of reforms that would improve teaching. But it too is opposed to public funding for private schools.

[20] Connaught Coyne Marshner, *Blackboard Tyranny* (New Rochelle: Arlington House, 1978), p. 53.

21 Bill Boynton and John Lloyd, *Who's Running Our Schools* (Washington D.C.: Save Our Schools Research and Education Foundation, 1986), p. 40.

22 Chester Finn, "Guess Who Spells Disaster for Education?" *Reader's Digest* (May 1984), p. 92.

23 Johnson's quote appears in advertising for Samuel Blumenfeld's book, *NEA: Trojan Horse in American Education*, already cited.

24 Blumenfeld, op. cit., p. x.

25 Robert W. Kagan, "A Relic of the New Age: The National Education Association," *The American Spectator* (Feb. 1982).

26 Quoted by Chester Finn, "Guess Who Spells Disaster for Education?" op. cit., p. 91.

27 For example, in 1984, the NEA spent $2.4 million to elect its candidates. See *Who's Running Our Schools*, op. cit., p. 86.

28 Blumenfeld., p. xii.

29 Ibid.

30 Ibid., p. 218. Blumenfeld refers directly to the NEA publication, *Today's Education*, 1983–84 Annual edition.

31 Ibid., p. 219.

32 Ibid., p. 220. A further example of this attitude is given in *Who's Running Our Schools?* op. cit., p. 51, in a description of a new funding law put into place in Alabama. Although called a merit pay system, it was put together by a committee controlled by the NEA's state organization (nineteen of thirty-five members were from the NEA). The new state-wide Educator Performance Review Committee which will determine standards for pay raises is also dominated by NEA members (Five of the ten members were appointed by the union, the other five by the state superintendent of education with the approval of the union). The merit pay structure set its standards so low that virtually every teacher got a raise.

33 Ibid., p. 211.

34 *NEA Today*, Vol. 6, No. 10 (May/June 1988), p. 26.

35 Blumenfeld, op. cit., pp. 216–17.

36 *NEA Resolutions*, 1988–89.

37 The pragmatist label results from the perception that Dewey was following in the train of earlier pragmatists like C. D. Pierce and William James. This greatly oversimplified view ignores important differences between Dewey and the pragmatists. It's best not to refer to his system as a version of pragmatism.

38 *Instrumentalism* is the preferable term to use when referring to Dewey's position. The reasons for this will become apparent in the exposition of Dewey's thought.

39 *Experimentalism* is an acceptable term because of Dewey's total confidence in the scientific method and the central role the experimental method had in his analysis of human belief and conduct.

[40] Quoted by Susan D. Rose in her book, *Keeping Them Out of the Hands of Satan: Evangelical Schooling in America* (New York: Routledge, 1988), p. 39. No source is provided for the quote. The reader should note that Rose's book is not written as a defense of Christianity, but as a critique of evangelical schools. The title could be misleading.

[41] Richard M. Weaver, *Visions of Order* (Baton Rouge, La.: Louisiana State University Press, 1964). The quotations that follow come from pages 115 and 116 of Weaver's book.

[42] Ibid., p. 117.

[43] Ibid. When Weaver wrote this material, higher education was still largely safe from the influences of the educational philosophy he describes. As much of this book makes clear, the same attitudes and values are now dominant in most colleges and universities as well.

Chapter 6 *Four Essential Steps*

[1] Ernest L. Boyer, "The Third Wave of School Reform," *Christianity Today* (22 September 1989), p. 18.

[2] Ibid.

[3] J. Gresham Machen, *Education, Christianity, and the State*, ed. John W. Robbins (Jefferson, Md.: The Trinity Foundation, 1987), p. 8.

[4] It was partly to provide help for situations like this that I wrote my book, *Faith and Reason*, op. cit.

[5] Allan Bloom, *The Closing of the American Mind*, op. cit., p. 57.

[6] Ibid., p. 58.

[7] Ibid., p. 64.

[8] Ibid.

[9] Herbert J. Walberg, Michael J. Bakalis, Joseph L. Bast, and Steven Baer, *We Can Rescue Our Children: The Cure for Chicago's Public School Crisis* (Chicago: The Heartland Institute, 1988).

[10] Ibid., p. 95. The authors of the Heartland book cite a number of works that support the claims in this paragraph. See R. G. Bridge, C. M. Judd, and P. R. Moock, *The Determinants of Educational Outcomes* (Cambridge, Mass.: Ballinger, 1979); G. V. Glass, L. Cahen, H. A. Averch, S. J. Caroll, T. S. Donaldson, J. J. Kriesling, and J. Pincus, *How Effective is Schooling? A Critical Review and Synthesis of Research Findings* (Santa Monica, Calif.: The Rand Corporation, 1972).

[11] Ibid., p. 111.

[12] See Rockne McCarthy, et. al., *Society, State and Schools* (Grand Rapids, Mich.: Eerdmans, 1981); also, James Skillen, *Christians Organizing for Political Service* (Washington, D.C.: Association for Public Justice, 1980). Parents can write to Focus on the Family, Pomona, Calif., 91799 for information on the Washington D.C.-based Family Research Council, or for subscription information on Focus on the Family *Citizen*.

[13] Home schools are enjoying a groundswell of popularity among Christian parents. I am not familiar enough with this movement to

give adequate service to an in-depth discussion of it myself. However, let me recommend the book, *Schooling Choices*, H. Wayne House, editor (Portland: Multnomah Press, 1988) for a look at the home school option. Parents may make an informed decision on the basis of the discussion in that book.

14 John E. Chubb and Terry M. Moe, "Give Choice a Chance," a paper delivered at Florida State University in March 1989, p. 1.

15 Ibid.

16 Herbert L. Walbert and Joseph L. Bast, "How to Improve the Public Schools," a report issued by the Heartland Institute of Chicago, 6 September 1989, p. 2.

17 Ibid., p. 3.

18 Pete du Pont, "Education in America: The Opportunity to Choose," in *An American Vision*, ed. Edward H. Crane and David Boaz (Washington: Cato Institute, 1989), p. 245.

19 Ibid., pp. 248–249.

20 Compare the following: "What the public school establishment likes most about such 'choice' [choice only among public schools] is what conservatives should like least: It continues to treat religious Americans as second-class citizens. Like the status quo, it forces families to entrust their children to institutions that are artificially stacked against traditional values and in favor of the counter-culture." Lawrence A. Uzzell, "Why No 'Choice' Exists for Private Schools," *Human Events* (12 August 1989), p. 11.

21 Stephen Arons, *Compelling Belief: The Culture of American Schooling* (New York:McGraw-Hill, 1983), p. 92.

Chapter 7 *The Separation of Church and State*

1 Barnard Bailyn, *Education in the Forming of American Society* (Chapel Hill, N.C.: University of North Carolina Press, 1960), p. 11.

2 Rockne McCarthy, Ronald Oppewal, Walfred Peterson, Gordon Spykman (Coordinator), *Society, State and Schools* (Grand Rapids, Mich.: Eerdmans, 1981), p. 80.

3 Ibid.

4 Ibid., p. 81.

5 Richard Baer, "American Public Education and the Myth of Neutrality," in *Democracy and the Renewal of Public Education*, ed. Richard John Neuhaus (Grand Rapids, Mich.: Eerdmans, 1987), p. 21.

6 McCarthy, p. 105. The McCarthy book provides much helpful information about the key Supreme Court decisions. See pages 92–106.

7 Ibid., p. 169.

8 Richard John Neuhaus, "Establishment is Not the Issue," *The Religion and Society Report*, June 1987, p. 1.

9 Ibid. For an excellent discussion that reaches a similar conclusion, see: Daniel L. Dreisbach, *Real Threat and Mere Shadow: Religious Liberty and the First Amendment* (Westchester, Ill.: Crossway, 1987).

[10] McCarthy, op. cit., p. 106.

[11] Ibid.

[12] Ibid., p. 107.

[13] Ibid., p. 134.

[14] Their book is cited in earlier notes.

[15] McCarthy, op. cit., p. 134.

[16] Ibid., p. 135.

[17] Ibid., pp. 136–44.

[18] Ibid., p. 144.

[19] Ibid.

[20] Ibid., p. 166.

[21] Ibid., pp. 167–68.

[22] Ibid., p. 168.

[23] Connaught Coyne Marshner, *Blackboard Tyranny* (New Rochelle, N.Y.: Arlington House, 1979), p. 289.

[24] Ibid., p. 268.

[25] McCarthy, op. cit., p. 176.

[26] Ibid. The McCarthy book discusses the constitutionality of a voucher system; see pp. 178ff.

[27] Marshner, op. cit., pp. 269–270.

[28] Ibid., p. 272.

[29] McCarthy, op. cit., p. 174.

[30] Marshner, op., p. 273.

[31] For an analysis of this dilemma, see Ronald Nash, *Freedom, Justice and the State* (Lanham, Md.: University Press of America, 1980) and Ronald Nash, *Social Justice and the Christian Church* (Lanham, Md.: University Press of America, 1990).

[32] Richard Baer, op. cit., p. 17.

Chapter 8 *The Christian School Movement*

[1] Susan D. Rose, *Keeping Them Out of the Hands of Satan: Evangelical Schooling in America* (New York: Routledge, 1988), p. 35.

[2] Kenneth Gangel, *Schooling Choices*, H. Wayne House, ed. (Portland, Oreg.: Multnomah, 1988), p. 93.

[3] Connaught Coyne Marshner, *Blackboard Tyranny* (New Rochelle, N.Y.: Arlington House, 1978), p. 27.

[4] Gangel, op. cit., p. 93.

[5] Rose, op. cit.

[6] Ibid., p. 1.

[7] Gangel, op. cit., p. 120.

[8] Peter Skerry, *Christian Schools, Racial Quotas, and the IRS* (Washington, D.C.: Ethics and Public Policy Center, 1980), p. 1. See also Thomas W. Vitullo-Martin "The Impact of Taxation Policy on Public and Private Schools," in *The Public School Monopoly*, edited by Robert B. Everhart (Cambridge, Mass.: Ballinger, 1982), p. 445.

[9] Rose, op. cit., p. 203.

[10] Ibid., p. 212.

[11] Ibid., pp. 205–206.

[12] James Coleman, *Public and Private Schools* (Washington, D.C.: National Center for Education Statistics, 1981), p. 2.

[13] For analyses of these subcultures, see Ronald Nash, *Evangelicals in America* (Nashville, Tenn.: Abingdon, 1987) and Ronald Nash, ed., *Evangelical Renewal in the Mainline Churches* (Westchester, Ill.: Crossway, 1987).

[14] See the notes to this book and the For Further Reading list.

Chapter 9 *American Higher Education and the Radical Left*

[1] See Paul Hollander, *The Survival of the Adversary Culture* (New Brunswick, N.J.: Transaction Books, 1988).

[2] See Georgie Anne Geyer, "Marxists on Campus," a nationally syndicated column, published on August 29, 1989.

[3] Hollander, op. cit., p. 14.

[4] William E. Simon, "To Reopen the American Mind," *The Wall Street Journal* (8 July 1988).

[5] Bill Anderson, "Stanford's Mind Games: On Christian Campuses, Too?" *World* (25 February 1989), p. 11.

[6] Georgie Anne Geyer, op. cit.

[7] Gregory Wolfe, "The Humanities in Crisis: A Symposium," *The Intercollegiate Review* vol. 23 (Fall 1987), p. 3.

[8] Lee Congdon, "The Marxist Chameleon," *The Intercollegiate Review*, vol. 23 (Fall 1987), p. 15.

[9] Ibid. For a critical analysis of Herbert Marcuse, see any of the following: Ronald Nash, "A Note on Marcuse and 'Liberation,'" *The Intercollegiate Review*, vol. 14 (Fall 1978), pp. 55–57; Ronald Nash, *Freedom, Justice and the State* (Lanham, MD: University Press of America, 1980), pp. 140–145; Ronald Nash, *Social Justice and the Christian Church* (Lanham, Md.: University Press of America, 1990), pp. 97–102.

[10] Ibid., pp. 15–16.

[11] Ibid., p. 16.

[12] Ibid.

[13] While no book can discuss everything, deconstructionism is a subject important enough to require analysis. That analysis appears later in the chapter.

[14] Ibid., pp. 16–17.

[15] Ibid., p. 17.

[16] Ibid., p. 18.

[17] Ibid., p. 19.

[18] Ibid., p. 23.

[19] The story of this grim episode in the history of American Christendom is recounted in Lloyd Billingsley, *The Generation that Knew Not Josef* (Portland, Oreg.: Multnomah Press, 1985).

20 For analyses of liberation theology, see Ronald Nash, ed., *Liberation Theology* (Grand Rapids: Baker, 1988), and Nash *Poverty and Wealth* (Westchester, Ill.: Crossway, 1987).

21 Jose Miguez-Bonino, *Christians and Marxists* (Grand Rapids, Mich.: Eerdmans, 1976).

22 Ibid., p. 76.

23 Ibid., p. 77.

24 Peter Berger, "Underdevelopment Revisited," *Commentary*, July 1984, p. 43.

25 Bonino, op. cit., p. 90.

26 All of my quotations from Ericson come from that editorial which appears on pages 2–4 of the issue.

27 Bill Anderson, op. cit. All of the quotes that follow are taken from pages 11–12 of his article.

28 Paul Johnson, *Intellectuals* (New York: Harper and Row, 1988), pp. 67–68. Johnson's book is a fascinating and revealing study of many heroes of the Left. Their hypocrisy is summed up by Bertrand Russell who, upon being criticized for his inconsistency in advocating socialism and accumulating all the wealth he could, replied: "I said I was a socialist; I never said I was a Christian!"

29 Among other books, see Sidney Hook, editor, *Marx and the Marxists* (Princeton, N.J.: D. Van Nostrand, 1955); Klaus Bockmuehl, *The Challenge of Marxism* (Colorado Springs, Colo.: Helmers and Howard, 1988); and Ronald Nash, *Poverty and Wealth* (Westchester, Ill.: Crossway, 1987).

30 Nash, *Poverty and Wealth*, already cited.

31 Paul Hollander, *Political Pilgrims* (New York: Oxford University Press, 1981), pp. 416–17.

32 Ibid., p. 417.

33 Peter Berger, "Underdevelopment Revisited," already cited, p. 41. Subsequent quotes come from page 43 of the article.

34 Allan Bloom, *The Closing of the American Mind*, op. cit., p. 379.

35 Murray N. Rothbard, "The Hermeneutical Invasion of Philosophy and Economics," *The Review of Austrian Economics* 3 (1989):45. Rothbard's article appears on pages 45–59 of this volume.

36 Ibid., p. 46.

37 Bloom, op. cit., p. 379.

38 I borrow the phrase from Jonathan Barnes' review of two books by Gadamer in the *London Review of Books*, 6 November 1986, pp. 12–13.

39 Rothbard, op. cit., p. 49.

40 Ibid., p. 53.

Chapter 10 *Strengths and Weaknesses of the Evangelical College*

1 Christian College Coalition, *Consider a Christian College* (Princeton, N.J.: Peterson's Guides, 1988), p. 7.

2 Ibid.

[3] Arthur F. Holmes, *The Idea of a Christian College*, revised edition (Grand Rapids, Mich.: Eerdmans, 1987), p. 5.

[4] Ibid., p. 4.

[5] Ibid., p. 38.

[6] Ibid., p. 6.

[7] Richard Quebedeaux, *The Worldly Evangelicals* (San Francisco: Harper and Row 1978), p. 38.

[8] Carl F. H. Henry, *Evangelicals in Search of Identity* (Waco, Tex.: Word, 1976), p. 4.

[9] Bill Anderson, "Stanford's Mind Games: On Christian Campuses, Too?" *World*, 25 February 1989, p. 11.

[10] Quebedeaux, op. cit., p. 93.

[11] Ibid.

[12] Ibid., p. 166.

[13] Neo-orthodoxy is, among other things, a refusal to recognize the Bible as the revealed Word of God. Neo-orthodox professors want students to believe that the Bible (which they sometimes describe as a totally human and fallible book) *becomes* the Word of God under "certain circumstances." We must never, they insist, confuse the Bible with the Word of God. For more on this complex movement, see Ronald Nash, *The Word of God and the Mind of Man* (Grand Rapids, Mich.: Zondervan, 1982).

[14] Carl F. H. Henry, "The Crisis of the Campus: Shall We Flunk the Educators?" *Faculty Dialogue*, Number 11 (Spring 1989), p. 4. Henry's article appears on pp. 33–46.

[15] Ibid., p. 166.

[16] Carl F. H. Henry, "The Christian Scholar's Task in a Stricken World," *Faculty Dialogue*, Number 11 (Spring 1989), p. 65.

[17] Timothy Smith, Introduction to *Making Higher Education Christian*, edited by Joel A. Carpenter and Kenneth W. Shipps (Grand Rapids, Mich.: Eerdmans, 1987), p. 4.

[18] Ibid., pp. 4–5.

[19] See Richard Perkins, "The Place of Ideology in Christian Liberal Arts: Why We Need More 'Ought' and Less 'Is'," *Faculty Dialogue*, Number Seven (Fall/Winter 1986–87), p. 60. The article appears on pages 53–70.

[20] James L. Sauer, "Transmitting Wisdom: The Necessity of Conservative Ideology in Christian Teaching," *Faculty Dialogue*, Number Eight (Spring/Summer 1987), p. 144. The article appears on pages 143–46.

[21] I discuss some of the arguments of the Christian Left in my book, *Social Justice and the Christian Church*, already cited.

[22] Different journals in this list support their own agenda of leftist causes. *The Other Side* frequently speaks as an apologist for the homosexual life-style. One will never find the *Daughters of Sarah* expressing concern about the rights of the unborn; and so on.

[23] Sauer, op. cit., p. 144.

[24] A mountain of support for the claims of this last paragraph can be found in such books as the following: Ronald Nash, *Poverty and Wealth* (Westchester, Ill.: Crossway, 1986); Ronald Nash, *Social Justice and the Christian Church* (Lanham, Md.: University Press of America, 1990); Ronald Nash, *Freedom, Justice and the State* (Lanham, Md.: University Press of America, 1980); Marvin Olasky and others, *Freedom, Justice and Hope* (Westchester, Ill.: Crossway, 1988); E. Calvin Beisner, *Prosperity and Poverty* (Westchester, IL: Crossway, 1988); Doug Bandow, *Beyond Good Intentions* (Westchester, Ill.: Crossway, 1988); George Grant, *Bringing in the Sheaves* (Brentwood, Tenn.: Wolgemuth & Hyatt, 1988).

[25] See *The Reformed Journal*, August 1985.

[26] Perkins makes this point on page 67 of his article in *Faculty Dialogue*, already cited. All of the quotations that follow are taken from pages 67–68 of his article.

[27] I examine attempts like this in my book, *Poverty and Wealth*, already cited.

[28] However, in an astounding postscript, he admits that he has not yet figured out how to politicize mathematics. Here, he could learn from the Nicaraguan Sandinistas whose teaching tools go something like this: "One gun plus one knife equals two dead Contras."

[29] Sauer, op. cit., p. 143.

[30] Ibid., pp. 145–46.

[31] Sauer, op. cit., p. 146.

[32] Richard Perkins, *Looking Both Ways: Exploring the Interface Between Christianity and Sociology* (Grand Rapids, Mich.: Baker, 1987).

Chapter 11 *Renewing Christianity's Links to its Past*

[1] Richard John Neuhaus, *The Catholic Moment* (San Francisco: Harper and Row, 1987), pp. 81-82.

[2] Ibid., p. 79.

[3] Ibid., pp. 172–73.

[4] See Neuhaus, p. 173 for interesting observations about the publications of Orbis Books. Documentation of the deviant theology that accompanies so much liberation theology is available in a number of places. See, for example, Emilio A. Nunez, *Liberation Theology* (Chicago: Moody, 1985); and Ronald Nash, ed., *Liberation Theology* (Grand Rapids, Mich.: Baker, 1988).

[5] For answers to this charge about a Hellenistic influence on first century Christianity, see my books, *Christianity and the Hellenistic World* (Dallas: Probe Books/Word, 1990) and *The Concept of God* (Grand Rapids, Mich.: Zondervan, 1983).

[6] Detailed support for this claim can be found in *Process Theology*, ed. Ronald Nash (Grand Rapids, Mich.: Baker, 1988).

[7] Neuhaus, op. cit., p. 284.

[8] Ibid., p. 99.

[9] For one of many arguments on behalf of the historical authenticity of the New Testament's record of what Jesus did and taught, see my *Christian Faith and Historical Understanding* (Dallas: Probe Books/Word, 1989), ch. 4.

[10] Herbert Butterfield, *Christianity and History* (London: Bell, 1949), p. 3.

[11] Ibid., p. 119.

[12] One of many books that argue for the reasonableness of belief in the Incarnation and the Resurrection is my *Faith and Reason* (Grand Rapids, Mich.: Zondervan, 1988).

[13] Christopher Derrick, *Escape from Skepticism* (LaSalle, Ill.: Sherwood Sugden, 1977), p. 64.

[14] James Orr, *The Christian View of God and the World*, 7th ed. (New York: Scribners, 1904), p. 20.

[15] The development of this attack is traced in the author's book, *The Word of God and the Mind of Man* (Grand Rapids, Mich.: Zondervan, 1982).

[16] Gordon D. Kaufman, *God the Problem* (Cambridge, Mass.: Harvard University Press, 1972), p. 95.

[17] Ibid.

[18] Neuhaus, op. cit., p. 76.

[19] Ibid., p. 82.

[20] While these substitutes have their own important role to play in the Christian's faith and life, they must never be allowed to replace truth, sound doctrine, and cognitive knowledge.

[21] See the expanded discussion in *The Word of God and the Mind of Man*, op. cit.

[22] See the elaboration of this claim in chapter 4 of *Christian Faith and Historical Understanding*, op. cit.

[23] See *Faith and Reason*, op. cit., for one presentation of these arguments.

Chapter 12 *Reopening the American Heart and Mind*

[1] Joseph Baldacchino, Forward to Irving Babbitt's *Literature and the American College* (Washington, D.C.: National Humanities Institute, 1986), p. x.

[2] Ibid.

[3] See William J. Bennett, "Moral Literacy and the Formation of Character," *Faculty Dialogue*, Number Eight (Spring/Summer 1987), p. 22. the entire article appears on pages 21–31.

[4] Charles Colson, *Against the Night* (Ann Arbor, Mich.: Servant, 1989), p. 85.

[5] Ibid.

[6] Bennett, op. cit., p. 24.

[7] Ibid., p. 22.

[8] Ibid., p. 23.

[9] Ibid., p. 24.

[10] Ibid., p. 22.

[11] Paul Vitz, *Censorship*, op. cit., p. 91.

[12] Colson, *Against the Night*, op. cit., p. 125.

[13] Ibid., 125–26. Colson's quote comes from Russell Kirk's *Beyond the Dreams of Avarice* (Chicago: Henry Regnery, 1956), p. 155.

[14] Ibid., p. 127.

[15] Ibid.

[16] Ibid.

[17] Ibid., p. 128.

[18] Ibid., pp. 128–29.

[19] Ibid., p. 130.

[20] For a picture of some of these churches, see Ronald Nash, ed., *Evangelical Renewal in the Mainline Churches* (Westchester, Ill.: Crossway, 1987).

[21] "Ichabod" means "The glory has departed." See 1 Samuel 4:21.

[22] For those who don't get the point, see Revelation 3:16.

[23] Russell Kirk, Introduction to Irving Babbitt's *Literature and the American College*, op. cit., p. 7.

[24] Bennett, op, cit., p. 25.

[25] Ibid.

[26] Ibid., p. 26.

[27] Ibid.

[28] Gary Weaver, "The Treason of the English Teachers," *The Reformed Journal*, September 1989, pp. 26–27.

[29] Ibid., p. 27.

[30] Ibid. While Weaver's comments appear in the course of a review of Joseph Baldacchino's *Educating for Virtue*, cited earlier, these quotes reflect points of agreement with the book he reviews.

[31] Russell Kirk, *Enemies of the Permanent Things* (La Salle, Ill.: Sherwood Sugden and Co., 1984), p. 41.

[32] Bennett, op. cit., p. 27.

[33] Ibid.

[34] Ibid., p. 28.

[35] Ibid.

[36] Ibid., p. 29.

[37] Ibid.

[38] Ibid., p. 30.

[39] Ibid.

[40] Colson, op. cit., pp. 10–11.

For Further Reading

Part One

This first section identifies well over one hundred deservedly famous pieces of literature that illustrate how easily great literature can be used to increase students' moral literacy. This list was first published in the book, *Literature Under the Microscope* by Lou Whitworth (Dallas, Tex.: Probe Books, 1984). It is used here with the permission of Probe Books. Certainly, there is no suggestion that this particular list is either complete or constitutes the best of all possible lists. Its purpose is to illustrate the ready availability of such literature.

The Bible. Recommended version: The New International Version.
Augustine of Hippo/Saint Augustine (345–430)
   Confessions
   The City of God
Blackmore, R. D. (1825–1900)
   Lorna Doone
Boswell, James (1740–1795)
   The Life of Samuel Johnson
Bronte, Charlotte (1816–1855)
   Jane Eyre
Bronte, Emily (1818–1848)
   Wuthering Heights
Bunyan, John (1628–1688)
   Pilgrim's Progress
   The Holy War
John Calvin (1509–1564)
   The Institutes of the Christian Religion (two volumes)
Carroll, Lewis (1832–1898)
   Alice in Wonderland
Cervantes, Miguel de (1547–1616)
   Don Quixote
Chesterton, G. K. (1874–1936)
   Everlasting Man
   The Man Who Was Thursday
   Any of the Father Brown stories
Cooper, James Fenimore (1789–1851)
   The Last of the Mohicans
   The Prairie
   The Deerslayer
   The Pilot

Crane, Stephen (1871–1900)
The Red Badge of Courage
Dante Alighieri (1265–1321)
Divine Comedy
Defoe, Daniel (ca. 1659–1731)
Robinson Crusoe
Dickens, Charles (1812–1870)
Oliver Twist
A Tale of Two Cities
David Copperfield
Christmas stories:
The Chimes
The Cricket on the Hearth
A Christmas Carol
Donne, John (1575–1631)
Devotions Upon Emergent Occasions
Sermons (highlights or selections from)
Miscellaneous poems:
"A Hymn to Christ, at the Author's Last Going into Germany"
"Hymns to God, My God, in My Sickness"
"A Hymn to God the Father"
"Renunciation"
"No Man is an Island"
Dostoevski, Feodor (1821–1881)
Crime and Punishment
The Brothers Karamazov
Dumas, Alexandre (1802–1870)
The Count of Monte Cristo
The Three Musketeers
Eliot, T. S. (1888–1965)
Pre-conversion poetry:
The Wasteland
The Hollow Men
The Love Song of J. Alfred Prufrock
Post-conversion poetry/drama
Ash Wednesday
Four Quartets
Murder in the Cathedral
Family Reunion
The Cocktail Party
The Confidential Clerk
Foxe, John (1516–1587)
Foxe's Book of Martyrs (selections from)
Golding, William (1911–   )
Lord of the Flies
The Spire

Gray, Thomas (1716–1771)
"Elegy Written in a Country Churchyard"
Hardy, Thomas (1840–1928)
Far from the Madding Crowd
Return of the Native
The Mayor of Casterbridge
Hawthorne, Nathaniel (1804–1864)
The Scarlet Letter
The House of Seven Gables
Short stories:
 "Rappaccini's Daughter"
 "Ethan Brand"
 "The Birthmark"
Herbert, George (1593–1633)
The Temple (selections)
Homer (ca. 850 B.C.)
Iliad
Odyssey
Kipling, Rudyard (1865–1936)
Captains Courageous
Kim
The Jungle Book
The Second Jungle Book
Just So Stories
Law, William (1686–1761)
A Serious Call to a Devout and Holy Life
Lewis, C. S. (1898–1963)
At least:
 Mere Christianity
 The Abolition of Man
 Screwtape Letters
 The Problem of Pain
 Miracles
 The Chronicles of Narnia
 Space Trilogy:
  Out of the Silent Planet
  Perelandra
  That Hideous Strength
Luther, Martin (1483–1546)
"Preface to the Epistle of St. Paul to the Romans"
The Freedom of the Christian
The Pagan Servitude of the Church (Also called *The Babylonian Captivity
 of the Church*)
The Bondage of the Will
MacDonald, George (1824–1905)
The Princess and the Goblin

The Princess and Curdie
Lilith
Phantastes
Sir Gibbie
The Golden Key
Gifts of the Christ Child

Marlowe, Christopher (1564–1593)
The Tragical History of the Life and Death of Dr. Faustus

Melville, Herman (1819–1891)
Moby Dick
Short stories:
    "Bartleby the Scrivener"
    "Bill Bud, Foretopman"
    "Benito Cereno"

Milton, John (1608–1674)
Major works:
    Paradise Lost
    Paradise Regained
    Samson Agonistes
Sonnets:
    VII "How Soon Hath Time"
    XVII "On the Last Massacre in Piedmont"
    XIX "When I Consider How My Light is Spent"
    XXIII "Methought I Saw My Late Espoused Saint"
Miscellaneous poetry:
    "On the Morning of Christ's Nativity"
    "The Hymn"
    Lycidas

Pascal, Blaise (1623–1662)
Pensees (Thoughts)

Sayers, Dorothy (1893–1957)
Whose Body?
Gaudy Night
Christian Letters to a Post-Christian World
The Mind of the Maker
The Man Born to be King
The Whimsical Christian

Scott, Sir Walter (1771–1832)
Adventure stories in verse:
    The Lay of the Last Minstrel
    Marmion
    The Lady of the Lake
Novels:
    Waverly
    Old Mortality
    Rob Roy

The Heart of Midlothian
Ivanhoe
Kenilworth

Shakespeare, William (1546–1616)
At least:
King Lear
Hamlet
Othello
Macbeth
Romeo and Juliet
Julius Caesar
Anthony and Cleopatra

Solzhenitsyn, Aleksandr (1918–   )
The First Circle
Cancer Ward
The Gulag Archipelago in three volumes
One Day in the Life of Ivan Denisovich
"We Never Make Mistakes"

Stevenson, Robert Louis (1850–1894)
Treasure Island
Kidnapped
Dr. Jekyll and Mr. Hyde

Swift, Jonathan (1667–1745)
Gulliver's Travels

Thomas a' Kempis (ca. 1380–1471)
The Imitation of Christ

Tolkien, J. R. R. (1892–1973)
The Hobbit
The Lord of the Rings, a trilogy
The Silmarillion

Twain, Mark (1835–1910)
Tom Sawyer
Huckleberry Finn

Virgil (70–19 B.C.)
Aeneid

Wallace, Lew (1827–1905)
Ben Hur: A Tale of the Christ

Walton, Izaak (1593–1683)
The Compleat Angler
The Life of Dr. John Donne

Williams, Charles (1886–1945)
Many Dimensions
All Hallows' Eve

Part Two

All of the books in this section of the bibliography are relevant to issues discussed in the book. Some of them provide important statistical or background information; some explore issues in greater depth than was possible for this book. Many of them contain their own bibliographies that point to additional sources.

Bloom, Allan. *The Closing of the American Mind*. New York: Simon and Schuster, 1987.

Even though most readers seem to find the second half incomprehensible and even though Bloom's own solution for the education crisis is ultimately unsatisfying, this is still required reading.

Blumenfeld, Samuel. *NEA: Trojan Horse in American Education*. Boise, Idaho: Paradigm Co., 1984.

A scathing indictment of the National Education Association.

Clark, Gordon H. *A Christian Philosophy of Education*, revised ed. Jefferson, Md.: The Trinity Foundation, 1988.

Clark's book, first published in the late 1940s, was perhaps the best treatment of the philosophy of education by an evangelical at that early stage of its development. It is still worth reading.

Colson, Charles. *Against the Night*. Ann Arbor, Mich.: Servant, 1989.

Colson has written a wide-ranging criticism of the new Dark Ages into which American society has fallen. The book contains a discussion of the education crisis.

Damerell, Reginald G. *Education's Smoking Gun: How Teachers' Colleges Have Destroyed Education in America*. New York: Freundlich, 1985.

The subtitle says it all.

Hirsch., E. D. *Cultural Literacy: What Every American Needs to Know*. Boston: Houghton Mifflin, 1987.

While the book can be faulted in some respects, it remains the place to begin one's study of cultural literacy.

House, H. Wayne, ed. *Schooling Choices*. Portland, Oreg.: Multnomah, 1988.

Evangelical educators who work in public schools, Christian schools, and the home school movement defend their own territory and criticize the others.

Johnson, Paul. *Intellectuals*. New York: Harper and Row, 1988.

A great book that is especially interesting for anyone who wants the inside information on what many intellectual heroes of the Left were really like.

Johnson, Paul. *Modern Times: The World from the Twenties to the Eighties.* New York: Harper and Row, 1983.

A distinguished historical account of the middle decades of the twentieth century. It shows how a great historian can make history exciting. It is full of material for teachers interested in using history to enhance the moral literacy of their students.

Kirk, Russell. *Decadence and Renewal in the Higher Learning.* South Bend, Ind.: Gateway, 1978.

Ten years before Allan Bloom wrote his *The Closing of the American Mind*, Russell Kirk wrote a better book on the same subject. This is it.

Lewis, C. S. *The Abolition of Man.* New York: Macmillan, 1947.

Lewis's book is still one of the most powerful criticisms of relativism in education.

Lockerbie, Bruce. *Who Educates Your Child?* Garden City, N.Y.: Doubleday & Co., 1980.

As the nuclear family has broken down in American culture, school has become a more important area where our children spend their time. This book shows why Christian education is the preferable option for parents who consider the place of the teacher as role model as important.

McCarthy, Rockne, Ronald Oppewal, Walfred Peterson, and Gordon Spykman (Coordinator). *Society, State and Schools.* Grand Rapids, Mich.: Eerdmans, 1981.

Except for one major flaw, this is an excellent discussion of the case for the private school movement. That weakness, so common among Reformed thinkers in Michigan and Iowa, is a total misunderstanding of political individualism.

Nash, Ronald. *Choosing a College.* Brentwood, Tenn.: Wolgemuth & Hyatt, 1989.

In addition to giving the kind of advice one would expect in a book with the title, the book discusses the strengths and weaknesses of evangelical colleges over against secular schools. It also contains a treatment of the effect higher education has on religious faith.

———. *Christian Faith and Historical Understanding.* Dallas: Probe Books/Word, 1989.

The book explores dimensions of history that are usually ignored and then discusses the impact that various theories about history have had on Christian thought.

————. *Christianity and the Hellenistic World*. Dallas: Probe Books/Word, 1990.

Provides a look at ancient philosophy and religion from a Christian perspective. The book is especially interested in answering charges that first-century Christianity borrowed essential beliefs from the pagan systems of the time.

————. *Evangelicals in America*. Nashville, Tenn: Abingdon, 1987.

A primer for anyone interested in knowing more about American evangelicals.

————. *Faith and Reason: Searching for a Rational Faith*. Grand Rapids, Mich.: Zondervan, 1988.

An up-to-date discussion of current issues in apologetics and the philosophy of religion. The book also contains a lengthy examination of the Christian world view.

————. *Freedom, Justice and the State*. Lanhan, Md.: University Press of America, 1980.

The same kind of statism that has helped create America's educational crisis has turned efforts to enhance freedom and justice into disasters. The book's treatment of individualism is an important corrective to the mistaken views found in the McCarthy book.

————. *Liberation Theology*. Grand Rapids, Mich.: Baker 1987.

Liberation theology continues to increase its influence in evangelical seminaries and colleges. This collection of essays explains what the movement is and identifies its weaknesses.

————. *Poverty and Wealth*. Westchester, Ill.: Crossway, 1986.

Among other things, this book serves as an introduction to economics from a Christian perspective. It argues that economics deals with much more than the making and spending of money. The book contains criticisms of liberal economic policies that are justified because of their supposed help for the poor; it shows that such policies end up injuring the poor.

————. *Process Theology*. Grand Rapids, Mich.: Baker, 1987.

Process theology is a sub-Christian or anti-Christian movement presently making headway on the campuses of many Christian colleges and seminaries. The movement is explained and critiqued by thirteen American scholars.

————. *Social Justice and the Christian Church*. Lanham, Md.: University Press of America, 1990.

The religious Left usually justifies its activity by appeals to "social justice." This book points out the weaknesses in this appeal and offers an analysis of "justice" that is more faithful to Scripture.

————. *The Word of God and the Mind of Man*. Grand Rapids, Mich.: Zondervan, 1982.

Another weakness of evangelical higher education is its increasing flirtation with a neo-orthodox view of the Bible. This book explains what neo-orthodoxy is, identifies some of its evangelical proponents, and offers criticisms.

Neuhaus, Richard John, ed. *Democracy and the Renewal of Public Education*. Grand Rapids, Mich.: Eerdmans, 1986.

Covers much of the same material as the McCarthy book. But the information is obviously more up-to-date, even though the end result seems less satisfying.

Peterson, Michael. *Philosophy of Education*. Downers Grove, Ill.: Inter-Varsity Press, 1986.

Next to Gordon Clark's book, this is probably the best place to examine the philosophy of education as viewed by an evangelical author.

Ravitch, Diane, and Chester E. Finn, Jr., eds. *What Do Our 17-Year-Olds Know?* New York: Harper and Row, 1987.

Here is all the horrifying and depressing information anyone needs to know about the cultural illiteracy of America's high school students.

Silber, John. *Shooting Straight*. New York: Harper and Row, 1989.

The president of Boston University covers America's problems from "A" to "Z". The book is full of important observations about American education.

Sykes, Charles J. *Profscam: Professors and the Demise of Higher Education*. Washington, D.C.: Regnery-Gateway, 1988.

While the author's journalistic style occasionally gets in the way of his argument, this is a powerful indictment of America's academic elitists.

Vitz, Paul C. *Censorship: Evidence of Bias in our Children's Textbooks*. Ann Arbor, Mich.: Servant, 1986.

Liberals often accuse Christians of wanting to censor school books. Vitz shows that people who live in glass houses shouldn't throw stones. The real censors in America are the liberals who control the content of our children's textbooks.

Index of Persons and Works

Adler, Mortimer, 63
Adorno, Theodor W., 145
Against the Night, 194
Anderson, William, 143, 151–52
Apple, Michael, 135
Aristotle, 26–27, 30, 35
Arnold, Matthew, 56
   Dover Beach, 57–59
Arons, Stephen, 111
Augustine, St., 34

Babbitt, Irving, 33–34
Baer, Richard, 116, 125
Bailyn, Barnard, 114
Baldacchino, Joseph, 20–21, 26–27, 29, 33–34
Bast, Joseph L., 108–9
Beichman, Arnold, 143
Bellah, Robert
   Habits of the Heart, 35–37
Bennett, William J., 48, 190–92, 194, 197–201
Berger, Peter, 149, 154
Block, Ernst, 145
Bloom, Allan, 62, 155–56
   The Closing of the American Mind, 21, 23–29, 31, 35, 101, 103
Blumenfeld, Samuel, 19, 45, 47, 79, 86–89
Boyer, Ernest L., 98
Boynton, Bill, 86
Bultmann, Rudolf, 186
Butterfield, Herbert, 182

Calvin, John, 37
Capital, 152
Cavazos, Lauro F., 110–11
Ceausescu, Nicolae, 153
Christianity and Crisis, 168
Christians and Marxists, 149

Chubb, John E., 107–8
Citizen, 168
Clark, Gordon, 28, 79
The Closing of the American Mind, 21, 23–29, 31, 35, 101, 103
Coleman, James, 134
Colson, Charles, 190–91, 194–97, 201–2
   Against the Night, 194
Congdon, Lee, 144–48
Cultural Literacy, 48

Damerell, Reginald, 81–83, 85
Daughters of Sarah, 168
Derrick, Christopher, 182–83
Derrida, Jacques, 156
Devine, Donald J., 25
Dewey, John, 50–51, 90–95
Dobson, James, 106
   Citizen, 168
Dover Beach, 57–59
du Pont, Pete, 109–10

Eliot, T. S., 34, 199
Ericson, Edward, Jr., 150–51, 170

Finn, Chester E., Jr., 46, 51, 82, 86
   What Do Our 17-Year-Olds Know?, 48–49
Foucault, Michel, 156
Futrell, Mary, 87

Gadamer, Hans-Georg, 156
Gangel, Kenneth, 55–56, 128, 130–31
The Gay Science, 70
Geyer, Georgie Anne, 143–44
Gorgias, 10
Gramsci, Antonio, 145–46

Habits of the Heart, 35–37
Hegel, Georg, 25
Heidegger, Martin, 156, 186
Henry, Carl F. H., 163–66
Heraclitus, 9
Herberg, Will, 53, 61–62, 65, 67–
     68, 70, 74
Hirsch, E. D., Jr., 47–48
     Cultural Literacy, 48, 50–51
Hollander, Paul, 141–42, 153
Holmes, Arthur, 161–62

Intellectuals, 152

Jameson, Frederick, 145–46
Jaspers, Karl, 186
Johnson, Paul
     Intellectuals, 152
Johnson, W. A. John, 86

Kaiser, Walter, 165–66
Kaufman, Gordon D., 183–84
*Keeping Them Out of the Hands of
     Satan*, 130–36
Kesler, Charles, 25, 28
Kirk, Russell, 22–23, 34, 52, 59,
     195, 198–99
Koerner, James B., 82
Korsch, Karl, 145

Lenin, Vladimir, 152
Lewis, C. S., 34, 138, 203
Lloyd, John, 86
Looking Both Ways, 173–76
Lukacs, George, 145

Machen, J. Gresham, 98
Mann, Horace, 115–16
Marcuse, Herbert, 145–46
Marsden, George, 165
     Reforming Fundamentalism,
     164
Marshner, Connaught Coyne,
     85, 123–24, 128
Marx, Karl, 152–53, 157
     Capital, 152

McCarthy, Rockne
     Society, State and Schools, 38,
     69–70, 106, 114, 116–24
McClay, Wilfred, 35–37
Miguez-Bonino, Jose, 150
     Christians and Marxists, 149
Miller, Edward, 64–65
Moe, Terry M., 107–8
Moral Education, 54
Moreland, J. P., 66

Nash, Ronald
     Poverty and Wealth, 174
     *Social Justice and the Christian
     Church*, 174
Neuhaus, Richard John, 69, 116–
     17, 178–81, 184
Nietzsche, Friedrich, 25, 70–74
     The Gay Science, 70

Orr, James, 183
The Other Side, 148, 168

Parmenides, 9
Perkins, Richard, 167–68, 170–72
     Looking Both Ways, 173–76
Peterson, Michael, 43–44
Plato, 26–27, 30–31, 34, 92, 138,
     203
Poverty and Wealth, 174
Protagoras, 10

Quebedeaux, Richard, 164
     The Worldly Evangelicals, 163

Ratzsch, Del, 66–67
Ravitch, Diane, 51
     *What Do Our 17-Year-Olds
     Know?*, 48–49
Reforming Fundamentalism, 164
Ricoeur, Paul, 156
Robbins, John, 28
Rose, Susan D., 128
     *Keeping Them Out of the
     Hands of Satan*, 130–36
Rothbard, Murray, 155–58

Rousseau, Jean Jacques, 50, 90
Ruether, Rosemary Radford, 184

Sartre, Jean-Paul, 73, 186
Sauer, James L., 167–68, 172
Schaeffer, Francis, 39–40
Segundo, Juan Luis, 184
Shapiro, Karl, 46
Shooting Straight, 53
Sider, Ronald, 151
Silber, John, 77, 83–85
   Shooting Straight, 53
Simon, Sidney, 55
Simon, William, 142
Sizer, Nancy F. and Theodore
   Moral Education, 54
Smith, Timothy, 166–67
Social Justice and the Christian
   Church, 174
Society, State and Schools, 38, 69,
   106, 114, 116–17, 119–22,
   124
Socrates, 10, 25, 30–31
Sojourners, 148, 151, 168
Sommers, Christina Hoff, 54–55
Sophocles, 57

Sowell, Thomas, 82
Stace, W. T., 65
Stalin, Josef, 148
Stott, John, 149
Sykes, Charles J., 20

Tillich, Paul, 37, 186

Visions of Order, 93
Vitz, Paul C., 52, 69, 192–93

Walbert, Herbert J., 108–9
Wallis, Jim, 151
We Can Rescue Our Children,
   103–5
Weaver, Gary, 198–99
Weaver, Richard M., 78, 93, 95
   Visions of Order, 93
*What Do Our 17-Year-Olds
   Know?*, 48–49
The Wittenburg Door, 168
Wolfe, Gregory, 144
The Worldly Evangelicals, 163

Zylstra, Henry, 38–39

ABOUT PROBE MINISTRIES

Probe Books are published by Probe Ministries, a nonprofit corporation whose mission is to reclaim the primacy of Christian thought and values in Western culture through media, education, and literature. In seeking to accomplish this mission, Probe provides perspective on the integration of the academic disciplines and historic Christianity. The members and associates of the Probe team are actively engaged in research as well as lecturing and interacting with students and faculty in thousands of university classrooms throughout the United States and Canada on topics and issues vital to the university student.

In addition, Probe acts as a clearing house, communicating the results of its research to the church and society as well.

Further information about Probe's materials and ministries may be obtained by writing to Probe Ministries International, P.O. Box 801046, Dallas, Texas 75204.

OTHER PROBE BOOKS
Strengthening the Christian Mind

Christian Faith and Historical Understanding $11.99
Ronald H. Nash   ISBN 094-5241-070

Existentialism:
The Philosophy of Despair and the Quest for Hope   8.99
C. Stephen Evans   ISBN 094-5241-038

Human Rights & Human Dignity   14.99
John Warwick Montgomery   ISBN 094-5241-02X

Measuring Morality:
A Comparison of Ethical Systems   9.99
Erwin W. Lutzer   ISBN 094-5241-046

The Natural Limits to Biological Change   12.99
Lane P. Lester & Raymond G. Bohlin   ISBN 094-5241-062

The Roots of Evil   8.99
Norman Geisler   ISBN 094-5241-054

Values-Driven People:
A Christian Approach to Management   4.99
Sharon G. Johnson   ISBN 094-5241-011

Look for PROBE BOOKS at your local Christian bookstore

Retailers should order PROBE BOOKS from Word Publishing (1-800-433-3340 or in Texas at 1-800-792-3270). Individuals may write directly to Probe Ministries (P.O. Box 801046, Dallas, Texas 75204 or call 1-214-480-0240).